COMING OF AGE IN AMERICA

COMING OF AGE IN AMERICA

A Multicultural Anthology

●●●●◉◉◎◎●●●●

EDITED BY

Mary Frosch

FOREWORD BY

Gary Soto

The New Press · New York

For Tom, Daniel, and Jonathan—always

Permissions acknowledgments appear on pp. 272–274.

Copyright © 1994 by Mary Frosch

Published in the United States by The New Press, New York
Distributed by W. W. Norton & Company, Inc., 500 Fifth Avenue, New York, NY 10110

Library of Congress Cataloging-in-Publication Data

Coming of age in America: a multicultural anthology / edited by Mary Frosch; foreword by Gary Soto.
    p.   cm.
  Includes bibliographical references (p.).
  ISBN 1–56584–146–8
  1. Children of minorities—United States—Literary collections.
2. Ethnic Groups—United States—Literary collections. 3. American literature—Minority authors. I. Frosch, Mary.
PS509.M5C66 1994
813.008'0920693—dc20   93–46921
                                          CIP

Book design by Paul Chevannes
Production by Kim Waymer

Established in 1990 as a major alternative to the large, commercial publishing houses, The New Press is the first full-scale nonprofit American book publisher outside of the university presses. The Press is operated editorially in the public interest, rather than for private gain; it is committed to publishing in innovative ways works of educational, cultural, and community value that, despite their intellectual merits, might not normally be "commercially" viable. The New Press's editorial offices are located at the City University of New York.

Printed in the United States of America.

Contents

Foreword

Once, after an argument with my stepfather—about a portion of the reseeded lawn that had yellowed—I had to take a stiff brush and a ten-gallon can of industrial white, and whack the fence until it looked reasonably fresh, even cheerful, against the backdrop of our dilapidated neighborhood. It was summer, the mid-sixties, and my hometown, Fresno, was dead of wind or any sweet promise. Nothing was going to happen. I slapped angrily at the pickets, never once feeling like Tom Sawyer with a cowlick gracing my head or a smart-alecky trick up my rolled sleeve. But after a while I took off my shirt and painted that fence with gusto, humming and getting into a swinging rhythm with my brush, when my mom came out in her housecoat. She sat down at the redwood picnic table and wedged a knife into a lemon and then lodged her elbows in the lemon halves—her home remedy for cutting away years of dirt and disgust. Instead of asking about the lemons, I dipped

my brush, which drooled idiotic paint, and kept working until my mom called out, "*Mi'jo,* you look like your grandpa."
I turned to her, squinting and confused. I was twelve and
awkward-looking, my huge adolescent head wagging over
bony shoulders. How could I look like grandpa? It was when
she pulled a long strand of her mussed-up hair that it came to
me. She meant my hair, misted white with paint and looking
prematurely gray.

Perhaps at that moment my mother saw what I would learn
only later. Childhood doesn't seem to go away no matter how
we age or how far we move from the source of our anger and
joy. We think we are clever. We smother ourselves beneath
beards, dye our hair, and put on rings of fat. We take on other
people's last names, learn new languages, and, with a facade
of new words, argue over the merits of a French or California
wine. We hide behind books written by dead philosophers
and read books by living philosophers, our wisdom caught up
in the tiny wrinkles around our eyes. We are smarter, possibly
better off, and able to lope along contentedly until . . . Christmas arrives and old stories fall from the closet like a vacuum
cleaner. This actually happens to me. My brothers and sister
count off on their fingers a litany of charges: "Hey, *menso,* you
remember when I told you to polish your shoes with peanut
butter?" Laughter from the kitchen to the living room. "Dude,
I thought you understood I was just joking when I told you to
jump off the roof." Laughter from my grandma, who's hard of
hearing. "Man, I can't believe you went door to door selling
panties!" Laughter from guests coming in the door. I have no
choice but to laugh along with them and sip my wine, a pi-
quant yet pleasant Chardonnay with a touch of chagrin.

We can slide through life incognito, hoping that no one will
remember us as we were. Certainly we have enough pain in
our adult years. Why make it worse? We are more sophisticated, or at least older than when we were living purely
through our bodies, without a battery of thought inside our
heads. Yes, we think we're pretty delightful . . . until the
cousin who fell in love with us gives us a call. Until the bully

we knew as a child shows up in our dreams. Until we have coffee with our parents and remember with wonder the love-making that carried through bedsheets and flimsy walls. Until the name of a nursemaid comes up in conversation and we remember her funeral. Until we witness a kid snatching candies, just as we snatched fistfuls of Tootsie Rolls. Until we gas up near midnight and remember the suck of siphoned gas. The reminders come back to strip away any pretense of maturity.

Perhaps I have leaked some of the story lines in this tenderly shaped, multicultural anthology. But I haven't given away the language or surprises that make this gathering remarkable. Nothing is predictable here. I draw on Gish Jen's remembrance of a popular eighth grader's first kiss with a boy with braces. The kiss was an exchange of tongues and—surprise—one of the rubber bands shot into the girl's mouth. These small gems of observation are what make this collection a page-turner.

Whether we are Jews or Catholic Chicanas, grew up on a corn farm or the oil-dark lot of a radiator shop in East Los Angeles, we come to age in the same human ways. There is no mystery to our human responses. We know enough to recognize greed, jealousy, love, slighted love, boredom, fear, and excitement. We react in similar ways to similar emotions.

Mary Frosch provides a literary map of our country that goes beyond the boundaries of established territory. That this book includes established writers such as Mary Gordon and Tobias Wolff as well as emerging writers such as Julia Alvarez and Cynthia Kadohata makes no difference to a reader ready to sit down with a good story. Let the reader settle in with Nicholasa Mohr, Chaim Potok, and Dorothy Allison, now popular writers—or discover such overlooked writers as Frank Chin, Wanda Coleman, and Eugenia Collier. I'm glad for the new discoveries in Reginald McKnight and Spiro Athanas and for the celebration of the late Arturo Islas.

For these writers, the memory of youth won't let go. It tugs at their sleeves, and they have to walk with gimpy knees, trying to keep up.

Gary Soto

Preface

Nothing stimulates the memory or the imagination more than coming-of-age stories. When I first began teaching, more than twenty years ago, my students enjoyed hearing my stories almost as much as I enjoyed hearing theirs. If memory failed to provide a scintillating detail, the imagination would kick in with the might-have-been, or felt-as-if moment. I was struck then, as I have been in compiling this anthology, by the common threads binding our coming-of-age stories together. No matter what the difference in age, race, or ethnicity might be, no matter what social or economic group may claim us, we seem to be connected through the awakening moments that move us toward adulthood—moments beyond boundaries.

The following selections, then, reflect our commonalities, while never completely subverting our differences. Our distinct ethnic backgrounds necessarily color the lens through which we view adulthood, and these collected stories provide different versions of our shared experience. In selecting these stories, I placed primary emphasis on the quality of the story and its originality in addressing the experience we all share— growing up.

In organizing the stories into categories, I considered the process involved in coming of age. For many, the first concern of self-identification is "fitting in" to a world where many decisions about us are imposed on us from the outside. Whether or not these decisions bring us close to ugliness, as in Gary Soto's brilliant evocation of a much-hated yet well-worn guacamole-colored jacket, or to racial, sexual, religious, or class discrimination, as depicted in the tales of Reginald McKnight, Peter Cameron, Nicholasa Mohr, and Mary Gordon, or to the success of Theodore Weesner's Glen Whalen, they help clarify who we set out to be, early definitions of ourselves.

The second step in this process of coming of age is wading through the often poignant and fragile relationships we have with our families. Siblings, such as those in Durango Mendoza's "Summer Water and Shirley"; parents or step-parents, like those in the stories of Dorothy Allison, Adam Schwartz, and Cynthia Kadohata; or a caregiver, like Arturo Islas's Maria, all contend for places in our hearts and thoughts and memories. Once we have established a few signposts in these relationships, we begin to reach toward other, more tenuous relationships; and if these relationships can be painful and embarrassing, like those depicted by D'Arcy McNickle and Sylvia Watanabe, they can also be humorous and gentle, as revealed in Frank Chin's hilarious correspondence between two cousins and Gish Jen's lovely, awkward cross-cultural romance between a Chinese-American girl and a Japanese foreign-exchange student.

Last, we come to the critical moments that can change our lives, moments that force us to confront what is unbecoming, even ugly about ourselves, as Tobias Wolff's Jack does when he cannot work out an apology for an acknowledged wrong-doing; or confront a kind of rejection that is not typically part of the adolescent package, such as that experienced by Wanda Coleman's Buzz; or the hopelessness that comes with inevitable loss, as felt by Spiro Athanas's Nikos, for example; or the humiliation that Julia Alvarez's Carla experiences; or Chaim Potok's buttressing of sandcastles against despair, and Eugenia Collier's crushed dreams—moments of crisis. Perhaps nothing tells us more about ourselves and the adults we are striving to be than these moments.

I must stress that the selection of stories in this anthology reflects my own tastes—stories I have enjoyed reading, as well as stories that I have enjoyed or would enjoy teaching, stories that have added to my own memories of coming of age. For that reason I have collected mostly contemporary views of growing up, though there are several entries harkening back to earlier "modern" times. Many stories I love could not be included in this collection; they are listed at the back of this book as "Suggestions for Further Reading."

Some of us remain perpetual voyagers on the journey from childhood to adulthood. I suspect there are many more voyagers than there are those who reach an acceptable destination. I therefore hope this anthology will appeal not only to the busy young travelers, but also to those who remember these moments, or moments like them, because we still experience from time to time what Eugenia Collier has called the conflicting tugs of compassion and innocence.

Acknowledgments

I would like to thank Edes Gilbert, Patricia Ranard, and The Spence School for granting me sabbatical time to undertake this project. Many colleagues, students, and friends helped me through their encouragement and advice, especially Annette Liberson, Verne Oliver, Susan Hinkle, Joan Dimancescu, Barbara Minakakis, Matthew Stuart, Lou Frederick, Steve Bender, Christine Schutt, and Louis Phillips. A special thanks goes to my dear friend Michele Krauthamer, who has accompanied me in every step of this book.

Three great influences on my thinking and reading over the years have been Jane Calvin, Annette Frosch, and Alice Woodrow.

The patience, diplomacy, and integrity of my editor at The New Press, Dawn Davis, have been invaluable, and I would also like to thank the remarkable New Press staff for all of their suggestions and contributions, especially to the selection process. Thanks also to Anne Sandhorst for her help with permissions.

Most of the reading work done for this anthology could not have taken place without the collections of the following libraries: the New York Public Library, the Great Neck Public Library, the Queens College Library, and the UCLA Library.

Finally, I would like to thank my sons, Daniel and Jonathan, for their willingness to reveal all that I might have forgotten about the teenage reader; and I owe more than I can say here to my husband, Tom, whose intellectual generosity and moral support have seen me through.

FITTING IN

The Jacket

●◉◉◉

GARY SOTO

My clothes have failed me. I remember the green coat that I wore in fifth and sixth grade when you either danced like a champ or pressed yourself against a greasy wall, bitter as a penny toward the happy couples.

When I needed a new jacket and my mother asked what kind I wanted, I described something like bikers wear: black leather and silver studs, with enough belts to hold down a small town. We were in the kitchen, steam on the windows from her cooking. She listened so long while stirring dinner that I thought she understood for sure the kind I wanted. The next day when I got home from school, I discovered draped on my bedpost a jacket the color of day-old guacamole. I threw my books on the bed and approached the jacket slowly, as if it were a stranger whose hand I had to shake. I touched the vinyl sleeve, the collar, and peeked at the mustard-colored lining.

From the kitchen mother yelled that my jacket was in the closet. I closed the door to her voice and pulled at the rack of clothes in the closet, hoping the jacket on the bedpost wasn't for me but my mean brother. No luck. I gave up. From my bed, I stared at the jacket. I wanted to cry because it was so ugly and so big that I knew I'd have to wear it a long time. I was a small kid, thin as a young tree, and it would be years before I'd have a new one. I stared at the jacket, like an enemy, thinking bad things before I took off my old jacket, whose sleeves climbed halfway to my elbow.

I put the big jacket on. I zipped it up and down several times and rolled the cuffs up so they didn't cover my hands. I put my hands in the pockets and flapped the jacket like a bird's wings. I stood in front of the mirror, full face, then profile, and then looked over my shoulder as if someone had called me. I sat on the bed, stood against the bed, and combed my hair to see what I would look like doing something natural. I looked ugly. I threw it on my brother's bed and looked at it for a long time before I slipped it on and went out to the backyard, smiling a "thank you" to my mom as I passed her in the kitchen. With my hands in my pockets I kicked a ball against the fence, and then climbed it to sit looking into the alley. I hurled orange peels at the mouth of an open garbage can, and when the peels were gone I watched the white puffs of my breath thin to nothing.

I jumped down, hands in my pockets, and in the backyard, on my knees, I teased my dog, Brownie, by swooping my arms while making bird calls. He jumped at me and missed. He jumped again and again, until a tooth sunk deep, ripping an L-shaped tear on my left sleeve. I pushed Brownie away to study the tear as I would a cut on my arm. There was no blood, only a few loose pieces of fuzz. Damn dog, I thought, and pushed him away hard when he tried to bite again. I got up from my knees and went to my bedroom to sit with my jacket on my lap, with the lights out.

That was the first afternoon with my new jacket. The next day I wore it to sixth grade and got a D on a math quiz. During the morning recess Frankie T., the playground terrorist, pushed me to the ground and told me to stay there until recess was over. My best friend, Steve Negrete, ate an apple while looking at me, and the girls turned away to whisper on the monkey bars. The teachers were no help: they looked my way and talked about how foolish I looked in my new jacket. I saw their heads bob with laughter, their hands half covering their mouths.

Even though it was cold, I took off the jacket during lunch and played kickball in a thin shirt, my arms feeling like braille from goose bumps. But when I returned to class I slipped the jacket on and shivered until I was warm. I sat on my hands, heating them up, while my teeth chattered like a cup of crooked dice. Finally warm, I slid out of the jacket but put it back on a few minutes later when the fire bell rang. We paraded out into the yard where we, the sixth graders, walked past all the other grades to stand against the back fence. Everybody saw me. Although they didn't say out loud, "Man, that's ugly," I heard the buzz-buzz of gossip and even laughter that I knew was meant for me.

And so I went, in my guacamole-colored jacket. So embarrassed, so hurt, I couldn't even do my homework. I received C's on quizzes and forgot the state capitals and the rivers of South America, our friendly neighbor. Even the girls who had been friendly blew away like loose flowers to follow the boys in neat jackets.

I wore that thing for three years until the sleeves grew short and my forearms stuck out like the necks of turtles. All during that time no love came to me—no little dark girl in a Sunday dress she wore on Monday. At lunchtime I stayed with the ugly boys who leaned against the chainlink fence and looked around with propellers of grass spinning in our mouths. We saw girls walk by alone, saw couples, hand in hand, their heads like bookends pressing air together. We saw them and spun our propellers so fast our faces were blurs.

I blame that jacket for those bad years. I blame my mother for her bad taste and her cheap ways. It was a sad time for the heart. With a friend I spent my sixth-grade year in a tree in the alley, waiting for something good to happen to me in that jacket, which had become the ugly brother who tagged along wherever I went. And it was about that time that I began to grow. My chest puffed up with muscle and, strangely, a few more ribs. Even my hands, those fleshy hammers, showed bravely through the cuffs, the fingers already hardening for the coming fights. But that L-shaped rip on the left sleeve got bigger; bits of stuffing coughed out from its wound after a hard day of play. I finally Scotch-taped it closed, but in rain or cold weather the tape peeled off like a scab and more stuffing fell out until that sleeve shriveled into a palsied arm. That winter the elbows began to crack and whole chunks of green began to fall off. I showed the cracks to my mother, who always seemed to be at the stove with steamed-up glasses, and she said that there were children in Mexico who would love that jacket. I told her that this was America and yelled that Debbie, my sister, didn't have a jacket like mine. I ran outside, ready to cry, and climbed the tree by the alley to think bad thoughts and watch my breath puff white and disappear.

But whole pieces still casually flew off my jacket when I played hard, read quietly, or took vicious spelling tests at school. When it became so spotted that my brother began to call me "camouflage," I flung it over the fence into the alley. Later, however, I swiped the jacket off the ground and went inside to drape it across my lap and mope.

I was called to dinner: steam silvered my mother's glasses as she said grace; my brother and sister with their heads bowed made ugly faces at their glasses of powdered milk. I gagged too, but eagerly ate big rips of buttered tortilla that held scooped-up beans. Finished, I went outside with my jacket across my arm. It was a cold sky. The faces of clouds were piled up, hurting. I climbed the fence, jumping down with a grunt. I started up the alley and soon slipped into my jacket, that green ugly brother who breathed over my shoulder that day and ever since.

The Neighborhood

❧❧❧❧

MARY GORDON

My mother has moved from her house now; it was her family's for sixty years. As she was leaving, neighbors came in shyly, family by family, to say good-bye. There weren't many words; my mother hadn't been close to them; she suspected neighborly connections as the third-rate PR of Protestant churches and the Republican party, the substitute of the weak, the rootless, the disloyal, for parish or for family ties. Yet everyone wept; the men she'd never spoken to, the women she'd rather despised, the teenagers who'd gained her favor by taking her garbage from the side of the house to the street for a dollar and a half a week in the bad weather. As we drove out, they arranged themselves formally on either side of the driveway, as if the car were a hearse. Through the rearview mirror, I saw the house across the street and thought of the Lynches, who'd left almost under cover, telling nobody, saying good-bye to no one, although they'd lived there seven years and when they'd first arrived the neighborhood had been quite glad.

The Lynches were Irish, Ireland Irish, people in the neighborhood said proudly, their move from the city to Long Island having given them the luxury of bestowing romance on a past their own parents might have downplayed or tried to hide. Nearly everybody on the block except my family and the Freeman sisters had moved in just after the war. The war, which the men had fought in, gave them a new feeling of legitimate habitation: they had as much right to own houses on Long Island as the Methodists, if not, perhaps, the old Episcopalians. And the Lynches' presence only made their sense of seigneury stronger: they could look upon them as exotics, or as foreigners, and tell themselves that after all now there was nothing they had left behind in Brooklyn that they need feel as a lack.

Each of the four Lynch children had been born in Ireland, although only the parents had an accent. Mr. Lynch was hairless, spry, and silent: the kind of Irishman who seems preternaturally clean and who produces, possibly without his understanding, child after child, whom he then leaves to their mother. I don't know why I wasn't frightened of Mrs. Lynch; I was the sort of child to whom the slightest sign of irregularity might seem a menace. Now I can place her, having seen drawings by Hogarth, having learned words like *harridan* and *slattern*, which almost rhyme, having recorded, in the necessary course of feminist research, all those hateful descriptions of women gone to seed, or worse than seed, gone to some rank uncontrollable state where things sprouted and hung from them in a damp, lightless anarchy. But I liked Mrs. Lynch. Could it have been that I didn't notice her wild hair, her missing teeth, her swelling ankles, her ripped clothes, her bare feet when she came to the door, her pendulous ungirded breasts? Perhaps it was that she was different and my fastidiousness was overrun by my romanticism. Or perhaps it was that she could give me faith in transformation. If, in the evenings, on the weekends, she could appear barefoot and unkempt, on Monday morning she walked out in her nurse's aide's uniform, white-stockinged and white-shod, her hair pinned under a starched cap, almost like any of my aunts.

But I am still surprised that I allowed her to be kind to me. I never liked going into the house; it was the first dirty house that I had ever seen, and when I had to go in and wait for Eileen, a year younger than I, with whom I played emotionlessly from the sheer demand of her geographical nearness and the sense that playing was the duty of our state in life, I tried not to look at anything and I tried not to breathe. When, piously, I described the mechanisms of my forbearance to my mother, she surprised me by being harsh. "God help Mrs. Lynch," she said, "four children and slaving all day in that filthy city hospital, then driving home through all that miserable traffic. She must live her life dead on her feet. And the oldest are no help."

Perhaps my mother's toleration of the Lynches pointed the response of the whole neighborhood, who otherwise would not have put up with the rundown condition of the Lynches' house and yard. The neighbors had for so long looked upon our family as the moral arbiters of the street that it would have been inconceivable for them to shun anyone of whom my mother approved. Her approvals, they all knew, were formal and dispensed *de haut en bas*. Despising gossip, defining herself as a working woman who had no time to sit on the front steps and chatter, she signaled her approbation by beeping her horn and waving from her car. I wonder now if my mother liked Mrs. Lynch because she too had no time to sit and drink coffee with the other women; if she saw a kinship between them, both of them bringing home money for their families, both them in a kind of widowhood, for Mr. Lynch worked two jobs every day, one as a bank guard, one as a night watchman, and on Saturdays he drove a local cab. What he did inside the house was impossible to speculate upon; clearly, he barely inhabited it.

My father died when I was seven, and from then on I believed the world was dangerous. Almost no one treated me sensibly after his death. Adults fell into two categories: they hugged me and pressed my hand, their eyes brimming over with unshed tears, or they slapped me on the back and urged me to get out in the sunshine, play with other children, stop brooding, stop reading, stop sitting in the dark. What they would not do was leave me alone, which was the only thing I wanted. The children understood that, or perhaps they had no patience; they got tired of my rejecting their advances, and left me to myself. That year I developed a new friendship with Laurie Sorrento, whom I never in the ordinary run of things would have spoken to since she had very nearly been left back in the first grade. But her father had died too. Like mine, he had had a heart attack, but his happened when he was driving his truck over the Fifty-Ninth Street Bridge, at five o'clock, causing a traffic jam of monumental stature. My father had a heart attack in the Forty-Second Street Library. He died a month later in Bellevue. Each evening during that month my mother drove into the city after work, through the Midtown Tunnel. I had supper with a different family on the block each evening, and each night some mother put me to bed and waited in my house until my mother drove into the driveway at eleven. Then, suddenly, it was over, that unreal time; the midnight call came, he was dead. It was as though the light went out in my life, and I stumbled through the next few years trying to recognize familiar objects which I had known but could not seem to name.

I didn't know if Laurie lived that way, as I did, in half darkness, but I enjoyed her company. I only remember our talking about our fathers once, and the experience prevented its own repetition. It was a summer evening, nearly dark. We stood in her backyard and started running in circles shouting, "My father is dead, my father is dead." At first it was the shock value, I think, that pleased us, the parody of adult expectation of our grief, but then the thing itself took over and we began running faster and faster and shouting louder and louder. We made ourselves dizzy and we fell on our backs in the grass, still shouting "My father is dead, my father is dead," and in our dizziness the grass toppled the sky and the rooftops slanted dangerously over the new moon, almost visible. We looked at each other, silent, terrified, and walked into the house, afraid we might have made it disappear. No one was in the house, and silently, Laurie fed me Saltine crackers, which I ate in silence till I heard my mother's horn honk at the front of the house, and we both ran out, grateful for the rescue.

But that Christmas, Laurie's mother remarried, a nice man who worked for Con Edison, anxious to become the father of an orphaned little girl. She moved away and I was glad. She had accepted normal life and I no longer found her interesting. This meant, however, that I had no friends. I would never have called Eileen Lynch my friend; our sullen, silent games of hopscotch or jump rope could not have been less intimate, her life inside her filthy house remained a mystery to me, as I hoped my life in the house where death had come must be to her. There was no illusion of our liking one another; we were simply there.

Although I had no friends, I was constantly invited to birthday parties, my tragedy giving me great cachet among local mothers. These I dreaded as I did the day of judgment (real to me; the wrong verdict might mean that I would never see my father), but my mother would never let me refuse. I hated the party games and had become phobic about the brick of vanilla, chocolate, and strawberry ice cream always set before me and the prized bakery cake with its sugar roses. At every party I would run into the bathroom as the candles were being blown out and be sick. Resentful, the mothers would try to be kind, but I knew they'd felt I spoiled the party. I always spent the last hour in the birthday child's room, alone, huddled under a blanket. When my mother came, the incident would be reported, and I would see her stiffen as she thanked the particular mother for her kindness. She never said anything to me, though, and when the next invitation came and I would remind and warn her, she would stiffen once again and say only, "I won't be around forever, you know."

But even I could see there was no point trying to get out of

Eileen Lynch's party. I didn't say anything as I miserably dressed and miserably walked across the street, my present underneath my arm, a pair of pedal pushers I was sure Eileen wouldn't like.

Superficially, the Lynches' house was cleaner, though the smell was there, the one that always made me suspect there was something rotting, dead, or dying behind the stove or the refrigerator. Eileen's older sisters, whose beauty I then felt was diminished by its clear sexual source, were dressed in starched, high dresses; their shoes shone and the seams in their stockings were perfect. For the first time, I felt I had to admire them, although I'd preferred their habitual mode of treatment —the adolescent's appraisal of young children as deriving from a low and altogether needless caste—to their false condescending warmth as they offered me a party hat and a balloon. Eileen seemed unimpressed by all the trouble that had been gone to for her; her distant walk-through of Blind Man's Bluff and Pin the Tail on the Donkey I recognized as springing from a heart as joyless as my own.

Throughout the party, Mrs. Lynch had stayed in the kitchen. After the presents had been opened, she appeared, wearing her nurse's uniform and her white hose, but not her cap, and said to all of us, "Will ye come in and have some cake, then?"

It was the cake and ice cream I had known from all the other birthday parties and I closed my eyes and tried to think of other things—the ocean, as my mother had suggested, the smell of new-mown grass. But it was no good. I felt the salty rising behind my throat: I ran for the bathroom. Eileen's guests were not from my class, they were a year younger than I, so I was spared the humiliation of knowing they'd seen all this a dozen times before. But I was wretched as I bent above the open toilet, convinced that there was nowhere in the world that I belonged, wishing only that I could be dead like my father in a universe which had, besides much else to recommend it, incorporeality for its nature. There was the expected knock on the door. I hoped it would be Mrs. Lynch instead of one of Eileen's sisters whose contempt I would have found difficult to bear.

"Come and lay down, ye'll need a rest," she said, turning her back to me the way the other mothers did. I followed, as I always had, into the indicated room, not letting my glance fall toward the eating children, trying not to hear their voices.

I was surprised that Mrs. Lynch had led me, not into the child's room but into the bedroom that she shared with Mr. Lynch. It was a dark room, I don't think it could have had a window. There were two high dressers and the walls were covered with brown, indistinguishable holy images. Mrs. Lynch moved the rose satinish coverlet and indicated I should lie on top of it. The other mothers always turned the bed down for me, and with irritation, smoothed the sheets. Mrs. Lynch went into the closet and took out a rough brown blanket. She covered me with it, and it seemed as though she were going to leave the room. She sat down on the bed, though, and put her hand on my forehead, as if she were checking for fever. She turned the light out and sat in the chair across the room in the fashion, I now see, of the paid nurse. Nothing was said between us. But for the first time, I understood what all those adults were trying to do for me. I understood what was meant by comfort. Perhaps I was able to accept it from Mrs. Lynch as I had from no other because there was no self-love in what she did, nothing showed me she had one eye on some mirror checking her posture as the comforter of a grief-stricken child. She was not congratulating herself for her tact, her understanding, her tough-mindedness. And she had no suggestions for me; no sense that things could change if simply I could see things right, could cry, or run around the yard with other children. It was her sense of the inevitability of what had happened, and its permanence, its falling into the category of natural affliction, that I received as such a gift. I slept, not long I know—ten minutes, perhaps, or twenty—but it was one of those afternoon sleeps one awakes from as if one has walked out of the ocean. I heard the record player playing and sat up. It was the time of the party for musical chairs.

"Ye'd like to join the others then?" she asked me, turning on the light.

I realized that I did. I waited till the first round of the game was over, then joined in. It was the first child's game I can remember enjoying.

My mother didn't come for me in the car, of course. I walked across the street, so she and Mrs. Lynch never exchanged words about what had happened. "I had a good time," I said to my mother, showing her the ring I'd won.

"The Lynches are good people," my mother said.

I'd like to say that my friendship with Eileen developed or that I acknowledged a strong bond with her mother and allowed her to become my confidante. But it wasn't like that; after that time my contacts with the Lynches dwindled, partly because I was making friends outside the neighborhood and partly because of the older Lynch children and what happened to their lives.

It was the middle fifties and we were, after all, a neighborhood of second-generation Irish. Adolescence was barely recognized as a distinct state; it was impossible to imagine that adolescent rebellion would be seen as anything but the grossest breach of the social contract, an incomprehensible one at that. *Rebel Without a Cause* was on the Legion of Decency condemned list; even Elvis Presley was preached against on the Sunday mornings before he was to appear on "The Ed Sullivan Show." So how could my neighborhood absorb the eldest Lynch kids: Charlie, who left school at sixteen and had no job, who spent his afternoons in the driveway, souping up his car. Or Kathy, who'd got in trouble in tenth grade and then married, bringing her baby several times a week, assuming that Eileen, at ten, would be enchanted to take care of it. She wasn't, of course; she viewed the child with the resentful gaze she cast on everything in life and refused to change its diapers. Rita, the third daughter, had gone to beautician school and seemed on her way to a good life, except that she spent all her evenings parked with different young men in different cars—

we all could see that they were different, even in the darkness
—in front of the Lynch house.

I was shocked by the way the Lynches talked to their parents. In the summer everyone could hear them, "Ma, you
stupid asshole," "Pop, you're completely full of shit." "For
Christ sake, this is America, not fucking Ireland." Once in the
winter, Charlie and Mrs. Lynch picked Eileen and me up from
school when it was raining a gray, dense, lacerating winter
rain. In the backseat, I heard Mrs. Lynch and Charlie talking.

"Ye'll drop me at the supermarket, then."

"I said I'd pick these kids up. That was all."

"I just need a few things, Charlie. And I remember asking
ye this morning and ye saying yes."

He slammed the brakes on and looked dangerously at his
mother. "Cut the crap out, Ma. I said I have things to do and
I have them. I mean it now."

Mrs. Lynch looked out the window, and Charlie left us off
at the Lynch house, then drove away.

People said it was terrible the way the Lynches sat back,
staring helplessly at their children like Frankenstein staring at
his monster. My mother's interpretation was that the Lynches
were so exhausted simply making ends meet that they didn't
have the strength left to control their children, and it was a
shame that children could take such advantage of their parents'
efforts and hard lot. The closest she would come to criticizing
them was to say that it might have been easier for them in the
city, where they didn't have the responsibility of a house and
property. And such a long commute. But it was probably the
kids they did it for, she said. Knowing how she felt, nobody
said "shanty Irish" in front of my mother, although I heard it
often on the street, each time with a pang of treachery in my
heart as I listened in silence and never opened my mouth to
defend.

Everyone for so long had predicted disaster for the Lynches
that no one was surprised when it happened; their only surprise was that it happened on such a limited scale. It was a

summer night; Charlie was drunk. His father had taken the keys to the car and hidden them so Charlie couldn't drive. We could hear him shouting at his father, "Give them to me, you fucking son of a bitch." We couldn't hear a word from Mr. Lynch. Finally, there was a shot, and then the police siren and the ambulance. Charlie was taken off by the police, and Mr. Lynch was wheeled out on a stretcher. We later found out from Joe Flynn, a cop who lived down the street, that Mr. Lynch was all right; Charlie'd only shot him in the foot. But Charlie was on his way to jail. His parents had pressed charges.

Then the Lynches were gone; no one knew how they'd sold the house; there was never a sign in front. It was guessed that Mr. Lynch had mentioned wanting to sell to someone in the cab company. Only the U-Haul truck driven by Kathy's husband and the new family, the Sullivans, arriving to work on the house, told us what had happened. Jack Sullivan was young and from town and worked for the phone company; he said he didn't mind doing the repairs because he'd got the house for a song. His father helped him on the weekends, and they fixed the house up so it looked like all the others on the street. His wife loudly complained, though, about the filth inside; she'd never seen anything like it; it took her a week to get through the kitchen grease, she said, and they'd had to have the exterminator.

Everyone was awfully glad when they were finally moved in. It was a relief to have your own kind, everybody said. That way you knew what to expect.

The Kind of Light That Shines on Texas

●●●●

REGINALD McKNIGHT

I never liked Marvin Pruitt. Never liked him, never knew him, even though there were only three of us in the class. Three black kids. In our school there were fourteen classrooms of thirty-odd white kids (in '66, they considered Chicanos provisionally white) and three or four black kids. Primary school in primary colors. Neat division. Alphabetized. They didn't stick us in the back, or arrange us by degrees of hue, apartheidlike. This was real integration, a ten-to-one ratio as tidy as upper-class landscaping. If it all worked, you could have ten white kids all to yourself. They could talk to you, get the feel of you, scrutinize you bone deep if they wanted to. They seldom wanted to, and that was fine with me for two reasons. The first was that their scrutiny was irritating. How do you comb your hair—why do you comb your hair—may I please touch your hair—were the kinds of questions they asked. This is no way to feel at home. The second reason was Marvin. He embarrassed me. He smelled bad, was at least two grades behind, was hostile, dark-skinned, homely, close-mouthed. I feared him for his size, pitied him for his dress, watched him all the time. Marveled at him, mystified, astonished, uneasy.

He had the habit of spitting on his right arm, juicing it down till it would glisten. He would start in immediately after taking his seat when we'd finished with the Pledge of Allegiance, "The Yellow Rose of Texas," "The Eyes of Texas Are upon You," and "Mistress Shady." Marvin would rub his spit-flecked arm with his left hand, rub and roll as if polishing an ebony pool cue. Then he would rest his head in the crook of his arm, sniffing, huffing deep like black-jacket boys huff bagsful of acrylics. After ten minutes or so, his eyes would close, heavy. He would sleep till recess. Mrs. Wickham would let him.

There was one other black kid in our class, a girl they called Ah-so. I never learned what she did to earn this name. There was nothing Asian about this big-shouldered girl. She was the tallest, heaviest kid in school. She was quiet, but I don't think any one of us was subtle or sophisticated enough to nickname our classmates according to any but physical attributes. Fat kids were called Porky or Butterball; skinny ones were called Stick or Ichabod. Ah-so was big, thick, and African. She would impassively sit, sullen, silent as Marvin. She wore the same dark-blue pleated skirt every day, the same ruffled white blouse every day. Her skin always shone as if worked by Marvin's palms and fingers. I never spoke one word to her, nor she to me.

Of the three of us, Mrs. Wickham called only on Ah-so and me. Ah-so never answered one question, correctly or incorrectly, so far as I can recall. She wasn't stupid. When asked to read aloud she read well, seldom stumbling over long words, reading with humor and expression. But when Wickham asked her about Farmer Brown and how many cows, or the capital of Vermont, or the date of this war or that, Ah-so never spoke. Not one word. But you always felt she could have answered those questions if she'd wanted to. I sensed no tension, embarrassment, or anger in Ah-so's reticence. She simply refused to speak. There was something unshakable about her, some core so impenetrably solid, you got the feeling that if you stood too close to her she could eat your thoughts like a black star eats light. I didn't despise Ah-so as I despised Marvin. There was nothing malevolent about her. She sat like a great icon in the back of the classroom, tranquil, guarded, sealed up, watchful. She was close to sixteen, and it was my guess she'd given up on school. Perhaps she was just obliging the wishes of her family, sticking it out till the law could no longer reach her.

There were at least half a dozen older kids in our class. Besides Marvin and Ah-so there was Oakley, who sat behind me, whispering threats into my ear; Varna Willard with the large breasts; Eddie Limon, who played bass for a high school rock band; and Lawrence Ridderbeck, who everyone said had a kid and a wife. You couldn't expect me to know anything about Texan educational practices of the 1960s, so I never knew why there were so many older kids in my sixth-grade class. After all, I was just a boy and had transferred into the school around midyear. My father, an air force sergeant, had been sent to Vietnam. The air force sent my mother, my sister Claire, and me to Connolly Air Force Base, which during the war housed "unaccompanied wives." I'd been to so many different schools in my short life that I ceased wondering about their differences. All I knew about the Texas schools is that they weren't afraid to flunk you.

Yet though I was only twelve then, I had a good idea why Wickham never once called on Marvin, why she let him snooze in the crook of his polished arm. I knew why she would press her lips together, and narrow her eyes at me whenever I correctly answered a question, rare as that was. I knew why she badgered Ah-so with questions everyone knew Ah-so would never even consider answering. Wickham didn't like us. She wasn't gross about it, but it was clear she didn't want us around. She would prove her dislike day after day with little stories and jokes. "I just want to share with you all," she would say, "a little riddle my daughter told me at the supper table th'other day. Now, where do you go when you injure your knee?" Then one, two, or all three of her pets would say for the rest of us, "We don't know, Miz Wickham," in that skin-chilling way suck-asses speak, "where?" "Why, to Africa," Wickham would say, "where the knee grows."

The thirty-odd white kids would laugh, and I would look across the room at Marvin. He'd be asleep. I would glance back at Ah-so. She'd be sitting still as a projected image, staring down at her desk. I, myself, would smile at Wickham's stupid jokes, sometimes fake a laugh. I tried to show her that at least one of us was alive and alert, even though her jokes hurt. I sucked ass, too, I suppose. But I wanted her to understand more than anything that I was not like her other nigra children, that I was worthy of more than the nonattention and the negative attention she paid Marvin and Ah-so. I hated her, but never showed it. No one could safely contradict that woman. She knew all kinds of tricks to demean, control, and punish you. And she could swing her two-foot paddle as fluidly as a big-league slugger swings a bat. You didn't speak in Wickham's class unless she spoke to you first. You didn't chew gum, or wear "hood" hair. You didn't drag your feet, curse, pass notes, hold hands with the opposite sex. Most especially, you didn't say anything bad about the Aggies, Governor Connolly, LBJ, Sam Houston, or Waco. You did the forbidden and she would get you. It was that simple.

She never got me, though. Never gave her reason to. But she could have invented reasons. She did a lot of that. I can't be sure, but I used to think she pitied me because my father was in Vietnam and my uncle A. J. had recently died there. Whenever she would tell one of her racist jokes, she would always glance at me, preface the joke with, "Now don't you nigra children take offense. This is all in fun, you know. I just want to share with you all something Coach Gilchrest told me th'other day." She would tell her joke, and glance at me again. I'd giggle, feeling a little queasy. "I'm half Irish," she would chuckle, "and you should hear some of those Irish jokes." She never told any, and I never really expected her to. I just did my Tom thing. I kept my shoes shined, my desk neat, answered her questions as best I could, never brought gum to school, never cursed, never slept in class. I wanted to show her we were not all the same.

I tried to show them all, all thirty-odd, that I was different. It worked to some degree, but not very well. When some article was stolen from someone's locker or desk, Marvin, not I, was the first accused. I'd be second. Neither Marvin nor Ahso nor I were ever chosen for certain classroom honors— "Pledge leader," "flag holder," "noise monitor," "paper passer-outer," but Mrs. Wickham once let me be "eraser duster." I was proud. I didn't even care about the cracks my fellow students made about my finally having turned the right color. I had done something that Marvin, in the deeps of his never-ending sleep, couldn't even dream of doing. Jack Preston, a kid who sat in front of me, asked me one day at recess whether I was embarrassed about Marvin. "Can you believe that guy?" I said. "He's like a pig or something. Makes me sick."

"Does it make you ashamed to be colored?"

"No," I said, but I meant yes. Yes, if you insist on thinking us all the same. Yes, if his faults are mine, his weaknesses inherent in me.

"I'd be," said Jack.

I made no reply. I was ashamed. Ashamed for not defending Marvin and ashamed that Marvin even existed. But if it had occurred to me, I would have asked Jack whether he was ashamed of being white because of Oakley. Oakley, "Oak Tree," Kelvin "Oak Tree" Oakley. He was sixteen and proud of it. He made it clear to everyone, including Wickham, that his life's ambition was to stay in school one more year, till he'd be old enough to enlist in the army. "Them slopes got my brother," he would say. "I'mna sign up and git me a few slopes. Gonna kill them bastards deader'n shit." Oakley, so far as anyone knew, was and always had been the oldest kid in his family. But no one contradicted him. He would, as anyone would tell you, "snap yer neck jest as soon as look at you."

Not a boy in class, excepting Marvin and myself, had been able to avoid Oakley's pink bellies, Texas titty twisters, moon pie punches, or worse. He didn't bother Marvin, I suppose, because Marvin was closer to his size and age, and because Marvin spent five-sixths of the school day asleep. Marvin probably never crossed Oakley's mind. And to say that Oakley hadn't bothered me is not to say he had no intention of ever doing so. In fact, this haphazard sketch of hairy fingers, slash of eyebrow, explosion of acne, elbows, and crooked teeth, swore almost daily that he'd like to kill me.

Naturally, I feared him. Though we were about the same height, he outweighed me by no less than forty pounds. He talked, stood, smoked, and swore like a man. No one, except for Mrs. Wickham, the principal, and the coach, ever laid a finger on him. And even Wickham knew that the hot lines she laid on him merely amused him. He would smile out at the classroom, goofy and bashful, as she laid down the two, five, or maximum ten strokes on him. Often he would wink, or surreptitiously flash us the thumb as Wickham worked on him. When she was finished, Oakley would walk so cool back to his seat you'd think he was on wheels. He'd slide into his chair, sniff the air, and say "Somethin's burnin. Do y'all smell smoke? I swanee, I smell smoke and fahr back here." If he had made these cracks and never threatened me, I might have grown to admire Oakley, even liked him a little. But he hated me, and took every opportunity during the six-hour school day to make me aware of this. "Some Sambo's gittin his ass broke open one of these days," he'd mumble. "I wanna fight somebody. Need to keep in shape till I git to Nam."

I never said anything to him for the longest time. I pretended not to hear him, pretended not to notice his sour breath on my neck and ear. "Yep," he'd whisper. "Coonies keep ya in good shape for slope killin." Day in, day out that's the kind of thing I'd pretend not to hear. But one day when the rain dropped down like lead balls, and the cold air made your skin look plucked, Oakley whispered to me, "My brother tells me it rains like this in Nam. Maybe I ought a go out at recess and break your ass open today. Nice and cool so you don't sweat. Nice and wet to clean up the blood." I said nothing for at least half a minute, then I turned half right and said, "Thought you said your brother was dead." Oakley, silent himself, for a time, poked me in the back with his pencil and hissed, "*Yer* dead." Wickham cut her eyes our way, and it was over.

It was hardest avoiding him in gym class. Especially when we played murderball. Oakley always aimed his throws at me. He threw with unblinking intensity, his teeth gritting, his neck veining, his face flushing, his black hair sweeping over one eye. He could throw hard, but the balls were squishy and harmless. In fact, I found his misses more intimidating than his hits. The balls would whizz by, thunder against the folded bleachers. They rattled as though a locomotive were passing through them. I would duck, dodge, leap as if he were throwing grenades. But he always hit me, sooner or later. And after a while I noticed that the other boys would avoid throwing at me, as if I belonged to Oakley.

One day, however, I was surprised to see that Oakley was throwing at everyone else but me. He was uncommonly accurate, too; kids were falling like tin cans. Since no one was throwing at me, I spent most of the game watching Oakley cut this one and that one down. Finally, he and I were the only ones left on the court. Try as he would, he couldn't hit me, nor I him. Coach Gilchrest blew his whistle and told Oakley and me to bring the red rubber balls to the equipment locker. I was relieved I'd escaped Oakley's stinging throws for once. I was feeling triumphant, full of myself. As Oakley and I approached Gilchrest, I thought about saying something friendly to Oakley: Good game, Oak Tree, I would say. Before I could speak, though, Gilchrest said, "All right boys, there's five minutes left in the period. Y'all are so good, looks like, you're gonna have to play like men. No boundaries, no catch outs, and you gotta hit your opponent three times in order to win. Got me?"

We nodded.

"And you're gonna use these," said Gilchrest, pointing to three volleyballs at his feet. "And you better believe they're pumped full. Oates, you start at that end of the court. Oak Tree, you're at th'other end. Just like usual, I'll set the balls at midcourt, and when I blow my whistle I want y'all to haul your cheeks to the middle and th'ow for all you're worth. Got me?" Gilchrest nodded at our nods, then added, "Remember, no boundaries, right?"

I at my end, Oakley at his, Gilchrest blew his whistle. I was faster than Oakley and scooped up a ball before he'd covered three-quarters of his side. I aimed, threw, and popped him right on the knee. "One-zip!" I heard Gilchrest shout. The ball bounced off his knee and shot right back into my hands. I hurried my throw and missed. Oakley bent down, clutched the two remaining balls. I remember being amazed that he could palm each ball, run full out, and throw left-handed or right-handed without a shade of awkwardness. I spun, ran, but one of Oakley's throws glanced off the back of my head. "One-one!" hollered Gilchrest. I fell and spun on my ass as the other ball came sailing at me. I caught it. "He's out!" I yelled. Gilchrest's voice boomed, "No catch outs. Three hits. Three hits." I leapt to my feet as Oakley scrambled across the floor for another ball. I chased him down, leapt, and heaved the ball hard as he drew himself erect. The ball hit him dead in the face, and he went down flat. He rolled around, cupping his hands over his nose. Gilchrest sped to his side, helped him to his feet, asked him whether he was OK. Blood flowed from Oakley's nose, dripped in startlingly bright spots on the floor, his shoes, Gilchrest's shirt. The coach removed Oakley's T-shirt and pressed it against the big kid's nose to stanch the bleeding. As they walked past me toward the office I mumbled an apology to Oakley, but couldn't catch his reply. "You watch your filthy mouth, boy," said Gilchrest to Oakley.

The locker room was unnaturally quiet as I stepped into its steamy atmosphere. Eyes clicked in my direction, looked away. After I was out of my shorts, had my towel wrapped around me, my shower kit in hand, Jack Preston and Brian

Nailor approached me. Preston's hair was combed slick and plastic looking. Nailor's stood up like frozen flames. Nailor smiled at me with his big teeth and pale eyes. He poked my arm with a finger. "You fucked up," he said.

"I tried to apologize."

"Won't do you no good," said Preston.

"I swanee," said Nailor.

"It's part of the game," I said. "It was an accident. Wasn't my idea to use volleyballs."

"Don't matter," Preston said. "He's jest lookin for an excuse to fight you."

"I never done nothing to him."

"Don't matter," said Nailor. "He don't like you."

"Brian's right, Clint. He'd jest as soon kill you as look at you."

"I never done nothing to him."

"Look," said Preston, "I know him pretty good. And jest between you and me, it's cause you're a city boy—"

"Whadda you mean? I've never—"

"He don't like your clothes—"

"And he don't like the fancy way you talk in class."

"What fancy—"

"I'm tellin him, if you don't mind, Brian."

"Tell him then."

"He don't like the way you say 'tennis shoes' instead of sneakers. He don't like coloreds. A whole bunch of things, really."

"I never done nothing to him. He's got no reason—"

"And," said Nailor, grinning, "and, he says you're a stuck-up rich kid." Nailor's eyes had crow's feet, bags beneath them. They were a man's eyes.

"My dad's a sergeant," I said.

"You chicken to fight him?" said Nailor.

"Yeah, Clint, don't be chicken. Jest go on and git it over with. He's whupped pert near ever'body else in the class. It ain't so bad."

"'Might as well, Oates."

"Yeah, yer pretty skinny, but yer jest about his height. Jest git im in a headlock and don't let go."

"Goddamn," I said, "He's got no reason to—"

Their eyes shot right and I looked over my shoulder. Oakley stood at his locker, turning its tumblers. From where I stood I could see that a piece of cotton was wedged up one of his nostrils, and he already had the makings of a good shiner. His acne burned red like a fresh abrasion. He snapped the locker open and kicked his shoes off without sitting. Then he pulled off his shorts, revealing two paddle stripes on his ass. They were fresh red bars speckled with white, the white speckles being the reverse impression of the paddle's suction holes. He must not have watched his filthy mouth while in Gilchrest's presence. Behind me, I heard Preston and Nailor pad to their lockers.

Oakley spoke without turning around. "Somebody's gonna git his skinny black ass kicked, right today, right after school." He said it softly. He slipped his jock off, turned around. I looked away. Out of the corner of my eye I saw him stride off, his hairy nakedness a weapon clearing the younger boys from his path. Just before he rounded the corner of the shower stalls, I threw my toilet kit to the floor and stammered, "I—I never did nothing to you, Oakley." He stopped, turned, stepped closer to me, wrapping his towel around himself. Sweat streamed down my rib cage. It felt like ice water. "You wanna go at it right now, boy?"

"I never did nothing to you." I felt tears in my eyes. I couldn't stop them even though I was blinking like mad. "Never."

He laughed. "You busted my nose, asshole."

"What about before? What'd I ever do to you?"

"See you after school, Coonie." Then he turned away, flashing his acne-spotted back like a semaphore. "Why?" I shouted. "Why you wanna fight me?" Oakley stopped and turned, folded his arms, leaned against a toilet stall. "Why you wanna fight *me*, Oakley?" I stepped over the bench. "What'd I do? Why me?" And then unconsciously, as if scratching, as if breathing, I walked toward Marvin, who stood a few feet from Oakley, combing his hair at the mirror. "Why not him?" I said. "How come you're after *me* and not *him*?" The room froze. Froze for a moment that was both evanescent and eternal, somewhere between an eye blink and a week in hell. No one moved, nothing happened; there was no sound at all. And then it was as if all of us at the same moment looked at Marvin. He just stood there, combing away, the only body in motion, I think. He combed his hair and combed it, as if seeing only his image, hearing only his comb scraping his scalp. I knew he'd heard me. There's no way he could not have heard me. But all he did was slide the comb into his pocket and walk out the door.

"I got no quarrel with Marvin," I heard Oakley say. I turned toward his voice, but he was already in the shower.

I was able to avoid Oakley at the end of the school day. I made my escape by asking Mrs. Wickham if I could go to the restroom.

" 'Restroom,' " Oakley mumbled. "It's a damn toilet, sissy."

"Clinton," said Mrs. Wickham. "Can you *not* wait till the bell rings? It's almost three o'clock."

"No, ma'am," I said. "I won't make it."

"Well, I should make you wait just to teach you to be more mindful about . . . hygiene . . . uh things." She sucked in her cheeks, squinted. "But I'm feeling charitable today. You may go." I immediately left the building, and got on the bus. "Ain't you a little early?" said the bus driver, swinging the door shut. "Just left the office," I said. The driver nodded, apparently not giving me a second thought. I had no idea why I'd told her I'd come from the office, or why she found it a satisfactory answer. Two minutes later the bus filled, rolled and shook its way to Connolly Air Base.

When I got home, my mother was sitting in the living room, smoking her Slims, watching her soap opera. She absently asked me how my day had gone and I told her fine. "Hear from Dad?" I said.

"No, but I'm sure he's fine." She always said that when we

hadn't heard from him in a while. I suppose she thought I was
worried about him, or that I felt vulnerable without him. It
was neither. I just wanted to discuss something with my
mother that we both cared about. If I spoke with her about
things that happened at school, or on my weekends, she'd
listen with half an ear, say something like, "Is that so?" or "You
don't say?" I couldn't stand that sort of thing. But when I
mentioned my father, she treated me a bit more like an adult,
or at least someone who was worth listening to. I didn't want
to feel like a boy that afternoon. As I turned from my mother
and walked down the hall I thought about the day my father
left for Vietnam. Sharp in his uniform, sure behind his aviator
specs, he slipped a cigar from his pocket and stuck it in mine.
"Not till I get back," he said. "We'll have us one when we go
fishing. Just you and me, out on the lake all day, smoking and
casting and sitting. Don't let Mamma see it. Put it in y'back
pocket." He hugged me, shook my hand, and told me I was
the man of the house now. He told me he was depending on
me to take good care of my mother and sister. "Don't you let
me down, now, hear?" And he tapped his thick finger on my
chest. "You almost as big as me. Boy, you something else." I
believed him when he told me those things. My heart swelled
big enough to swallow my father, my mother, Claire. I loved,
feared, and respected myself, my manhood. That day I could
have put all of Waco, Texas, in my heart. And it wasn't till
about three months later that I discovered I really wasn't the
man of the house, that my mother and sister, as they always
had, were taking care of me.

   For a brief moment I considered telling my mother about
what had happened at school that day, but for one thing, she
was deep down in the halls of "General Hospital," and never
paid you much mind till it was over. For another thing, I just
wasn't the kind of person—I'm still not, really—to discuss my
problems with anyone. Like my father I kept things to myself,
talked about my problems only in retrospect. Since my father
wasn't around, I consciously wanted to be like him, doubly
like him, I could say. I wanted to be the man of the house in

some respect, even if it had to be in an inward way. I went to my room, changed my clothes, and laid out my homework. I couldn't focus on it. I thought about Marvin, what I'd said about him or done to him—I couldn't tell which. I'd done something to him, said something about him; said something about and done something to myself. *How come you're after me and not* him? I kept trying to tell myself I hadn't meant it that way. *That* way. I thought about approaching Marvin, telling him what I really meant was that he was more Oakley's age and weight than I. I would tell him I meant I was no match for Oakley. *See, Marvin, what I meant was that he wants to fight a colored guy, but is afraid to fight you cause you could beat him.* But try as I did, I couldn't for a moment convince myself that Marvin would believe me. I meant it *that* way and no other. Everybody heard. Everybody knew. That afternoon I forced myself to confront the notion that tomorrow I would probably have to fight both Oakley and Marvin. I'd have to be two men.

I rose from my desk and walked to the window. The light made my skin look orange, and I started thinking about what Wickham had told us once about light. She said that oranges and apples, leaves and flowers, the whole multicolored world, was not what it appeared to be. The colors we see, she said, look like they do only because of the light or ray that shines on them. "The color of the thing isn't what you see, but the light that's reflected off it." Then she shut out the lights and shone a white light lamp on a prism. We watched the pale splay of colors on the projector screen; some people ooohed and aaahed. Suddenly, she switched on a black light and the color of everything changed. The prism colors vanished, Wickham's arms were purple, the buttons of her dress were as orange as hot coals, rather than the blue they had been only seconds before. We were all very quiet. "Nothing," she said after a while, "is really what it appears to be." I didn't really understand then. But as I stood at the window, gazing at my orange skin, I wondered what kind of light I could shine on Marvin, Oakley, and me that would reveal us as the same.

I sat down and stared at my arms. They were dark brown

again. I worked up a bit of saliva under my tongue and spat on my left arm. I spat again, then rubbed the spittle into it, polishing, working till my arm grew warm. As I spat and rubbed, I wondered why Marvin did this weird, nasty thing to himself, day after day. Was he trying to rub away the black, or deepen it, doll it up? And if he did this weird, nasty thing for a hundred years, would he spit-shine himself invisible, rolling away the eggplant skin, revealing the scarlet muscle, blue vein, pink and yellow tendon, white bone? Then disappear? See through, all colors, no colors. Spitting and rubbing. Is this the way you do it? I leaned forward, sniffed the arm. It smelled vaguely of mayonnaise. After an hour or so, I fell asleep.

I saw Oakley the second I stepped off the bus the next morning. He stood outside the gym in his usual black penny loafers, white socks, high-water jeans, T-shirt, and black jacket. Nailor stood with him, his big teeth spread across his bottom lip like playing cards. If there was anyone I felt like fighting that day it was Nailor. But I wanted to put off fighting for as long as I could. I stepped toward the gymnasium, thinking that I shouldn't run, but if I hurried I could beat Oakley to the door and secure myself near Gilchrest's office. But the moment I stepped into the gym, I felt Oakley's broad palm clap down on my shoulder. "Might as well stay out here, Coonie," he said. "I need me a little target practice." I turned to face him and he slapped me, one-two, with the back, then the palm of his hand, as I'd seen Bogart do to Peter Lorre in *The Maltese Falcon*. My heart went wild. I could scarcely breathe. I couldn't swallow.

"Call me a nigger," I said. I have no idea what made me say this. All I know is that it kept me from crying. "Call me a nigger, Oakley."

"Fuck you, ya black ass slope." He slapped me again, scratching my eye. "I don't do what coonies tell me."

"Call me a nigger."

"Outside, Coonie."

"Call me one. Go ahead."

He lifted his hand to slap me again, but before his arm could swing my way, Marvin Pruitt came from behind me and calmly pushed me aside. "Git out my way, boy," he said. And he slugged Oakley on the side of his head. Oakley stumbled back, stiff-legged. His eyes were big. Marvin hit him twice more, once again to the side of the head, once to the nose. Oakley went down and stayed down. Though blood was drawn, whistles blowing, fingers pointing, kids hollering, Marvin just stood there, staring at me with cool eyes. He spat on the ground, licked his lips, and just stared at me, till Coach Gilchrest and Mr. Calderon tackled him and violently carried him away. He never struggled, never took his eyes off me.

Nailor and Mrs. Wickham helped Oakley to his feet. His already fattened nose bled and swelled so that I had to look away. He looked around, bemused, walleyed, maybe scared. It was apparent he had no idea how bad he was hurt. He didn't even touch his nose. He didn't look like he knew much of anything. He looked at me, looked me dead in the eye, in fact, but didn't seem to recognize me.

That morning, like all other mornings, we said the Pledge of Allegiance, sang "The Yellow Rose of Texas," "The Eyes of Texas Are upon You," and "Mistress Shady." The room stood strangely empty without Oakley, and without Marvin, but at the same time you could feel their presence more intensely somehow. I felt like I did when I'd walk into my mother's room and could smell my father's cigars or cologne. He was more palpable, in certain respects, than when there in actual flesh. For some reason, I turned to look at Ah-so, and just this once I let my eyes linger on her face. She had a very gentle-looking face, really. That surprised me. She must have felt my eyes on her because she glanced up at me for a second and smiled, white teeth, downcast eyes. Such a pretty smile. That surprised me too. She held it for a few seconds, then let it fade. She looked down at her desk, and sat still as a photograph.

The Body Politic

⬤⬤⬤⬤

THEODORE WEESNER

Five-five and one-twelve, thirteen years old, out of an obscure elementary school, a complete unknown, Glen Whalen walks into the boys' locker room to spin the dial of his combination lock. Emerson Junior High. It's a school with a double gym with a whiskey-colored floor upon which street shoes are never allowed.

The occasion: seventh-grade basketball tryouts.

Glen removes items from his gym bag and places them on the bench. Two pairs of white wool socks, white high-top sneakers, gym shorts, T-shirt, jock. All but the T-shirt are new. He has to remove staple and paper label from a pair of socks, the jock from the box. The new sneakers, a once-a-year event, promise speed, new squeak-grips on the polished wooden floor, sudden turns, spring. This pair, he has told himself, he'll keep strictly for indoor use, a promise he made to himself in sixth grade too, only to break it during a sunny February thaw to the more immediate promise of running outdoors with seeming lightning speed.

The gym bag is new too, his first, navy blue with brown leather handles, a spontaneous gift from his father as they shopped on Saturday. Except for the sneakers, P. F. Flyers, and the jock, a Bike—a slight necessity, but his first and thus no slight event after all—the items are free of racing stripes and product names, as apparently uncomplicated as other forces at work in the era in which this otherwise unnoticed chapter in sports history is quietly unfolding.

Glen and his father, Red Whalen—the two live alone together in an apartment on Buick Street, in the obscure elementary school district, just up the hill from Buick Plant Three where Red works the second shift—picked out the items at Hubbard's Hardware & Sporting Goods Store downtown. Glen's list from school did not include a gym bag, and he imagined carrying everything in a paper bag, much as his father always had a bottle in a paper bag nearby, in glove compartment, trunk, under the driver's seat. But his father had already tipped one of those bags a few times by midday Saturday, the last a sizable snort as they parked in the alley behind Hubbard's, and there were the gym bags on a shelf before them.

"How you going to carry all that gear?"

Glen, looking in the same direction, did not say.

"Let's do it right," his father said. "Fight them to the end. On land, in the air, on the sea." There was that reddish glow in his cheeks, the film over his eyes, his Mona Lisa grin.

Blue is the wrong color, though, Glen realizes when a string of five boys—tall, renowned Ray Peaks among them—enters the locker room, each carrying a kelly green gym bag. The school colors are green and white, Glen knows, alas, in this moment, even as he knew it all along. Green and white, fight fight! "Shoot!" he says aloud.

"Belly high . . . without a rubber," one of the five boys sings out as they turn into a nearby aisle.

Glen's plain white T-shirt also identifies him as an outsider.
It's true that other white T-shirts are present in the gathering
of twenty-five or thirty, but each is worn by a boy who handles
a basketball with his elbows out, or one who cannot get his
feet, in concert with his hands, to comprehend the concept of
steps. Then two more boys wearing white T-shirts walk in, but
the two—they have to be twins—are blubbery with jelly rolls
around their middles, with near-breasts, and each wears knee
guards, elbow guards, and wire cages over glasses. Otherwise
most of the boys wear kelly green basketball jerseys, although
no such item was included on the mimeographed list. One boy
wears a flowered bathing suit that he had outgrown perhaps a
year earlier.

Coach Bass walks into the gym carrying a new ball, blowing
his whistle, shouting at them to return the balls to the ball bin,
to *never* take a ball from that bin unless he says to! Appearing
then, making a jogging entrance from the tunnel onto the
glossy floor, are the boys of the green gym bags. The five, Glen
notices, wear uniform gray sweatshirts—over green sleeveless
jerseys, it will turn out—above white gym shorts and, laced in
a military staircase braid into their white sneakers, matching
green shoelaces. They are the ones, everything about them
seems to say, who know the score, who already have it made
at Emerson Junior High.

Coach Bass, ball under his arm, tweets his whistle, tells
them to sit down. He paces to and fro before them, shifts the
new ball hand to hand as he talks. He introduces the locker-
room man, "Slim," who stands at the tunnel entrance watching. The best players and hardest workers will make the travel-
ing squad of ten, he tells them. That's the way it is. This
isn't elementary school anymore and that is the black-and-blue
reality of competitive sports. A list will be posted on the bulletin board outside his office after practice on Friday. BUT, he
adds, raising a finger. That's not all. Any boy—any one of
them who has the desire. Who is willing to do the work. Can
continue to attend practices. AND—from among THOSE boys

—TWO alternates will be selected to dress for each home game.

Glen sits watching and wondering. Two alternates for each home game. It means everyone has a chance. Sort of. But does the Coach mean the *same two*, or two *new* ones each time? There are so many students here in junior high—hundreds more than in the small brick elementary school he attended last year. Building and grounds cover acres. And any number of ninth-grade boys actually have mustaches, are over six feet tall. And some of the girls—wow!

The Coach blows his whistle again. He snaps, "On your feet!" and they jump, almost as one, as if the process of selection is related to how quickly one can get upright. All but Ray Peaks, Glen notices. Ray Peaks—his arms appear to reach his knees—pushes up from one hand and is the last to stand. Still he is the first to receive a pass, as the Coach snaps the new ball to him and tells him to lead a line along the wall of folding doors.

Glen follows into the line and performs as instructed. He joins rows of five, back-pedals, sidesteps side to side, starts and stops. However anxious he feels, he does not have the problems of any number of boys who move left when they should move right, cross their feet when they should sidestep, stop when they should start. He dribbles in and around strategically placed folding chairs. He exchanges passes along a line of others and takes his place at the other end. He follows through one line to shoot a lay-up, and another to rebound and pass off. He begins to perspire, to breathe more deeply, to relax a little, and begins to observe the others in their turns as he waits in lines. And, like others, he glances to the Coach now and then, to see if he can see whatever it is the man is taking in.

Junior-high basketball. For home games the panels will be folded away, bleachers will unfold from either side, and the space and glossy floor—the surface is no less than beautiful, precious, an expanse of fixed lacquer upon which to perform

—will offer a dimension that is possibly magical. Ray Peaks, Glen hears in one of the moving lines, could play with the senior team if he wanted.

Glen tries harder, tries to concentrate. However new he is to organized drills and dashes, shouts and whistles, it is becoming increasingly apparent that he is far from the worst. For while the gang of five seems to know all of the moves, any number of others, here and there, now and again, continue to reveal various shortcomings. And—that most promising sign —going in on a bounce pass down the middle, to go UP! and lay the ball over the front edge of the rim without crashing into the Coach where he is positioned just under the backboard, Glen hears at his back that phrase which shoots him through with sudden hope. "Nice shot there."

Friday waits before them as the week moves along, but Glen goes about life and school in his usual ways. He has never *made* anything like a team before, and even as he entertains his degree of hope, he hardly takes on any of the anxieties of expectation. Good things come home when you don't stand at the door waiting, his father has told him, and Glen gives little thought to what it will mean if he does or does not make the team. He will probably keep trying, he thinks, on the chance of dressing as an alternate.

He begins to eat lunch with Norman Van Slyke, who sits in front of him in homeroom. Glen's father leaves him a dollar on the kitchen table every morning for lunch and on his own Glen has fallen into a habit of walking three blocks from school to a small corner grocery he spotted sometime previously. Cold weather has yet to arrive, and at the store—Sam Jobe's Market—he stands inside near a red pop case to eat, or he sits outside in the sun. Lunch is a packaged pie, usually pineapple but sometimes cherry, a Clark bar or two, and from a glass-bowl machine, five or six pennies' worth of Spanish peanuts to feed into his bottle of Hire's root beer, which salty beetles, as he thinks of them—perhaps Japanese, which are popular at the time, although he has never seen one—he pops to oblivion between his teeth as he drinks his root beer.

Norman Van Slyke's looks made Glen smile the first time he saw him in homeroom. Sparse hairs sprout already from the short, thin boy's upper lip, just under his adhesive-tape-hinged glasses, and his extensive nose projects in the midst of this confusion like an animal reaching its head from a hole in the ground. Norman's features twitch; the periscope that is his nose seems to look around at times, to glance up and down and to the side.

Glen calls him Rat Nose at once, and the name brings immediate snickers of pleasure from the other boy. In turn, Rat Nose identifies Glen as Weasel, and they take on the names and wear them along the street as easily as old sweatshirts.

After-school practices continue. Each morning, coming out of Civics and turning right, headed for Geometry, Glen discovers that he passes Ray Peaks going the other way. On Thursday morning, the lanky boy utters, "Say," in passing, and on Friday, when Glen speaks first, says, "Hi," to the school's already famous athlete, Ray Peaks winks in a natural and friendly way that reminds Glen of his father's winks.

Glen also hears or learns in the days passing that the boys of the kelly green gym bags all attended the elementary school attached to the very end of Emerson Junior High. So it is that they had used the glossy hardwood double gymnasium all those years, stopped by after school to see home games, and, as it also comes out, played together for two years as teammates in a Saturday-morning league. In practices, when teams are identified, and when they scrimmage, the five boys, Ray Peaks ever the nucleus, move as one.

Glen's basketball experience was different. His elementary school, near Buick Plants Two and Three along a branch of the city river, had neither gymnasium nor coach. A basement classroom served as a gym, under the guidance of the gym teacher, Mrs. Roland. Painted blackish brown, its high windows and ceiling light fixtures caged, the room offered a single netless rim fixed flush to the wall, eight or nine feet from the floor and perhaps eighteen inches from the ceiling. The clearance was enough for either lay-ups or line drives.

No matter, Glen always thought, for in gym class they only played little kid games in circles anyway and only once was basketball ever given a try. Mrs. Roland, whistle around her neck, glasses on a separate lanyard, demonstrated—to introduce that one game—by hoisting the cumbersome ball from her side with both hands, kicking up one ankle as she tossed it at the basket, hitting the *bottom* of the rim. Then she selected teams—which selections for any real sport, indoors or out, were always maddening to Glen, as she chose captains and teams by height rather than ability. And she officiated the year's single basketball game by calling one jump ball after another, the contest lasting three minutes or less, concluding on a score of 2–0.

Tall boys will always be given the breaks, Mrs. Roland seemed to say. And if your last name starts with W, your place will always be at the end of the line.

Glen did play outdoors. At least a year earlier, as an eleven-year-old, he paused on a sidewalk beside a cement driveway at the side of a church along Buick Avenue and discovered not Jesus but basketball. The church was First Nazarene and the boys playing under the outdoor hoop were high-school age. Glen stood and watched, and when a loose ball came his way, he shagged it and walked it back several steps to throw it to the boy walking toward him.

"Wanna play, come on," the boy said.

Glen was too thrilled to be able to say. He did walk toward the action, though, nodding, although he had just a moment ago touched a basketball for the first time in his life. "You're on my side," the boy said. "Gives us three on a side."

Anxious, Glen moved into the area as instructed. The boy who had invited him—who was pointing out the sides, treating him as some actual person he had never known himself to be—turned out to be the seventeen-year-old son of the church's minister. Glen had never encountered a generous teenager before, and his wonder was such that he might have been a possible convert to nearly anything, but no such strings were attached. The seventeen-year-old boy was merely that rarest of individuals in Glen's life, a teenager who wasn't mean.

The game—Twenty-one—progressed, and passes were sent Glen's way as if he knew what to do. He did not. He passed the ball back each time, another time bounced it once and passed it back, and no one said anything critical, nor cast any critical glances, and the minister's son, who was already a memorable figure to Glen, said at last, when Glen single-dribbled again and return-passed the ball, "That's the way."

It would seem that Glen was being indulged, but something in the way the game was managed made it no less real as a contest. The minister's son had Glen put the ball in play each time it was his team's turn to do so, and in time he said to him, "Don't be afraid to take a shot," and when Glen passed off instead, he said, "Go ahead, take a shot or you'll never learn." A chance came again, and even as it may not have been the best opportunity, Glen pushed the ball two-handed toward the basket, only to see it fall short by two or three feet.

His teammates recovered the ball, passed and circled, and the boy said to him, "That's okay, good try, try it again." In time there came another opportunity, closer in, and this time the ball hit on the rim, hesitated, and, alas, dropped through, and the boy said only, "There you go, that's the way," as if it were just another basket among all that might pass through such a metal ring and not Glen Whalen's very first. Glen continued with the game, too, as if nothing out of the ordinary had happened. But by the time evening air was descending he had grown so happy a glow was in his eyes, and for the first time in his life he was falling in love with something.

He had to be told to go home. When the sky was so dark the ball could be spotted only directly overhead, a black moon against the night sky, and three of the other boys had drifted away, the minister's son finally said to him that he had better head on home, it was getting late. As Glen started off, though, the boy called after him, said they played every night at that time, to stop by again, and if he wanted to shoot by himself, the ball would be just inside that side door and he was welcome to use it just so he put it back when he was done.

Glen shot baskets, hours on end, entering into any number of imaginary schemes and games, and that summer and fall alone, until snow and ice covered the driveway, he played away a hundred or more evenings with the older boys, game after game, unto darkness. The games were three-on-three, although there were evenings when enough boys showed up to make three or four teams and, to continue to play, a threesome had to win or go to the end of the line. Glen loved it; he learned most of the moves and absorbed them into his system as one does. And so it is, on Friday after school, when practice ends and he follows along with the others to the bulletin board between gym and locker room and reads the typed list there between shoulders, reads it from the top—*Raymond Peaks*—down, the tenth name on the list is *Glen Whalen*.

●

He is invited to lunch. In school on Monday, outside his homeroom, one of the boys of the green gym bags—Keith Klett, also a guard—appears at Glen's side and doesn't ask him but tells him to meet them out front at lunchtime. His house is only two blocks away, the boy adds; it's where they go to eat.

Seeing Rat Nose later, Glen mentions that he is going to eat lunch with the basketball team, and he experiences but the slightest twinge of betrayal. When he gathers with the others by the mailbox, though, there are only six of them who cross the street to walk along the residential sidestreet, and Glen realizes, for whatever reason, that he is being selected by the five as a sixth man. He is being taken in. And he is not so naive that he doesn't know the reason; basketball is at the heart of it, and some one person or another, or the Coach, has to have noted, as the line goes, that he is good.

Four of the five—all but Keith Klett—carry home-packed lunches in paper bags, and Glen is asked about the whereabouts of his own. "You can make a sandwich at my house," Keith Klett says. "No charge."

So Glen does—nutty peanut butter on fluffy Wonder Bread —in a large kitchen and large house which if not elegant are far more middle-class than any house he has ever visited in a similar way. He is impressed by the space; there seem to be so many rooms, rooms of such size, a two-car garage outside, a sun porch, a den; then, up a carpeted turning stairway to a second floor, Keith Klett's bedroom is larger than the living room in the four-room walk-up apartment he and his father have called home for the last couple years.

No less noticeable to Glen's eyes are the possessions, the furnishings and appliances, a boy's bedroom seemingly as filled with sports equipment as Hubbard's Hardware, and, on a counter, a globe that lights and an aquarium with bubbles but no fish—"the dumb jerk peed in the tank and they all croaked," Ray Peaks says—and model planes, ships, tanks, a desk with a lampshade shaped like a basketball, and, in its own bookcase, an *Encyclopaedia Britannica* set just like the set in the junior-high Reference Room. And—the reason they can troop through the house at will, the reason to troop here for lunch in the first place—Keith Klett's parents are both at work.

Making a sandwich in the kitchen, following each of Keith Klett's steps, including the pouring of a glass of milk, Glen follows into the den where the others sit around eating. Hardly anything has been said about basketball, and some joke seems to be in the air, but Glen has yet to figure out what it is. Sandwich packed away in two or three bites, two-thirds of his glass of milk poured in after, Keith Klett, smiling, is soon on his feet, saying to Glen, "There's something you have to see," slipping away to run upstairs as Ray Peaks calls after him, "Keith, leave that crap alone, it makes me sick."

There is no response.

"What's he doing?" Glen asks.

"You'll see—it'll make you toss your cookies."

Reappearing, a grin on his face, holding something behind

his back, Keith Klett moves close before Glen where he sits chewing a mouthful of peanut-butter sandwich. The others titter, giggle, offer expressions of sickness, as Keith Klett hangs near Glen's face and sandwich a white rectangle of gauze blotched at its center with a blackish red stain. Even as Glen doesn't know exactly what it is, he has an idea and pulls his neck back enough, turtle-fashion, not to be touched by the daintily held object.

"Get out of here, Keith!" Gene Elliott says, adding to Glen, to them all, "Anybody who gets a charge out of that has to be a pervert."

Not entirely certain of the function of the pad of gauze, Glen decides not to ask. As Keith returns upstairs, white object in a pinch of fingertips, Glen finishes his sandwich, drinks away his milk, and carries the glass to the kitchen sink where he rinses it out, as he does at home. Perhaps it has to do with his father working second shift, leaving him to spend his evenings generally alone, or maybe it has to do with his not having brothers or sisters with whom to trade jokes and stories, but Glen has a sense, realized for probably the first time, as he and the others are walking back to school, that maybe he is shy or maybe he doesn't have much that he wishes to say. It's a disappointing realization in its way, and he is disappointed too, in some attic area of thoughts, with the group of five that has decided to take him in. He had imagined something else. And a twinge continues in him over Rat Nose going off on his own. One thing Glen does seem to see; he is a person. Each of them is a person, and each of them is different, and so is he, which is something he had never thought about before.

The season's first game is away, Friday after school. Lowell Junior High.

Thursday, at the end of practice, they are issued green satin trunks and white jerseys with green satin letters and numbers. Glen will always remember that first digital identity, Number 5, will feel a kinship with all who wear it. Cheerleaders and a busload of students are scheduled to leave at 3 P.M. the next day, the Coach, clipboard in hand, tells them as they check the uniforms for size. Team members are to gather at the rear door at exactly 2:30.

"You have a parent who can drive?" the Coach all at once asks Glen.

"No," Glen says, feeling that old rush of being from the wrong side of something.

"You don't—your mother can't drive?"

"I just live with my father," Glen says.

"He can't drive?"

"Works second shift."

The Coach makes a mark on his clipboard, goes on to question others. In a moment, in the midst of assigning rides, he says, "Keep those uniforms clean now, and be sure to bring clean socks and a towel."

Four cars, including the Coach's own, will be making the drive, he announces at last. "Two-thirty on the button," he adds. "If you're late, you miss the game. And no one will change cars. Everybody will come back in the same car they go in."

●

The next afternoon, entering the strange school building across town, filing into a strange locker room, they select lockers to use and the Coach comes along, giving each of them a new pair of green shoelaces. Glen—he rode over in the Coach's car with two other silent second-stringers—continued more or less silent now, sitting on the bench, removing his still-clean white laces, placing them in his gym bag, replacing them with the green laces. He also unstaples his second new pair of wool socks, thinking that later he will remove the new green laces and save them and the second pair of socks for games only.

At last, dressed in the school uniform—Number 5; he loves the number already and tries, unsuccessfully, to glimpse it over his shoulder—and new socks and bright shoelaces, he stands up from the bench to shake things out, to see how he feels. Nervous, he realizes. Frightened, although of what exactly, he isn't sure. Goose-bumped in locations—along thighs, under biceps—where he has not known the chilled sensation to visit him before, he notices that one, and then another and another, all of them, have laced in the green laces in the stairway military pattern, while his make their way in X's. He feels himself a fool. Was there time to change? Should he say something?

The Coach holds up both hands. "Now I know you all want to play," he says. "Chances are you won't. Depends on how things go. One thing—I want each and every one of you to understand before we go out that door. You will listen to what I say and you will do as I tell you. There will be no debates. There will be no complaints during or after this game. Anyone who complains, about the game, or about teammates, or about anything, will find himself an ex-member of this team. Nor will there be any arguing with officials. No calls will be disputed. Remember: Losers complain and argue—men get the job done. They stand up to adversity. They win.

"Now, we're going to go out there and have a good warm-up. The starting five will be the starting five from practice, and Ray Peaks will be our captain for this game. Now: Let it be said of you that you tried your hardest, that you did your best. Now: Everyone pause, take a deep breath.

"Let's go! Green and White!"

●

Throughout the warm-up, throughout the entire first half, in a continuing state of awe and shock, Glen's goose bumps maintain their topography in unusual places. It is the first time he has ever performed or even moved before a group of people purposely assembled to watch and judge and count, and even as this occasions excitement in him, a roller-coaster thrill, his greater sense, sitting on the bench in the middle of the second-stringers, is one of high-wire anxiety. His eyes feel froglike, his neck has unforeseen difficulty turning in its socket, chills chase over his arms and legs like agitated sled dogs.

From folded-down bleachers on this side of the gym only—opposite is a wall with high, wire-covered windows—Lowell

Junior High students, teachers, and parents clap, cheer, and shout as the game moves along. Glen sits there. He looks around. His neck continues to feel stiff and sluggish. It occurs to him as he glances to the lighted score board at the left end of the gym that he does not know how long the halves are. Six minutes and departing seconds remain in the first half, then, all at once, five minutes and a new supply of seconds begin to disappear into some tunnel of time gone by.

To Glen's right, before the narrow width of bleachers next to the door that leads to their locker room, the cheerleaders from his school, half a dozen seventh-grade girls in green and white, work, against all odds, it seems, to do their job:

Peaks, Peaks—he's our man!
If he can't do it—nobody can! Yayyy!

Glen does not quite look at the cheerleaders; so carefully dressed, he feels he has gone to a dance of some kind when he has never danced a step in his life and would have declined the invitation if he had known it would lead to this. The seconds on the clock chase each other away; then, again, another fresh supply. Glen looks to the action out on the floor without knowing quite what is happening. Nor can he entirely grasp what it is he is doing sitting there on the bench. Even as he went through the warm-up drills, he did not look at any of the spectators; rather he looked ahead, or at the floor, or kept his eye on the ball as it moved here and there. How has it come to this? Where is he? His team, he realizes, is behind 17–11, and he could not tell anyone how this had come to pass.

No substitutions. As the first half ends and the Coach stands up, Glen moves with the other second-stringers to follow along with the starting five to the locker room. Glen feels no disappointment that he has spent this time sitting and watching, nor any urge to be put into the game. Sitting on the bench in that costume, getting his neck to swivel; it seemed contribution enough. As they pass before the group from their school, however, and names and remarks of encouragement are called out, he hears distinctly, "Go get 'em, Weasel," and looks over to see Rat Nose's face looking at him, smiling, pleased, and a pleasure of friendship leaps up in Glen's chest.

The Coach paces and talks and points. They are behind 19–11. He slaps a fist into an opened palm. Glen continues to feel overwhelmed by all that surrounds him, but on the thought of Rat Nose sitting out there, calling him Weasel, he has to stop himself from tittering and giggling out loud. For one moment, then another, it seems to be the funniest thing that has ever happened to him.

"Now we don't have much time," the Coach is saying. "We have to get the ball in to Ray Peaks. If we're going to pull this out, we have to get the ball in to Ray under the basket! Now let's get out there and do it. Green and white, fight—okay?" he inquires with some uncertainty.

On the floor, going through a confused warm-up, Glen glances back at the group from his school, looks to see Rat Nose there in particular, but the group is too far away and at such an angle that he cannot be sure. Then they're being herded back to their bench; maybe they aren't supposed to warm up for the second half—no one seems to know.

Glen sits in the middle of those on the bench and stares at the game as before. Five-on-five, two officials in black-and-white striped shirts. Whistles. The scrambled movement of basketball at ground level. Hands raised. Shouts from the bleachers. Yet again he has forgotten to check the beginning time. Nine minutes thirty seconds remain as he looks for the first time. The score? His next realization is that he has not been keeping score. He is too nervous for math, he thinks. Home 25/Visitors 16. The next time he looks, the clock shows eight minutes forty-four seconds. His team, he realizes, has scored but five points so far in the half. The other team's lead is increasing. It looks like his team is going to lose. That's what it looks like. There is Keith Klett snapping a pass to the side to

Gene Elliott as they move before the scrambled concentration of players at the far end, and Glen experiences a vague sense that they are somehow progressing in the wrong direction, and he experiences a vague sense, too, of hearing his name called out: "Whalen—Whalen!"

It is his name, in fact, and there is the Coach's face as he looks, his fingers indicating sharply that he is to move to his side. The next thing Glen seems to know, as if he had received a blast of frozen air, is that he is crouched, one hand on the floor, next to the Coach's knee. In this location the volume of the game, the cheers, and spectators, seems to have increased three times over. "Check in at the table, next whistle, for Klett, get that ball to Ray Peaks!" Glen hears, sees the Coach spit the words at him from the side of his mouth, all the time continuing to watch the action at the far end.

Stealing along in the same crouch, Glen reports in over the tabletop, says, "Whalen for Klett—I mean Number 5 for Number 7."

Taking a duck-step or two to the center line, Glen looks up to the scoreboard. Home 27/Visitors 16. Seven minutes thirty-one seconds.

A whistle blows out on the floor and at once a horn honks behind him, giving him so sudden a scare, he seems to lose some drops in his pants. "Substitution Emerson," the man calls.

Glen moves onto the floor, into the view of all, seeking Keith Klett; spotting him, he says, "In for you," and believing he is the object of all eyes, moves past him toward the end of the court where the other team is putting the ball in play, not knowing, in the blur of things, if it is the consequence of a basket or not.

Nor does he see Gene Elliott for the moment as, before him, an official hands the ball to a Lowell player. The boy passes it at once to a player who turns to start dribbling downcourt and Glen dashes toward him and the ball, slaps the ball away, chases it, grabs it in both hands, pivots, looks to find his fellow guard, to get rid of the ball, as he is poked in the wrist and forearm by someone's fingers and a whistle blows sharply, close by.

"Foul! Lowell! Number 13!" the official snaps. "One shot! Number 5!"

The players return, taking their positions. "That's the way! Way to go!" comes from Glen's teammates.

He stands waiting at the free-throw line. The others settle in, lean, wait. He has done this a thousand times, and never. The ball is handed over. "One shot," the official says. Glen looks to the distant hoop; he finds presence of mind enough to call up something of the endless shots in the church driveway, although the message remains elusive. He shoots, from the chest, as he had in the driveway, although they were taught in practice to shoot from between their legs. Hitting the rim with a thud, the ball holds, rolls, tries to get away to the side, cannot escape, falls through.

"Way to go, Whalen," a teammate remarks, passing him on the way down the floor. "That's the way," comes from another.

Glen moves toward the out-of-bounds line again, toward the other guard, as the ball is about to be put in play. He looks over for Gene Elliott again, but doesn't spot him, as the ball is passed in, and the guard receiving the ball, more alert this time, starts to dribble upcourt as Glen rushes him, explodes over him, somehow hits the ball as the boy swings it in both hands, knocks it loose, chases it, dribbles it once in the chase, looks again for his teammate as the Lowell player is on him, jumps, shoots—sees the ball hit the backboard, hit the rim, go through—and hears an explosion of applause from the other end of the gym.

At once he moves back in, pursuing the ball, as a teammate slaps his back, says, "Great shot!" and hears his coach call out, "Go ahead with that press, that's the way!" and hears the other team's coach, close by, snarl to his guards, "Keep it away from that guy will you?" and hears Gene Elliott, inches away, say, "Coach says to go ahead with the press."

There he is, poised, ready, so thrilled already that his eyes seem aflame, as the Lowell players are all back downcourt and are taking more time. He glances to the clock: seven minutes twenty seconds. In about ten seconds, he realizes, he has scored three points, which message keeps coming to him, that he has, in about ten seconds scored three points, that it is true, he has, and it is something, it is all things, and everything he has ever known in his life is different now.

The ball is moved along this time. At the other end, in their zone defense, the other team loses possession near the basket, and players run and lope past Glen as he circles back, and the ball is passed to him, and he dribbles along, eluding a Lowell player, passes off to Gene Elliott, sees Ray Peaks ranging to the right of the basket, and when the ball comes back to him—it will be his most satisfying play, one which is no way accidental, no way lucky—he immediately fires a long one-handed pass, more football than basketball, hard and high, and to his amazement Ray Peaks leaps high, arms extended, whips the ball out of the air with both hands, dribbles at once on a pivot-turn and lays it in neatly off the board, and there comes another explosion from behind them. And there is Ray Peaks seeking him out, grabbing his arm, hissing in a wild, feverish whisper, "That's the way to pass! Keep it up! Keep it up! We're going to beat these guys!"

The game progresses. Glen intercepts a pass and goes two-thirds of the court to put in a lay-up just over the front edge of the rim, as they were instructed, and he scores two more free throws, to go three for three, bringing his point total to seven, but his most satisfying play is the first long, high pass, and the most exciting experience of the game is the fever that infects them all, especially Ray Peaks, who scores any number of added baskets on his high, hard passes, and Gene Elliott, too, who passes harder, as they all become caught up in the fever, including the Coach, who is on his feet shouting, clapping, waving, and the group from their school, whose explosions of applause keep becoming louder and wilder, until, suddenly to Glen, both horn and whistle sound, and there comes another explosion of applause, and the Coach and play-

ers from the bench are on the floor, grabbing, slapping, shouting, for the game is over and they have won, and they know
things they had not known before, and none can quite get
enough, it seems, of what it is they have not known until this
very moment.

As they move and are being moved toward the locker room,
Ray Peaks is slapped and congratulated, and so is Glen. There
is the Coach, arm around Glen's shoulders, voice close, calling
to him, "That full-court press was the thing to do! You ignited
that comeback! You turned it around!"

The celebration continues in the locker room. The final
score: Home 29/Visitors 33. Locker doors are slammed, towels
are thrown around, there is the Coach congratulating Glen
again, slapping his shoulder, calling to them all, "That full-
court press turned it around!" Glen learns, too, in the melee,
that only two players on his team have scored, he and Ray
Peaks, seven points and twenty-six, and everything, all of it,
keeps occurring over again for him as a surprise, and as a
surprise all over again, and he lets it go on as it will, a dozen
Christmasses and birthdays combined, accepts the compli-
ments, knows in some part of himself already that he is
changed by what has happened, has been granted something,
knows these things, and does not volunteer in any way that at
the time he simply chased the ball because he was so confused
by all that was happening around him that he did not know,
otherwise, what it was that he was supposed to do.

Monday it is back to school and lunch hour as usual. After
school, though, as practice moves along, as they run through
drills with the dozen or so alternates, there comes a time for
the Coach to name squads of five, and the name *Glen Whalen*
is called to run out and join the first team, in place of Keith
Klett, who is left to stand with the others. It is not something
Glen anticipated—is a small surprise—but as it happens the
logic is not unreasonable to him. Nor is anything unreasonable
to the other four, who congratulate him in small ways as he
takes his place on the floor.

Keith Klett stands among the others, retreats, Glen notices, to the back row. His eyes appear not to focus on anything in particular as he stands looking ahead, glancing around.

They come face to face after practice in the locker room. Glen, sitting on the bench to untie his shoes, looks to the end of his aisle and sees Keith Klett staring at him. "You suck-ass," the boy says.

Keith Klett walks on. Glen doesn't say anything. He sits looking that way for a moment and doesn't know what to say or do.

Nor does he see the other boy when, undressed, towel around his waist, he walks along the main aisle to the shower. He wonders if they will fight, there in the locker room or out behind the school, and although the prospect of everyone streaming along uttering "Fight, fight," excites and terrifies him at once—he'll do it, he thinks—nothing of the kind happens. The remark stays within him like a speck; it stays and stays.

At home that night he thinks of resurrecting his friendship with Rat Nose and the thought appeals to him, as if to return home after having been away. Then he wonders if Rat Nose might turn his back on him—who would blame him?—and he worries about it until the next day when he encounters Rat Nose near his locker in the hall.

"Still go to Jobe's Market?" Glen asks.

"Sometimes," Rat Nose says.

"Wanna go?"

The Wrong Lunch Line

●◉◉◉

NICHOLASA MOHR

Early Spring 1946

The morning dragged on for Yvette and Mildred. They were anxiously waiting for the bell to ring. Last Thursday the school had announced that free Passover lunches would be provided for the Jewish children during this week. Yvette ate the free lunch provided by the school and Mildred brought her lunch from home in a brown paper bag. Because of school rules, free-lunch children and bag-lunch children could not sit in the same section, and the two girls always ate separately. This week, however, they had planned to eat together.

Finally the bell sounded and all the children left the classroom for lunch. As they had already planned, Yvette and Mildred went right up to the line where the Jewish children were filing up for lunch trays. I hope no one asks me nothing, Yvette said to herself. They stood close to each other and held hands. Every once in a while one would squeeze the other's hand in a gesture of reassurance, and they would giggle softly.

The two girls lived just a few houses away from one another. Yvette lived on the top floor of a tenement, in a four-room apartment which she shared with her parents, grandmother, three older sisters, two younger brothers, and baby sister. Mildred was an only child. She lived with her parents in the three small rooms in back of the candy store they owned.

During this school year, the two girls had become good friends. Every day after public school, Mildred went to a Hebrew school. Yvette went to catechism twice a week, preparing for her First Communion and Confirmation. Most evenings after supper, they played together in front of the candy store. Yvette was a frequent visitor in Mildred's apartment. They listened to their favorite radio programs together. Yvette looked forward to the Hershey's chocolate bar that Mr. Fox, Mildred's father, would give her.

The two girls waited patiently on the lunch line as they slowly moved along toward the food counter. Yvette was delighted when she saw what was placed on the trays: a hard-boiled egg, a bowl of soup that looked like vegetable, a large piece of cracker, milk, and an apple. She stretched over to see what the regular free lunch was, and it was the usual: a bowl of watery stew, two slices of dark bread, milk, and cooked prunes in a thick syrup. She was really glad to be standing with Mildred.

"Hey, Yvette!" She heard someone call her name. It was Elba Cruz, one of her classmates. "What's happening? Why are you standing there?"

"I'm having lunch with Mildred today," she answered, and looked at Mildred, who nodded.

"Oh yeah?" Elba said. "Why are they getting a different lunch from us?"

"It's their special holiday and they gotta eat that special food, that's all," Yvette answered.

"But why?" persisted Elba.

"Else it's a sin, that's why. Just like we can't have no meat on Friday," Yvette said.

"A sin? . . . Why—why is it a sin?" This time, she looked at Mildred.

"It's a special lunch for Passover," Mildred said.

"Passover? What is that?" asked Elba.

"It's a Jewish holiday. Like you got Easter, so we have Passover. We can't eat no bread."

"Oh . . ."

"You better get in your line before the teacher comes," Yvette said quickly.

"You're here!" said Elba.

"I'm only here because Mildred invited me," Yvette answered. Elba shrugged her shoulders and walked away.

"They gonna kick you outta there. . . . I bet you are not supposed to be on that line," she called back to Yvette.

"Dumbbell!" Yvette answered. She turned to Mildred and asked, "Why can't you eat bread, Mildred?"

"We just can't. We are only supposed to eat matzo. What you see there." Mildred pointed to the large cracker on the tray.

"Oh," said Yvette. "Do you have to eat an egg too?"

"No . . . but you can't have no meat, because you can't have meat and milk together . . . like at the same time."

"Why?"

"Because it's against our religion. Besides, it's very bad. It's not supposed to be good for you."

"It's not?" asked Yvette.

"No," Mildred said. "You might get sick. You see, you are better off waiting like a few hours until you digest your food, and then you can have meat or the milk. But not together."

"Wow," said Yvette. "You know, I have meat and milk together all the time. I wonder if my mother knows it's not good for you."

By this time the girls were at the counter. Mildred took one tray and Yvette quickly took another.

"I hope no one notices me," Yvette whispered to Mildred. As the two girls walked toward a long lunch table, they heard giggling, and Yvette saw Elba and some of the kids she usually ate lunch with pointing and laughing at her. Stupids, thought Yvette, ignoring them and following Mildred. The two girls sat down with the special lunch group.

Yvette whispered to Mildred, "This looks good!" and started to crack the eggshell.

Yvette felt Mildred's elbow digging in her side. "Watch out!" Mildred said.

"What is going on here?" It was the voice of one of the teachers who monitored them during lunch. Yvette looked up and saw the teacher coming toward her.

"You! You there!" the teacher said, pointing to Yvette. "What are you doing there?" Yvette looked at the woman and was unable to speak.

"What are you doing over there?" she repeated.

"I went to get some lunch," Yvette said softly.

"What? Speak up! I can't hear you."

"I said . . . I went to get some lunch," she said a little louder.

"Are you entitled to a free lunch?"

"Yes."

"Well . . . and are you Jewish?"

Yvette stared at her and she could feel her face getting hot and flushed.

"I asked you a question. Are you Jewish?" Another teacher Yvette knew came over and the lunchroom became quiet. Everyone was looking at Yvette, waiting to hear what was said. She turned to look at Mildred, who looked just as frightened as she felt. Please don't let me cry, thought Yvette.

"What's the trouble?" asked the other teacher.

"This child," the woman pointed to Yvette, "is eating lunch here with the Jewish children, and I don't think she's Jewish. She doesn't—I've seen her before; she gets free lunch, all right. But she looks like one of the—" Hesitating, the woman went on, "She looks Spanish."

"I'm sure she's not Jewish," said the other teacher.

"All right now," said the first teacher, "what are you doing here? Are you Spanish?"

"Yes."

"Why did you come over here and get in that line? You went on the wrong lunch line!"

Yvette looked down at the tray in front of her.

"Get up and come with me. Right now!" Getting up, she dared not look around her. She felt her face was going to burn up. Some of the children were laughing; she could hear the suppressed giggles and an occasional "Ooooh." As she started to walk behind the teacher, she heard her say, "Go back and bring that tray." Yvette felt slightly weak at the knees but managed to turn around, and going back to the table, she returned the tray to the counter. A kitchen worker smiled nonchalantly and removed the tray full of food.

"Come on over to Mrs. Ralston's office," the teacher said, and gestured to Yvette that she walk in front of her this time.

Inside the vice-principal's office, Yvette stood, not daring to look at Mrs. Rachel Ralston while she spoke.

"You have no right to take someone else's place." Mrs. Ralston continued to speak in an even-tempered, almost pleasant voice. "This time we'll let it go, but next time we will notify your parents and you won't get off so easily. You have to learn, Yvette, right from wrong. Don't go where you don't belong. . . ."

Yvette left the office and heard the bell. Lunchtime was over.

◉

Yvette and Mildred met after school in the street. It was late in the afternoon. Yvette was returning from the corner grocery with a food package, and Mildred was coming home from Hebrew school.

"How was Hebrew school?" asked Yvette.

"OK," Mildred smiled and nodded. "Are you coming over tonight to listen to the radio? 'Mr. Keene, Tracer of Lost Persons' is on."

"OK," said Yvette. "I gotta bring this up and eat. Then I'll come by."

Yvette finished supper and was given permission to visit her friend.

"Boy, that was a good program, wasn't it, Mildred?" Yvette ate her candy with delight.

Mildred nodded and looked at Yvette, not speaking. There was a long moment of silence. They wanted to talk about it, but it was as if this afternoon's incident could not be mentioned. Somehow each girl was afraid of disturbing that feeling of closeness they felt for one another. And yet when their eyes met they looked away with an embarrassed smile.

"I wonder what's on the radio next," Yvette said, breaking the silence.

"Nothing good for another half hour," Mildred answered. Impulsively, she asked quickly, "Yvette, you wanna have some matzo? We got some for the holidays."

"Is that the cracker they gave you this afternoon?"

"Yeah. We can have some."

"All right." Yvette smiled.

Mildred left the room and returned holding a large square cracker. Breaking off a piece, she handed it to Yvette.

"It don't taste like much, does it?" said Yvette.

"Only if you put something good on it," Mildred agreed, smiling.

"Boy, that Mrs. Ralston sure is dumb," Yvette said, giggling. They looked at each other and began to laugh loudly.

"Old dumb Mrs. Ralston," said Mildred, laughing convulsively. "She's scre . . . screwy."

"Yeah," Yvette said, laughing so hard tears began to roll down her cheeks. "Dope . . . dopey . . . M . . . Mi . . . Mrs. Ra . . . Ral . . . ston. . . ."

Jump or Dive

@@@@

PETER CAMERON

Jason, my uncle's lover, sat in the dark kitchen eating what sounded like a bowl of cereal. He had some disease that made him hungry every few hours—something about not enough sugar in his blood. Every night, he got up at about three o'clock and fixed himself a snack. Since I was sleeping on the living-room couch, I could hear him.

My parents and I had driven down from Oregon to visit my Uncle Walter, who lived in Arizona. He was my father's younger brother. My sister Jackie got to stay home, on account of having just graduated from high school and having a job at the Lob-Steer Restaurant. But there was no way my parents were letting me stay home: I had just finished ninth grade and I was unemployed.

My parents slept in the guest room. Jason and Uncle Walter slept together in the master bedroom. The first morning, when I went into the bathroom, I saw Jason sitting on the edge of the big unmade bed in his jockey shorts. Jason was very tan, but it was an odd tan: His face and the bottom three-quarters of his arms were much darker than his chest. It looked as if he was wearing a T-shirt.

The living-room couch was made of leather and had little metal nubs stuck all over it. It was almost impossible to sleep on. I lay there listening to Jason crunch. The only other noise was the air conditioner, which turned itself off and on constantly to maintain the same, ideal temperature. When it went off, you could hear the insects outside. A small square of light from the opened refrigerator appeared on the dining-room wall. Jason was putting the milk away. The faucet ran for a second, and then Jason walked through the living room, his white underwear bright against his body. I pretended I was asleep.

After a while, the air conditioner went off, but I didn't hear the insects. At some point in the night—the point that seems closer to morning than to evening—they stopped their drone, as though they were unionized and paid to sing only so long. The house was very quiet. In the master bedroom, I could hear bodies moving, and murmuring, but I couldn't tell if it was people making love or turning over and over, trying to get comfortable. It went on for a few minutes, and then it stopped.

We were staying at Uncle Walter's for a week, and every hour of every day was planned. We always had a morning activity and an afternoon activity. Then we had cocktail hour, then dinner, then some card game. Usually hearts, with the teams switching: some nights Jason and Walter versus my parents, some nights the brothers challenging Jason and my mother. I never played. I watched TV, or rode Jason's moped around the deserted roads of Gretna Green, which was the name of Uncle Walter's condominium village. The houses in Gretna Green were called villas, and they all had different names—some for gems, some for colors, and some for animals. Uncle Walter and Jason lived in Villa Indigo.

We started each morning on the patio, where we'd eat

breakfast and "plan the day." The adults took a long time planning the day so there would be less day to spend. All the other villa inhabitants ate breakfast on their patios, too. The patios were separated by lawn and rock gardens and pine trees, but there wasn't much privacy: Everyone could see everyone else sitting under uniformly striped umbrellas, but everyone pretended he couldn't. They were mostly old people, retired people. Children were allowed only as guests. Everyone looked at me as if I was a freak.

Wednesday morning, Uncle Walter was inside making coffee in the new coffee machine my parents had brought him. My mother told me that whenever you're invited to someone's house overnight you should bring something—a hostess gift. Or a host gift, she added. She was helping Uncle Walter make breakfast. Jason was lying on a chaise in the sun, trying to even out his tan. My father was reading the *Wall Street Journal*. He got up early every morning and drove into town and bought it, so he could "stay in touch." My mother made him throw it away right after he read it so it wouldn't interfere with the rest of the day.

Jason had his eyes closed, but he was talking. He was listing the things we could do that day. I was sitting on the edge of a big planter filled with pachysandra and broken statuary that Leonard, my uncle's ex-boyfriend, had dug up somewhere. Leonard was an archaeologist. He used to teach paleontology at Northern Arizona University, but he didn't get tenure, so he took a job with an oil company in South America, making sure the engineers didn't drill in sacred spots. The day before, I'd seen a tiny, purple-throated lizard in the vines, and I was trying to find him again. I wanted to catch him and take him back to Oregon.

Jason paused in his list, and my father said, "Uh-huh." That's what he always says when he's reading the newspaper and you talk to him.

"We could go to the dinosaur museum," Jason said.

"What's that?" I said.

Jason sat up and looked at me. That was the first thing I'd said to him, I think. I'd been ignoring him.

"Well, I've never been there," he said. Even though it was early in the morning, his brown forehead was already beaded with sweat. "It has some reconstructed dinosaurs and footprints and stuff."

"Let's go there," I said. "I like dinosaurs."

"Uh-huh," said my father.

My mother came through the sliding glass doors carrying a platter of scrambled eggs. Uncle Walter followed with the coffee.

"We're going to go to the dinosaur museum this morning," Jason said.

"Please, not that pit," Uncle Walter said.

"But Evan wants to go," Jason said. "It's about time we did something he liked."

Everyone looked at me. "It doesn't matter," I said.

"Oh, no," Uncle Walter said. "Actually, it's fascinating. It just brings back bad memories."

As it turned out, Uncle Walter and my father stayed home to discuss their finances. My grandmother had left them her money jointly, and they're always arguing about how to invest it. Jason drove my mother and me out to the dinosaur museum. I think my mother came just because she didn't want to leave me alone with Jason. She doesn't trust Uncle Walter's friends, but she doesn't let on. My father thinks it's very important we all treat Uncle Walter normally. Once he hit Jackie because she called Uncle Walter a fag. That's the only time he's ever hit either of us.

The dinosaur museum looked like an airplane hangar in the middle of the desert. Inside, trenches were dug into the earth and bones stuck out of their walls. They were still exhuming some of the skeletons. The sand felt oddly damp. My mother took off her sandals and carried them; Jason looked around quickly, and then went outside and sat on the hood of the car, smoking, with his shirt off. At the gift stand, I bought a small bag of dinosaur bone chips. My mother bought a 3-D panoramic postcard. When you held it one way, a dinosaur stood with a creature in its toothy mouth. When you tilted it, the creature disappeared. Swallowed.

On the way home, we stopped at a Safeway to do some grocery shopping. Both Jason and my mother seemed reluctant to push the shopping cart, so I did. In the produce aisle, Jason picked up cantaloupes and shook them next to his ear. A few feet away, my mother folded back the husks to get a good look at the kernels on the corncobs. It seemed as if everyone was pawing at the food. It made me nervous, because once, when I was little, I opened up a box of chocolate Ding Dongs in the grocery store and started eating one, and the manager came over and yelled at me. The only good thing about that was that my mother was forced to buy the Ding Dongs, but every time I ate one I felt sick.

A man in Bermuda shorts and a yellow cardigan sweater started talking to Jason. My mother returned with six apparently decent ears of corn. She dumped them into the cart. "Who's that?" she asked me, meaning the man Jason was talking to.

"I don't know," I said. The man made a practice golf swing, right there in the produce aisle. Jason watched him. Jason was a golf pro at a country club. He used to be part of the golf tour you see on television on weekend afternoons, but he quit. Now he gave lessons at the country club. Uncle Walter had been one of his pupils. That's how they met.

"It's hard to tell," Jason was saying. "I'd try opening up your stance a little more." He put a cantaloupe in our shopping cart.

"Hi," the man said to us.

"Mr. Baird, I'd like you to meet my wife, Ann," Jason said.

Mr. Baird shook my mother's hand. "How come we never see you down the club?"

"Oh . . ." my mother said.

"Ann hates golf," Jason said.

"And how 'bout you?" The man looked at me. "Do you like golf?"

"Sure," I said.

"Well, we'll have to get you out on the links. Can you beat your dad?"

"Not yet," I said.

"It won't be long," Mr. Baird said. He patted Jason on the shoulder. "Nice to see you, Jason. Nice to meet you, Mrs. Jerome."

He walked down the aisle and disappeared into the bakery section. My mother and I both looked at Jason. Even though it was cold in the produce aisle, he was sweating. No one said anything for a few seconds. Then my mother said, "Evan, why don't you go find some Doritos? And some Gatorade, too, if you want."

Back at Villa Indigo, my father and Uncle Walter were playing cribbage. Jason kissed Uncle Walter on the top of his semibald head. My father watched and then stood up and kissed my mother. I didn't kiss anyone.

Thursday, my mother and I went into Flagstaff to buy new school clothes. Back in Portland, when we go into malls, we separate and make plans to meet at a specified time and place, but this was different: It was a strange mall, and since it was school clothes, my mother would pay for them, and therefore she could help pick them out. So we shopped together, which we hadn't done in a while. It was awkward. She pulled things off the rack which I had ignored, and when I started looking at the Right Now for Young Men stuff she entered the Traditional Shoppe. We finally bought some underwear, and some orange and yellow socks, which my mother said were "fun."

Then we went to the shoe store. I hate trying on shoes. I wish the salespeople would just give you the box and let you try them on yourself. There's something about someone else doing it all—especially touching your feet—that embarrasses me. It's as if the person was your servant or something. And in this case the salesperson was a girl about my age, and I could tell she thought I was weird, shopping with my mother. My mother sat in the chair beside me, her pocketbook in her

lap. She was wearing sneakers with little bunny-rabbit tails
sticking out the back from her socks.

"Stand up," the girl said.

I stood up.

"How do they feel?" my mother asked.

"OK," I said.

"Walk around," my mother commanded.

I walked up the aisle, feeling everyone watching me. Then I
walked back and sat down. I bent over and unlaced the shoes.

"So what do you think?" my mother asked.

The girl stood there, picking her nails. "They look very
nice," she said.

I just wanted to get out of there. "I like them," I said. We
bought the shoes.

On the way home, we pulled into a gas station–bar in the
desert. "I can't face Villa Indigo without a drink," my mother
said.

"What do you mean?" I asked.

"Nothing," she said. "Are you having a good time?"

"Now?"

"No. On this trip. At Uncle Walter's."

"I guess so," I said.

"Do you like Jason?"

"Better than Leonard."

"Leonard was strange," my mother said. "I never warmed to
Leonard."

We got out of the car and walked into the bar. It was dark
inside, and empty. A fat woman sat behind the bar, making
something out of papier-mâché. It looked like one of those
statues of the Virgin Mary people have in their front yards.
"Hiya," she said. "What can I get you?"

My mother asked for a beer and I asked for some cranberry
juice. They didn't have any, so I ordered a Coke. The woman
got my mother's beer from a portable cooler like the ones you
take to football games. It seemed very unprofessional. Then
she sprayed Coke into a glass with one of those shower-head

things. My mother and I sat at a table in the sun, but it wasn't hot, it was cold. Above us, the air conditioner dripped.

My mother drank her beer from the long-necked green bottle. "What do you think your sister's doing right now?" she asked.

"What time is it?"

"Four."

"Probably getting ready to go to work. Taking a shower."

My mother nodded. "Maybe we'll call her tonight."

I laughed because my mother called her every night. She would always make Jackie explain all the noises in the background. "It sounds like a party to me," she kept repeating.

My Coke was flat. It tasted weird, too. I watched the woman at the bar. She was poking at her statue with a swizzlestick—putting in eyes, I thought.

"How would you like to go see the Petrified Forest?" my mother asked.

"We're going to another national park?" On the way to Uncle Walter's, we had stopped at the Grand Canyon and taken a mule ride down to the river. Halfway down, my mother got hysterical, fell off her mule, and wouldn't get back on. A helicopter had to fly into the canyon and rescue her. It was horrible to see her like that.

"This one's perfectly flat," she said. "And no mules."

"When?" I said.

"We'd go down on Saturday and come back to Walter's on Monday. And leave for home Tuesday."

The bar woman brought us a second round of drinks. We had not asked for them. My Coke glass was still full. My mother drained her beer bottle and looked at the new one. "Oh dear," she said. "I guess we look like we need it."

The next night, at six-thirty, as my parents left for their special anniversary dinner in Flagstaff, the automatic lawn sprinklers went on. They were activated every evening. Jason explained that if the lawns were watered during the day the beads of moisture would magnify the sun's rays and burn the grass. My parents walked through the whirling water, got in their car, and drove away.

Jason and Uncle Walter were making dinner for me—steaks, on their new electric barbecue. I think they thought steak was a good, masculine food. Instead of charcoal, their grill had little lava rocks on the bottom. They reminded me of my dinosaur bone chips.

The steaks came in packs of two, so Uncle Walter was cooking up four. The fourth steak worried me. Who was it for? Would we split it? Was someone else coming to dinner?

"You're being awfully quiet," Uncle Walter said. For a minute, I hoped he was talking to the steaks—they weren't sizzling—so I didn't answer.

Then Uncle Walter looked over at me. "Cat got your tongue?" he asked.

"What cat?" I said.

"The cat," he said. "The proverbial cat. The big cat in the sky."

"No," I said.

"Then talk to me."

"I don't talk on demand," I said.

Uncle Walter smiled down at his steaks, lightly piercing them with his chef's fork. "Are you a freshman?" he asked.

"Well, a sophomore now," I said.

"How do you like being a sophomore?"

My lizard appeared from beneath a crimson leaf and clicked his eyes in all directions, checking out the evening.

"It's not something you like or dislike," I said. "It's something you are."

"Ah," Uncle Walter said. "So you're a fatalist?"

I didn't answer. I slowly reached out my hand toward the lizard, even though I was too far away to touch it. He clicked his eyes toward me but didn't move. I think he recognized me. My arm looked white and disembodied in the evening light.

Jason slid open the terrace doors, and the music from the

stereo was suddenly loud. The lizard darted back under the foliage.

"I need a prep chef," Jason said. "Get in here, Evan."

I followed Jason into the kitchen. On the table was a wooden board, and on that was a tomato, an avocado, and an apple. Jason handed me a knife. "Chop those up," he said.

I picked up the avocado. "Should I peel this?" I asked. "Or what?"

Jason took the avocado and sliced it in half. One half held the pit and the other half held nothing. Then he pulled the warty skin off in two curved pieces and handed the naked globes back to me. "Now chop it."

I started chopping the stuff. Jason took three baked potatoes out of the oven. I could tell they were hot by the way he tossed them onto the counter. He made slits in them and forked the white stuffing into a bowl.

"What are you doing?" I asked.

"Making baked potatoes," he said. He sliced butter into the bowl.

"But why are you taking the potato out of the skin?"

"Because these are stuffed potatoes. You take the potato out and doctor it up and then put it back in. Do you like cheese?"

"Yes," I said.

"Do you like chives?"

"I don't know," I said. "I've never had them."

"You've never had chives?"

"My mother makes normal food," I said. "She leaves the potato in the skin."

"That figures," Jason said.

After dinner, we went to the driving range. Jason bought two large buckets and we followed him upstairs to the second level. I sat on a bench and watched Jason and my uncle hit ball after ball out into the floodlit night. Sometimes the balls arched up into the darkness, then reappeared as they fell.

Uncle Walter wasn't too good. A few times, he topped the ball and it dribbled over the edge and fell on the grass right below us. When that happened, he looked around to see who noticed, and winked at me.

"Do you want to hit some?" he asked me, offering his club.

"Sure," I said. I was on the golf team last fall, but this spring I played baseball. I think golf is an elitist sport. Baseball is more democratic.

I teed up a ball and took a practice swing, because my father, who taught me to play golf, told me always to take a practice swing. Always. My first shot was pretty good. It didn't go too far, but it went straight out and bounced a ways before I lost track of it in the shadows. I hit another.

Jason, who was in the next cubicle, put down his club and watched me. "You have a great natural swing," he said.

His attention bothered me, and I almost missed my next ball. It rolled off the tee. I picked it up and reteed it.

"Wait," Jason said. He walked over and stood behind me. "You're swinging much too hard." He leaned over me so that he was embracing me from behind, his large tan hands on top of mine, holding the club. "Now, just relax," he said, his voice right beside my cheek.

I tried to relax, but I couldn't. I suddenly felt very hot.

"OK," Jason said, "nice and easy. Keep the left arm straight." He raised his arms, and with them the club. Then we swung through, and he held the club still in the air, pointed out into the night. He let go of the club and ran his hand along my left arm, from my wrist up to my shoulder. "Straight," he said. "Keep it nice and straight." Then he stepped back and told me to try another swing by myself.

I did.

"Looking good," Jason said.

"Why don't you finish the bucket?" my uncle said. "I'm going down to get a beer."

Jason returned to his stall and resumed his practice. I teed up another ball, hit it, then another, and another, till I'd established a rhythm, whacking ball after ball, and all around me clubs were cutting the night, filling the sky with tiny white meteorites.

Back at Villa Indigo, the sprinklers had stopped but the insects were making their strange noise in the trees. Jason and I went for a swim while my uncle watched TV. Jason wore a bathing suit like the swimmers in the Olympics: red-white-and-blue, and shaped like underwear. We walked out the terrace doors and across the wet lawn toward the pool, which was deserted and glowed bright blue. Jason dived in and swam some laps. I practiced diving off the board into the deep end, timing my dives so they wouldn't interfere with him. After about ten laps, he started treading water in the deep end and looked up at me. I was bouncing on the diving board.

"Want to play a game?" he said.

"What?"

Jason swam to the side and pulled himself out of the pool. "Jump or Dive," he said. "We'll play for money."

"How do you play?"

"Don't you know anything?" Jason said. "What do you do in Ohio?"

"It's Oregon," I said. "Not much."

"I can believe it. This is a very simple game. One person jumps off the diving board—jumps high—and when he's at the very highest the other person yells either 'Jump' or 'Dive,' and the person has to dive if the other person yells 'Dive' and jump if he yells 'Jump.' If you do the wrong thing, you owe the guy a quarter. OK?"

"OK," I said. "You go first."

I stepped off the diving board and Jason climbed on. "The higher you jump, the more time you have to twist," he said.

"Go," I said. "I'm ready."

Jason took three steps and sprang, and I yelled, "Dive." He did.

He got out of the pool, grinning. "OK," he said. "Your turn."

I sprang off the board and heard Jason yell, "Jump," but I was already falling forward head first. I tried to twist backward, but it was still a dive.

"You owe me a quarter," Jason said when I surfaced. He was

standing on the diving board, bouncing. I swam to the side. "Here I go," he said.

I waited till he was coming straight down toward the water, feet first, before I yelled, "Dive," but somehow Jason somersaulted forward and dived into the pool.

We played for about fifteen minutes, until I owed Jason two dollars and twenty-five cents and my body was covered with red welts from smacking the water at bad angles. Suddenly the lights in the pool went off.

"It must be ten o'clock," Jason said. "Time for the geriatrics to go to bed."

The black water looked cold and scary. I got out and sat in a chair. We hadn't brought towels with us, and I shivered. Jason stayed in the pool.

"It's warmer in the water," he said.

I didn't say anything. With the lights off in the pool, the stars appeared brighter in the sky. I leaned my head back and looked up at them.

Something landed with a splat on the concrete beside me. It was Jason's bathing suit. I could hear him in the pool. He was swimming slowly underwater, coming up for a breath and then disappearing again. I knew that at some point he'd get out of the water and be naked, so I walked across the lawn toward Villa Indigo. Inside, I could see Uncle Walter lying on the couch, watching TV.

Later that night, I woke up hearing noises in the kitchen. I assumed it was Jason, but then I heard talking, and realized it was my parents, back from their anniversary dinner.

I got up off the couch and went into the kitchen. My mother was leaning against the counter, drinking a glass of seltzer. My father was sitting on one of the barstools, smoking a cigarette. He put it out when I came in. He's not supposed to smoke anymore. We made a deal in our family last year involving his quitting: My mother would lose fifteen pounds, my sister would take Science Honors (and pass), and I was supposed to brush Princess Leia, our dog, every day without having to be told.

"Our little baby," my mother said. "Did we wake you up?"

"Yes," I said.

"This is the first one I've had in months," my father said. "Honest. I just found it lying here."

"I told him he could smoke it," my mother said. "As a special anniversary treat."

"How was dinner?" I asked.

"OK," my mother said. "The restaurant didn't turn around, though. It was broken."

"That's funny," my father said. "I could have sworn it was revolving."

"You were just drunk," my mother said.

"Oh, no," my father said. "It was the stars in my eyes." He leaned forward and kissed my mother.

She finished her seltzer, rinsed the glass, and put it in the sink. "I'm going to bed," she said. "Good night."

My father and I both said good night, and my mother walked down the hall. My father picked up his cigarette. "It wasn't even very good," he said. He looked at it, then held it under his nose and smelled it. "It think it was stale. Just my luck."

I took the cigarette butt out of his hands and threw it away. When I turned around, he was standing by the terrace doors, looking out at the dark trees. It was windy.

"Have you made up your mind?" he asked.

"About what?"

"The trip."

"What trip?"

My father turned away from the terrace. "Didn't Mom tell you? Uncle Walter said you could stay here while Mom and I went down to see the Petrified Forest. If you want to. You can come with us otherwise."

"Oh," I said.

"I think Uncle Walter would like it if he had some time

alone with you. I don't think he feels very close to you anymore. And he feels bad Jackie didn't come."

"Oh," I said. "I don't know."

"Is it because of Jason?"

"No," I said.

"Because I'd understand if it was."

"No," I said, "it's not that. I like Jason. I just don't know if I
want to stay here. . . ."

"Well, it's no big deal. Just two days." My father reached up
and turned off the light. It was a dual overhead light and fan,
and the fan spun around some in the darkness, each spin
slower. My father put his hands on my shoulders and half
pushed, half guided me back to the couch. "It's late," he said.
"See you tomorrow."

I lay on the couch. I couldn't fall asleep, because I knew
that in a while Jason would be up for his snack. That kept me
awake, and the decision about what to do. For some reason, it
did seem like a big deal: going or staying. I could still picture
my mother, backed up against the wall of the Grand Canyon,
as far from the cliff as possible, crying, her mule braying, the
helicopter whirring in the sky above us. It seemed like a choice
between that and Jason swimming in the dark water, slowly
and nakedly. I didn't want to be there for either.

The thing was, after I sprang off the diving board I did hear
Jason shout, but my brain didn't make any sense of it. I could
just feel myself hanging there, above the horrible, bright blue
water, but I couldn't make my body turn, even though I was
dropping dangerously, and much too fast.

FAMILY
MATTERS

·····©©©©©·····

Bastard Out of Carolina

●●●●

DOROTHY ALLISON

"Don't you ever let me catch you stealing," Mama commanded
in one of her rare lectures, after Cousin Grey got caught running out of the White Horse Winn Dixie with a bargain quart
of RC Cola. "You want something, you tell me, and if it's worth
the trouble we'll find a way. But I an't gonna have no child of
mine caught stealing."

I took Mama at her word and hung around with my cousins
Garvey and Grey, planning not to get caught and not to tell
Mama. But one afternoon after I produced Tootsie Rolls for
Reese and me, Mama took my hands in hers like she was going
to cry.

"Where'd you get them?"

"Uncle Earle," I suggested.

"No." Mama dropped down a little so her face was close to
mine.

"Aunt Alma." Carefully, I made my face a mask.

"Don't lie too." The lines in her face looked as deep as the rivers that flowed south toward Charleston. "Tell me the truth."

I started to cry. "Downtown with Grey and Garvey this morning, at the Woolworth's counter."

Mama used her forefinger to wipe the tears off my cheeks. She wiped her own. "Is this all of it? How many did you take?"

"Two others, Mama. I ate one, gave Reese one."

Mama leaned back in her chair, dropping my hands. She shook a cigarette out of the pack and lit it carefully. I sat still, watching her, waiting. Tears kept collecting in the corners of my eyes, and I had to turn to wipe them away on my shoulder, but I kept watching Mama's face as she sat and smoked without looking at me. The fingers of her right hand rubbed together steadily like the legs of grasshoppers I had seen climbing up the long grass at Aunt Raylene's place. Her lips moved steadily too, as if she were sucking on her teeth or about to speak, but she was quiet a long time, just sitting there looking off through the open window smoking her cigarette.

"You know your cousin Tommy Lee? Aunt Ruth's oldest boy?"

I frowned, trying to remember their names. There was Dwight, I knew, Lucius, D. W., Graham, yeah, Tommy Lee, and Butch. Aunt Ruth had only two daughters and six boys, most of them married with boys of their own. All of them were so alike that I never could keep track of anyone but Butch, and I rarely saw him anymore since he had gone to live with Ruth's oldest girl, Mollie, in Oklahoma. The younger boys turned up occasionally to wrestle Reese and me, give us candy, or tell us stories. The older ones had the sunken eyes and planed faces of men, and they never gave us anything except nasty looks. I couldn't have said which of the older ones was Tommy Lee, though I'd heard people talk about him enough —about what a hardass he was, about his girlfriends and his dirty mouth, his stints in the county jail, and the fights he got into.

"He's bad," Mama said, her eyes still looking out the window. He's just bad all the way through. He steals from his mama. He's stolen from me. Don't dare leave your pocketbook around him, or any of your stuff that he could sell. He even took Deedee's green stamp books one time and traded them off for some useless thing." Her eyes drifted back to my face, the stunned brown of the pupils shining like mossy rocks under water.

"I remember when we were just kids and he was always stealing candy to give away. Thought people would like him if he gave them stuff, I suppose. Now he's always saying how he's been robbed, and he's got a story to account for everything he does. Beats his girlfriends up 'cause they cheat on him. Can't keep a job 'cause people tell lies about him. Steals 'cause the world's been so cruel to him. So much nonsense. He's just bad, that's all, just bad. Steals from his mama and sisters, steals from his own."

I dropped my head. I remembered Grey telling me how he learned to break locks from Tommy Lee, that Tommy Lee was the slickest piece of goods in Greenville. "Boy knows how to take care of himself for sure. Never owes nobody nothing." Grey's face had flushed with respect and envy when he said it, and I had felt a little of the same—wishing I too knew how to take care of myself and could break locks or start cars without a key or palm stuff off a counter so smoothly that no one would know I had done it. But to steal from your mama! My face felt stiff with shame and anger. I wasn't like that. I would never steal from Mama.

Mama's hand touched my chin, trailed along my cheek, and stroked my hair. "You're my pride. Do you know? You and your sister are all I really have, all I ever will have. You think I could let you grow up to be like that?"

I shook my head. The tears started again, and with them hiccups. Mama went and got a cool washcloth to wet my face. "Don't cry, honey. It'll be all right. We'll take care of it, it'll be all right." She put the Tootsie Rolls in a paper bag and gave me a handful of pennies to carry. She kept talking while she brushed my hair and then hers, called Reese in and told her to stay on the porch, turned the heat down on the beans that were cooking on the stove, and walked me out to the car. She told me about when she and Aunt Raylene were girls, how they had worked for this man out past Old Henderson Road, picking strawberries for pennies every day for weeks, going through the rows and pulling loose the red ripe ones for him to sell in his stand by the side of the road.

"Only the ripe ones, he kept telling us, but it was so hot and the dust was so thick, sometimes we'd pull up the ones that weren't quite ripe, you know—green ones, or half-green anyway. We'd hide them under the ripe ones when we set them up for him. People would buy a box and then get home to find those half-ripe ones, call him up to complain. He'd get so mad, but we were just kids, and his yelling didn't bother us so long as he kept paying us for the work."

"What'd he pay you?"

Mama waved her hand as if that didn't matter. "Not enough, you know, not enough. Strawberry picking is terrible work, hurts your back, your eyes. You get that juice all over you, get those little prickers in your hands. An't enough money in it even for children, even if you eat as many as you can. After a while you don't want any anyway." She laughed.

"Though Raylene sure could eat a lot. Faster than you could see, she'd swallow handfuls of berries. Only proof she'd been eating them was her red red tongue."

She stopped the car in front of the Woolworth's, cut the engine, and sat for a moment, her hands resting on the wheel. I looked out at the big display windows, where stacks of plastic picnic baskets, little tin office waste cans, and sleeveless cotton sundresses on hangers were squeezed behind ratty stuffed animals and tricycles with multicolored plastic streamers on the handlebars. The thought of going back in there with Mama made me feel sick to my stomach and almost angry at her. Why couldn't she just let me promise never to do it again?

Her hand on my shoulder made me jump. "Your granny found out what we'd been doing, 'cause we got lazy, you know, and started putting more and more green ones in the bottom of the boxes. Grandpa laughed about it, but your granny didn't laugh. She came over there one afternoon and turned half a dozen boxes upside down. Collected a bucket of green strawberries and paid the man for them. Took us home, sat us at the kitchen table, and made us eat every one of them. Raylene and I puked strawberries all night long."

"You must have hated her!"

Mama was quiet, and I got scared. I didn't want her to think I hated her. I didn't even want to be angry at her. I clamped my teeth tight and tried not to start crying again.

"There an't no other way to do it," she said quietly. "I hate it. You hate it. You might hate me for it. I don't know, and I can't say what might happen now. But I just don't know no other way to do it. We're gonna go in there and give the man back his candy, pay for what you ate, and that will be all there is to it. It will be over, and you'll be glad it's settled. We won't ever have to mention it again."

Mama opened the door briskly, and I followed her numbly. There was a flush on her cheeks as she walked me back to the candy counter, waited for the salesgirl to come over, and stood me right in front of her. "My daughter has something to tell you," she said, and gave me a little push. But I couldn't speak. I held out the bag and the pennies, and started to cry again, this time sobbing loud. The girl looked confused, but Mama wouldn't say anything else, just gave me another little push. I thought I'd strangle on my tongue when the manager walked over to us.

"What's this?" he said in a booming voice. "What's this? You got something for us, little girl?" He was a big man with a wide face and a swollen belly poking out from under a buttoned-up vest. He stopped down so that his face was right in front of me, so close I could smell the sharp alcohol scent of after-shave.

"You do, don'tcha, honey?" He looked like he was swallowing an urge to laugh at us. I was suddenly so angry at him my stomach seemed to curl up inside me. I shoved the bag at him, the pennies.

"I stole it. I'm sorry. I stole it."

Mama's hand squeezed my shoulder, and I heard the breath come out of her in a sigh. I closed my eyes for a moment, trying hard not to get as mad at her as I was at that man.

"Uh-huh," he said. "I see." I looked up at him again. He was rummaging in the bag, counting the Tootsie Rolls and nodding. "It's a good thing, ma'am," he said, still talking loudly, "that you caught this when you did." He nodded at me. "You're a fortunate little girl, truly fortunate. Your mama loves you. She doesn't want you to grow up to be a thief."

He stood back up and passed the pennies to the salesgirl. He stretched a hand out like he was going to put it on my head, but I stepped back so that he would have had to bend forward to reach me. "Son of a bitch," Grey would have called him, "slimy son of a bitch probably eats Tootsie Rolls all day long." If he reached for me again, I decided, I'd bite him, but he just looked at me long and carefully. I knew I was supposed to feel ashamed, but I didn't anymore. I felt outraged. I wanted to kick him or throw up on him or scream his name on the street. The longer he looked at me, the more I hated him. If I could have killed him with my stare, I would have. The look in his eyes told me that he knew what I was thinking.

"I'm gonna do your mama a favor." He smiled. "Help her to teach you the seriousness of what you've done." Mama's hand tightened on my shoulder, but she didn't speak.

"What we're gonna do," he announced, "is say you can't come back in here for a while. We'll say that when your mama thinks you've learned your lesson, she can come back and talk to me. But till then, we're gonna remember your name, what you look like." He leaned down again. "You understand me, honey?"

I understood. I understood that I was barred from the Woolworth's counters. I could feel the heat from my mama's hand through my blouse, and I knew she was never going to come near this place again, was never going to let herself stand in the same room with that honey-greased bastard. I looked around at the bright hairbrushes, ribbons, trays of panties and socks, notebooks, dolls, and balloons. It was hunger I felt then, raw and terrible, a shaking deep down inside me, as if my rage had used up everything I had ever eaten.

After that, when I passed the Woolworth's windows, it would come back—that dizzy desperate hunger edged with hatred and an aching lust to hurt somebody back. I wondered if that kind of hunger and rage was what Tommy Lee felt when he went through his mama's pocketbook. It was a hunger in the back of the throat, not the belly, an echoing emptiness that ached for the release of screaming.

Where Is It Written?

◉◉◉◉

ADAM SCHWARTZ

Three months before my thirteenth birthday, I persuaded my father to sue my mother for custody of me. This was in late August, near the end of a two-week visit with my father. I wrote my mother a letter informing her of my decision. I told her I knew she might be disappointed, but I wasn't rejecting her; I only wanted to spend more time with my father, to know and love him as well as I knew her. I also told her not to call me. We could discuss this when I returned home, if she wanted to.

She called the second the letter came. Phyllis, my father's wife, answered the phone. "Hold on, Sandra," she said, and held the phone out to me, her palm covering the receiver. I shook my head. Phyllis gave me an exasperated look, and told my mother I was busy. She called three more times in the next hour. I knew this was going to happen, but I was not even thirteen, and I wanted to forget how well I knew my mother.

Phyllis agreed to relay her messages to me: How long should she preheat the oven for my lemon-chicken recipe? Should she run hot or cold water when scrubbing the sink with Comet? What should she do if the washing machine stopped in mid-cycle? I had typed out three pages of instructions before I left, but the calls kept coming right through dinner. Could she use ammonia on Formica surfaces? Should she use tap or distilled water in the iron? Finally, Phyllis exclaimed, "Jesus, Sandra, we're eating. He'll be home in two days." Then I watched her face darken and imagined the blast my mother was delivering: "Don't you tell me when I can talk to my own son. I'm his mother, and when I tell you to get him, you jump—understand?" Phyllis hung up the phone and sat back down at the table, her lips drawn across her face like a thin white scar. Ten seconds later the phone rang again. My father and Phyllis looked at each other. I felt like Jonah hiding in the bowels of the ship, knowing the storm above was all his fault. No one moved. "Mommy, the phone is ringing," shouted Debbie, my little stepsister. "Maybe you should answer the phone, Sam," my father said. I stood up from the table very slowly, giving myself every chance that the phone might stop ringing before I reached it.

"What's the problem, Mom? I wrote everything down."

"You little bastard! Don't bother coming home. If I never see you again I'll die happy!"

My father wasn't enthusiastic when I asked him to sue. "Lawyers? Court? Not again." My parents divorced when I was four, and the episode still bothered him. He had wanted to work things out quietly, but my mother staged a grand opera. She asked for an exorbitant amount of alimony and minimal visitation rights for my father. She accused him of being an adulterer and a wife beater. My father was a rabbi in a small town on the New Jersey shore and brought in many members of his congregation as character witnesses. My mother had no witnesses on her behalf. She lost every point she argued for.

"But, Dad," I implored, "she's driving me *crazy*!"

He and I usually didn't have a lot to say to each other, but I expected the word *crazy* to explain everything, as if I were revealing to him that we shared the same inherited trouble, like gum disease or premature balding. I pitched my case to him, describing how she moaned during meals about her haywire menstrual cycle, how she slept on the couch every night, sometimes with a cigarette still burning in her hand.

"Do you know how dangerous that is, Dad?"

He pressed his palms up his cheeks, a gesture that always led me to imagine he was trying to stretch his beard over his eyes and forehead. I envisioned him doing the same thing the day he met my mother. When I had asked her, the year before, how they came together—a far more mysterious question to me than where I had come from—she answered, "In the shower." Both were on an archaeological dig in Israel. My father, recently ordained, was covered with soap in the primitive communal shower when my mother walked in, nineteen, naked, enthusiastic about everything. Several months later they were married, but my mother was bored by the life of a rabbi's wife. She had no interest in charity work or Sisterhood meetings. She saw an analyst five times a week and signed up for courses in Sanskrit and criminology. Once she planned a lecture at the synagogue on Gurdjieff's centers of consciousness. Three people came.

I told my father I was fed up with cooking and cleaning, washing and ironing.

"I thought you liked doing housework," he said.

"Not all the time. I want to have a normal life, Dad."

He touched his beard lightly, thoughtfully. I had found the right word.

"Sometimes her boyfriends sleep over. I see them on the sofa bed when I get up in the morning."

"All right, all right."

"Dad, I'm telling you, this is an open-and-shut case. I'm old enough to live with whoever I want. That's the law."

I knew about the law from my mother. She sued everyone. Landlords, universities, car dealers, plumbers, my father. She stayed up all night researching her cases and planning her strategies. In the morning I would see her asleep on the couch, openmouthed, beneath a blanket of ashes and law books and the sheets of legal paper on which she outlined her complex and futile arguments. Years later, after I graduated from law school and returned to New Jersey, many of the older lawyers around the courthouse told me that my mother indeed had a reputation as a compulsive but extremely knowledgeable and creative litigant. "I always thought the law was a metaphysical exercise for her," one of them said to me. " 'I can sue you: therefore I exist.' "

I also learned the art of exaggeration from my mother, the art of how to invent something when the truth is boring or makes you nervous. I had seen her on the sofa bed with a man only once. The year before, she had come into my bedroom very early one morning to tell me that Sy, her sometime boy-friend, had spent the night. "You don't mind that he's here?" she asked, sitting on the side of my bed. Her weight was comforting, as were her warm, heavy, sleepy odors. I told her I didn't mind. "I slept in the other room," she said anxiously. "But I'm going to lie down next to Sy for a couple of minutes."

"All right," I said, and went back to sleep. I knew she liked Sy. She had told me that he had always wanted a boy to raise, that he was personal friends with Joe Namath, that he had a home in Florida. He bought me books, bats, tickets to ball-games. In two years he would go to jail for fraud and income tax evasion, but that morning my mother and I both believed in him. When I went into the living room, he was asleep on his side. My mother was awake, pressed up against his back with an arm around his chest. She smiled at me, as if Sy were some wonderful secret between us, something valuable she had found.

My mother's explosion of telephone calls came on Thursday night; late Sunday afternoon I took the bus from my father's house to the Port Authority. My mother usually met me inside the terminal, but I didn't see her anywhere. I called home six times in the next hour, counting twenty-three rings on the last attempt. The next local bus across the river didn't leave for two hours. I found a bench at a far end of the terminal and, sitting with my suitcase between my knees, watched everyone going home, everyone except for the panhandlers, the proselytizers, the older men sleeping against walls, teenagers who had run away.

My mother wasn't in when I arrived home. She hadn't left a note, and by ten o'clock I still hadn't heard from her. I knew what she was doing. She was letting me know how it felt to be abandoned, to suddenly be alone. I knew she would return the next day, but still I was in tears by the time I was ready for bed. My room felt like the loneliest place in the world that night, so I pulled out the sofa bed. I had never slept in the living room before, and I couldn't orient myself, couldn't gauge the black space around me.

Gradually the darkness lightened into shadows and the shadows into a dull grayness. When I could see everything in the room clearly, I began preparing for the first day of school. I kept thinking, *Now he's brushing his teeth, now he's deciding which shirt to wear, now he's pouring milk over his cereal* . . . as if, without my mother in the house, I were inhabiting someone else's life. I was all ready by six-thirty. I lay back down on the couch and watched the clock for the next hour and forty-five minutes.

At eleven-thirty, during biology, the principal's secretary came to the classroom to tell me my mother had phoned. She told me I was to go right home because of an emergency. The year before, I'd been called out of class about once a month because of an "emergency" at home. Usually my mother had fought with a patient, or a married man she was seeing had stopped answering her calls, or her father had sent her another sanctimonious letter, or some judge had treated her in a cavalier manner.

I declined the secretary's offer of a ride and walked home. When I let myself into the apartment, my mother was sitting at the kitchen table. She held the letter I had written to her in one hand and was burning holes in it with her cigarette. She looked like a curious child torturing a small animal.

"I thought you saw a patient now," I finally said.

She was a psychologist, but had only four regular patients. She used her bedroom as an office, though she longed to have one in town. "Someplace beautiful," she would say. "Some place where I can really be myself."

"I canceled," she said, burning a chain of holes through my name.

"Canceled! What for? That's thirty-five dollars!"

She looked at me for the first time. "Would you please explain this, Sam?"

"I explained everything in the letter."

"Everything? Really? I can think of any number of things you didn't explain. Why you're leaving me, for instance. Can you explain that? Am I really that bad of a mother?"

"I told you I wasn't rejecting you."

"Look, Sam. Let's agree on one thing. Let's agree you're not going to treat me like I'm stupid." She said this slowly and rhythmically, as if I were the stupid one.

"Mom, I just don't want to live here anymore. That's all."

"That's all?"

"I explained. I want to live with my father."

"Tell me the last time he called."

"Maybe he doesn't call because he's afraid you'll sue if he says something you don't like over the phone."

"Oh, I see. Now it's my fault. I'm to blame because your father has no interest in you."

"I didn't say that."

"Then what are you saying? That I'm a failure as a mother?"

"No, Mom. You're not a failure. All right?"

"Then why? *Why* are you doing this to me?"

"God, Mom. I don't know! I just want to lead a normal life."

"*Normal!*" she cried. "What's not normal about the way we live?"

"Everything! The cooking, the cleaning, the shouting. Everything!"

"Who shouts?"

"You do. You're shouting now."

"Of course I am. My son tells me he doesn't want to live with me anymore. Can't I shout about that? Isn't that *normal*?"

"Mom, this conversation is retarded. I'm going back to school."

"And who asked you to cook and clean?" she shouted after me. "Not me. You love to cook. Or is that something else to blame me for?"

"Good-bye, Mom," I said, walking out the door.

"Don't come back, you lousy child! Just see how well you get along without me!"

Before I began cooking and cleaning, my clothing always came out of the wash shrunk and discolored, sending me into fits most mornings because I was embarrassed to wear wrinkled shirts to school and my mother refused to iron them.

"You iron them," she would say. "They're your shirts."

"But I don't know how!"

"Neither do I."

"Yes, you do! You're supposed to know!"

"I am? Where is it written that I'm supposed to know? Tell me! Where?"

For supper she usually boiled pouches of frozen food, and even that gave her problems. "Oh, puke!" I'd say, pursing up my face and coughing out a mouthful of half-frozen meat loaf.

Once, on my birthday, I bought her a cookbook and pleaded with her to learn some recipes.

"Oh, honey, I can't deal with recipes."

"But why?"

"Because nothing ever turns out the way it's supposed to for me."

I began with simple dishes—baked chicken and steamed vegetables, broiled lamb chops and rice. Then I moved on to lasagna, brisket in red wine sauce, curried shrimp, veal scallops with prosciutto, Grand Marnier soufflés, and poached peaches with raspberry puree. I prepared some of my most inspired meals when my mother entertained Sy.

"I don't know how you do it," she would say, anointing herself with perfume as she watched me work in the kitchen.

"It's easy, Mom. All you have to do is read the directions."

"Directions," she replied, "bore me."

❦

When my first day of school ended, I returned home as usual to begin dinner. Mrs. Gutman, my mother's four-thirty patient and close friend, was sitting on the couch. She was a stout Romanian woman with a collapsing beehive of rust-colored hair held vaguely together with hundreds of bobby pins. "Hello, darlink," she greeted me, her accent falling with a thud on the "darlink." I could tell by the sad cast of her eyes that she knew all about my letter.

Mrs. Gutman had been seeing my mother longer than any other patient. Three days a week for four years she had journeyed from her apartment in Staten Island to our apartment in Bergenfield, where her fifty-minute session lasted for hours. She would call at three and four in the morning when nightmares frightened her awake. The ringing phone always exploded in my ears. I sat up in bed, my heart beating violently, as if it were connected to the phone with jumper cables. I couldn't hear my mother's words very clearly, but I would lie awake for hours listening to the dim, low murmur of her voice, a sound as comforting as the patter of rain after an electrical storm.

Mrs. Gutman was the last scheduled patient of the day because her sessions went on so long. Usually I would be preparing dinner when they finished, and Mrs. Gutman would crowd into the tiny kitchen to sample and advise. Pressing her bosom against my rib cage, she stirred, tasted, lifted covers off pots and inhaled deeply. "No, darlink. You must do like dis one," she'd say, sprinkling paprika into a stew that I had delicately seasoned and simmered for hours.

"Great! Now you've ruined it," I'd say, hurling my wooden spoon into the sink.

"No, darlink, was too bland. Taste now."

"Don't call me that. I've told you my name is Sam."

"Yes, Sam, darlink."

Later, after Mrs. Gutman had left, my mother would say, "Why do you have to be so mean to her? Because she's my friend? Is that why?"

"I've told you not to analyze me. I'm not your patient."

"You can't give me credit for my successes, can you? You know how important I am to Mrs. Gutman, but you won't give me credit for it."

"Mom, she's your patient. She shouldn't be wandering into the kitchen. It's unprofessional."

"Mrs. Gutman is one of my dearest friends."

"Well, she shouldn't be. You're her therapist. You're not supposed to be her best friend, too."

"Where is it written that I can't be both? Tell me! If Mrs. Gutman values my friendship, who are you to tell me it's wrong?"

❦

That afternoon Mrs. Gutman stayed only for her scheduled time. When my mother came into the kitchen, I was already eating my dinner, poached turbot. She joined me at the table with peanut butter on stale white bread.

"That smells delicious," she said.

"It is."

"Can I have a taste?"

"No."

"Why not?"

"I'm seeing how well I get along without you."

"Oh, really? Who paid for that?"

I pushed my plate over to her.

"Look, honey, I'm sorry I said that. The truth is that I can't get along without you, either."

"Mom, I just want a change."

"But you don't have to leave. I can change. *I'll change*. You want me to cook? I'll learn to cook. I'll be the best cook in the world. You don't want me sleeping on the couch? I won't sleep on the couch. I'll rent an office in town. How's that? You'll never have to see any of my patients again. Just tell me what you don't like."

I was staring down at the table. Without looking up, I replied, "Mom, I've decided."

She yanked me by the elbow. "You think it's that simple? Do you think some judge is just going to send you to your father because you say you want a change?"

"Do you think there are any judges who don't know about you?"

"What is that supposed to mean?"

"I mean all the lawyers you've spent the night with."

She slapped me across the face. She had never hit me before, and she began to cry, holding her hand as if she had burned it on something.

"You're just like everyone else," she cried. "You're all the same."

I had hoped my mother would just boot me out, hurling suitcases and insults at me, and when she thought to call me back, to apologize and argue some more, I would already be ensconced at my father's house, too far away to hear a thing. But after my father sued, I barely heard her voice. At dinner she would occasionally glance up from her plate to look at me oddly, as if I were a stranger she had just found sitting at her table. If I attempted conversation, she'd either ignore me or say, "Ask your father." I felt sure her silence was purely strategic; I was certain that if I told her I was changing my mind, tears would well in her eyes, all would be forgiven, and she'd vow to change. Some nights, though, after I was in bed and she called up Mrs. Gutman, her voice sounded extremely faint, more so than usual. I kept changing the position of my head on the pillow, but I couldn't tune her in, and after a time she faded out like a voice on the radio during a long drive in the middle of the night.

●

At the end of September, my mother and I visited her father in Florida. He was a dentist, and we saw him twice a year to have our teeth fixed and to be reminded of things we were not supposed to do. I was not supposed to eat sweets because my teeth were low in calcium; my mother was not supposed to "use" cigarettes in public or tell anyone she was divorced. For some reason, he thought it was less embarrassing to introduce her as a widow.

"Your grandfather doesn't know about our problems," she said to me on the plane, "and I don't plan on telling him."

We always went to Florida at the wrong time—either in May or late September, when the air in New Jersey was most delicious, when the perspiration on your face was cooling as a breeze. Usually, we stayed only for two or three days, sunning by the pool of his condominium or accompanying him on the golf course for his daily 6 A.M. game. Neither my mother nor I played, but he was adamant that we come along, as if she and I might get into trouble if we were left alone. By the thirteenth hole she was desperate for a cigarette. She'd quickly light one up as my grandfather was bent over the ball. He'd catch a scent of it and stop his stroke. "Sandra, how many times have I asked you to refrain from doing that in public? Now, put it out." Once the cigarette was lit, she became calmer, drawing deeper into herself with each drag. "Sandra!" She let a long, elegant ash drop to the green.

"Sorry, Daddy," she'd say in a bored voice, as she grasped my shoulder for support and twisted the cigarette against the bottom of her shoe.

On this visit we went straight from the airport to the office. My mother's gums had ached for weeks, but she didn't have the money to see a local dentist. My grandfather ushered her into the chair and instructed her to remove her lipstick. She pressed her lips against a tissue, leaving a red O-shaped print, and then gave it to my grandfather as though she were handing over her mouth. "Sandra," he said over the hum of the drill, "have you heard from the Yoskowitzes' son?" Both his thumbs were in her mouth and she moved her head from side to side. I sat in the dental assistant's chair, where I had a direct view of the bloody saliva swirling underneath my mother's tongue.

"No? Maybe he'll call when you get back. I gave your number to Jack and Ruth to give to him. He lives in Jersey City and sells hospital equipment. They showed me a copy of his tax returns, so I know for certain that he earned $81,000 last year. He thinks you're a widow, so don't say anything to disappoint him. Understand?" Her eyes widened with hurt. I wanted to do something. Unclasp the towel from around her neck, give her back her mouth, and tell her, Run, I'll meet you at the airport. "Let's just hope," he continued, "he doesn't mind that your teeth are so stained with nicotine."

She raised her hand for him to stop. "Daddy, I really don't want to hear this today. My life has been a real shit-hole lately, and I just don't want to hear this." She never glanced at me.

My grandfather held the drill in the air and looked up, like someone about to begin conducting an orchestra. "Some days," he sighed, "I'm almost relieved that Rose is gone." I watched my mother's eyes brimming with tears. When my grandfather noticed, he reached for a needle and asked if she needed more Novocain.

A month before the hearing, and two weeks before my Bar Mitzvah, I went to see a court-appointed psychologist. Florence Fein's office, in a red Victorian house, was a large room crowded with old furniture, oriental rugs, stained glass, and antique lamps. She served me a cup of tea and then asked me what I would like to talk about. I told her I couldn't think of anything.

"Why do you think you're here?" she asked.

"Because I have an appointment."

"Perhaps you can tell me why you don't want to be here."

"Because there's nothing wrong with me."

"You don't have to have something wrong with you to come to a psychologist, Sam. Most people come here just to figure things out."

"But I don't have anything to figure out. I know I want to live with my father."

"No one is keeping you here. You're free to leave."

"Then you'll tell the judge I have to stay with my mother."

"Sam, I'm not here to penalize you for saying the wrong thing. If you really don't want to be here, I'll just write in my report that I couldn't draw any conclusions."

I was uncomfortable with Florence Fein because I knew I could never say a bad word about my mother to a stranger. For a second I wondered if my mother had anticipated this; maybe she hadn't booted me out because she knew I'd turn silent and recalcitrant with psychologists and judges.

"If I go right now, is my mother still going to have to pay for the time?"

"Why do you ask?"

"I feel bad about her spending money for nothing."

"Do you always feel bad about your mother's actions?"

"Sometimes."

"Do you think that would change if you lived with your father?"

"I don't know. . . . Don't you think people can change?"

"Of course. I wouldn't be in this business if I didn't think so." I believed her when she said this, as if change were a reliable commodity. I knew the word didn't hold the same meaning for my mother. When I thought of her pleading "I can change, I'll change!" the words sounded like *"I'm in pain, I'm in pain!"*

"Sam, you probably know that your parents' divorce was very bitter."

"So?"

"Do you think your father has put any subtle pressure on you to come live with him?"

"Did my mother say that?"

"Not at all. As a matter of fact, she argued that your father wasn't all that interested in having you live with him and that you might be deeply hurt once that became a reality for you."

"What else did she say?"

"She said she's failed at everything she's ever tried, and she doesn't want to fail as a parent."

We looked at each other for a long two or three seconds;

and in that moment I felt the whole weight of my mother's life, as if Florence Fein had placed in my cup a teaspoonful of matter from a black hole, weighing millions and millions of tons.

The day before my Bar Mitzvah, my mother informed me that she was planning on showing up. I acted surprised, but deep down I had expected it.

"You're not religious," I argued.

She was driving me to the Port Authority.

'You know this isn't a question of religion. You just don't want me to come. Admit it."

"But you're always saying that my father's friends are against you. You'll have to face all of them if you come."

"And so why should they be at my son's Bar Mitzvah and not me?"

"Mom, that's not a reason to go."

"Oh, and are your reasons any better? You just want all your father's friends to think you're more your father's son. You want them to think, My, hasn't he turned out so nice and polite despite his mother."

"I told you not to analyze me! I'm not your goddamned patient!"

We entered the Lincoln Tunnel, and I was truly afraid that she might stop the car in the middle of it and order me out. We hadn't talked that way in months. But she didn't say anything until we pulled up to the bus terminal. "Talk to your father that way sometime," she said, "and see how long he lets you live with him."

That evening Phyllis fixed a traditional Sabbath meal. My father invited six couples from his congregation to join us. My mother had warned me about all of them at one time or another. They were too interested and too familiar with me, as if I were a disfigured child and they were pretending not to notice. Before we had finished the soup and melon, they asked me which subject I liked the most in school (social studies), whether I was a Yankee or a Met fan (neither—the Dodgers), whether I, too, planned on becoming a rabbi (no, a gourmet chef). Everyone gave me a pained smile. I was thinking of the last elaborate meal I'd prepared for my mother and Sy, and how I loved standing in the kitchen with her, minutes before he came to the door. My mother and the pots rattled with expectancy: would this be the man to stay with her, to adjust our haphazard course? The kitchen smelled rich with promise, as if the scent of her perfume and the odors of my cooking held the power to transform our lives, to transport us from our crowded, chaotic apartment into a large house, where we all had our own rooms, where my mother would be calm, secure, loved.

After we returned from services that evening, I told my father and Phyllis that my mother would probably show up the next morning. They looked at each other.

"Oh, Sam," my father sighed. "Couldn't you have done something?"

"No, Dad. She wants to come."

"Doesn't she know how uncomfortable this is going to be?" Phyllis said.

"Mommy, who's coming?" Debbie asked.

"Nobody, dear. Nobody."

I didn't say anything, and I went to bed feeling just like everyone else.

The next morning, I stepped up to the Torah and saw my mother sitting in a row of empty seats. She waved at me like someone in a lifeboat attempting to flag a distant ship. Everyone's eyes moved from her to me. I brought my tallis to my lips and began chanting in a language I didn't understand. From behind me, the sun beamed through a stained-glass mural. The light washed over me and the colors skated back and forth across the parchment, echoing the manic movements of my heart.

After the service, she rushed over to the receiving line and reclaimed me with a long, long embrace. She had not held or kissed me in months. Several people waiting to greet me formed an uncomfortable semicircle around us. She tightened

her hold, as if I were a charm to ward off bad spirits. People
began to file away. Soon we were standing alone, like two
strangers who had wandered into the wrong celebration. Then
Phyllis came over to tell me that the photographer was set up
for a family portrait. My mother squeezed my elbow.

"You stay right here, Sam."

"We'll only be five minutes," Phyllis said impatiently.
"Come, Sam."

She reached for me and my mother slapped her hand away.
Phyllis looked at her hand as if she had never seen it before.

"I'm his family," my mother said. "If the photographer wants
a portrait, he can come over here."

"Crazy woman," Phyllis murmured, and turned away. My
mother caught her on the side of the head with her purse.
Phyllis whirled around, crying "Oh! Oh!" more in disbelief
than in pain. My mother lunged at her. Both women grabbed
at each other's hair and face. They teetered back and forth in
their high heels. I could hear nylons whispering against nylons. My father rushed over, his hand raised and his black
robes billowing. I ran out.

I kept running until I reached the beach, breathless. Each
gulp of the November air stung my lungs. I wrapped my tallis
around my neck and walked rapidly through the sand. Then I
heard my mother shout my name. I turned around. She was
perhaps a hundred yards behind me, her shoes in her hands.
She crossed them above her head, signaling me to stop. I
walked down to the shoreline.

I recalled how she and I used to come to this same beach
on winter afternoons when my parents were still married. She
hated the summer crowds, but liked the remoteness of the
beach in winter. Once we came with a helium balloon she had
bought me at a nearby amusement park. At the shoreline she
had bent down beside me and we placed our fingertips all over
its shiny red surface. "We're sending a message," she said, "to
your Nana Rose." I let go of the balloon, and we watched it
sail up into the brilliant blue air and disappear over the ocean.
She explained that when the balloon reached heaven Nana

Rose would recognize our fingerprints. Perhaps I looked at her quizzically, because she then said, "Trust me, sweetie. We're already on the moon."

I watched the waves explode and dash toward me, watched the froth top my shoes, and at almost the same moment felt my socks turn to ice.

"Sam, dear, why are you standing in the water?"

She was about five feet behind me. I didn't answer or turn around.

"Honey, you'll ruin your shoes."

"Good."

"You'll catch pneumonia."

"Good."

"Won't you at least step out of the water?"

"No."

"No?"

"Maybe I want to go for a swim."

I really didn't want to swim. I just wanted to lie down in the surf and close my eyes and drift, like a toy boat or a bottle, to the other side of the ocean, washing up on the shore of a new country.

"Darling, it's too cold to swim. Wait until June. Then you can go in the water."

"Don't talk to me like that!"

"Like what, sweetie?"

"Like I'm crazy. Like I'm about to jump out a window. You're the one who's crazy, not me."

"Oh, Sam, don't criticize. Not now. Not after what I've been through. Don't be like everyone else." I turned around, ready to shout, "Why can't you be like everyone else!" Then I saw how bad she looked. One eye was half closed and her nostrils were rimmed with blood. Angry red welts laced her windpipe. She dropped to her knees and began crying noiselessly into the sand.

I was only thirteen that day, but I knew my mother would never change. She would never have a beautiful office like Florence Fein's. She would never have more than three or four patients, people like Mrs. Gutman, who were as chaotic and pained as she was. I knew she would always feel like a stranger on the planet.

Two weeks later a judge sent me to live with my father. The fight with Phyllis, and the depositions provided by nearly everyone in my father's congregation, weighed heavily against my mother. I was sullen with the judge, though he was gentle with me. Perhaps I could have said something kind about my mother, but I was only thirteen, and I didn't know that love can be as obdurate as the changes you long for. Perhaps I could have told him that after I turned around and saw her bruised face, I lifted my mother to her feet. I pressed my tallis against her bloody nose. Then I rolled it up into a tight little ball, and we trekked back up the beach together.

Summer Water
and Shirley

●●●●

DURANGO MENDOZA

It was in the summer that had burned every stalk of corn and
every blade of grass and dried up the creek until it only flowed
in trickles across the ford below the house where in the pools
the boy could scoop up fish in a dishpan.

The boy lived with his mother and his sister, Shirley, and
the three smaller children eleven miles from Weleetka, and
near Lthwathlee Indian church where it was Eighth Sunday
meeting and everyone was there. The boy and his family stayed
at the camp house of his dead father's people.

Shirley and her brother, who was two years older and
twelve, had just escaped the deacon and were lying on the
brown, sun-scorched grass behind the last camp house. They
were out of breath and giggled as they peeped above the slope
and saw the figure of the deacon, Hardy Eagle, walking slowly
toward the church house.

"Boy, we sure out-fooled him, huh?" Shirley laughed lightly and jabbed her elbow in her brother's shaking side. "Whew!" She ran her slim hand over her eyes and squinted at the sky. They both lay back and watched the cloudless sky until the heat in their blood went down and their breath slowed to normal. They lay there on the hot grass until the sun became too much for them.

"Hey, let's go down to the branch and find a pool to wade in, okay?" She had rolled over suddenly and spoke directly into the boy's ear.

"I don't think we better. Mama said to stay around the church grounds."

"Aw, you're just afraid."

"No, it's just that—"

" 'Mama said to stay around the church grounds!' Fraidy-cat, I'll go by myself then." She sat up and looked at him. He didn't move and she sighed. Then she nudged him. "Hey." She nudged him again and assumed a stage whisper. "Looky there! See that old man coming out of the woods?"

The boy looked and saw the old man shuffling slowly through the high Johnson grass between the woods and the clearing for the church grounds. He was very old and still wore his hair in the old way.

"Who is he?" Shirley whispered. "Who is he?"

"I can't tell yet. The heat makes everything blurry." The boy was looking intently at the old man who was moving slowly in the weltering heat through the swaying grass that moved with the sound of light tinsel in the dry wind.

"Let's go sneak through the grass and scare him," Shirley suggested. "I bet that'd make him even run." She moved her arms as if she were galloping and broke down into giggles. "Come on," she said, getting to one knee.

"Wait!" He pulled her back.

"What do you mean, 'wait'? He'll be out of the grass pretty soon and we won't—" She broke off. "What's the matter? What're you doing?"

The boy had started to crawl away on his hands and knees and was motioning for her to follow. "Come on, Shirley," he whispered. "That's old Ansul Middlecreek!"

"Who's *he*?"

"Don't you remember? Mama said he's the one that killed Haskell Day—with witchcraft. He's a *stiginnee*!"

"A *stiginnee*? Aw, you don't believe that, do you? Mama says you can tell them by the way they never have to go to the toilet, and that's where he's been. Look down there." She pointed to the little unpainted house that stood among the trees.

"I don't care *where* he's been! Come on, Shirley! Look! Oh my gosh! He saw you pointing!"

"I'm coming," she said and followed him quickly around the corner of the camp house.

They sat on the porch. Almost everyone was in for the afternoon service and they felt alone. The wind was hot and it blew from the southwest. It blew past them across the dry fields of yellow weeds that spread before them up to the low hills that wavered in the heat and distance. They could smell the dry harshness of the grass and they felt the porch boards hot underneath them. Shirley bent over and wiped her face with the skirt of her dress.

"Come on," she said. "Let's go down to the creek branch before that deacon comes back." She pulled at his sleeve and they stood up.

"Okay," he said and they skirted the outer camp houses and followed the dusty road to the bridge, stepping from tuft to tuft of scorched grass.

Toward evening and suppertime they climbed out of the dry bed of the branch, over the huge boulders to the road and started for the camp grounds. The sun was in their eyes as they trudged up the steep road from the bridge. They had found no water in the branch so they had gone on down to the creek. For the most part it too was dry.

Suddenly they saw a shadow move into the dust before them. They looked up and saw old Ansul Middlecreek shuf-

fling toward them. His cracked shoes raised little clouds of
dust that rose around his ankles and made whispering sounds
as he moved along.

"Don't look when you go by," the boy whispered intently,
and he pushed her behind him. But as they passed by, Shirley
looked up.

"Hey, Ansul Middlecreek," she said cheerfully.
"*Henkschay!*"* Then with a swish of her skirt she grabbed her
brother and they ran. The old man stopped and the puffs of
dust around his feet moved ahead as he grumbled, his face
still in shadow because he did not turn around. The two didn't
stop until they had reached the first gate. Then they slowed
down and the boy scolded his sister all the way to their camp.
And all through supper he looked at the dark opening of the
door and then at Shirley who sat beside him, helping herself
with childish appetite to the heavy, greasy food that was set
before her.

"You better eat some," she told her brother. "Next meetin's
not 'til next month."

Soon after they had left the table she began to complain that
her head hurt and their mother got them ready to go home.
They took the two little girls and the baby boy from where
they were playing under the arbor and cleaned them up before
they started out. Their uncle, George Hulegy, would go with
them and carry the biggest girl. The mother carried the other
one while the boy struggled in the rear with the baby. Shirley
followed morosely behind them all as they started down the
road that lay white and pale under the rising moon.

She began to fall further behind and shuffled her bare feet
into the warm underlayer of dust. The boy gave to his uncle
the sleeping child he carried and took Shirley by the hand,
surprised that it was so hot and limp.

"Come on, Shirley, come on. Mama, Shirley's got a fever.
Don't walk so fast—we can't keep up. Come on, Shirley," he
coaxed. "Hurry."

---

* Hey, hello. A greeting.

They turned into their lane and followed it until they were on the little hill above the last stretch of road and started down its rocky slope to the sandy road below. Ahead, the house sat wanly under the stars, and Rey, the dog, came out to greet them, sniffing and wriggling his black body and tail.

George Hulegy and the mother were already on the porch as the boy led his sister into the yard. As they reached the porch they saw the lamp begin to glow orange in the window. Then Shirley took hold of the boy's arm and pointed weakly toward the back yard and the form of the storehouse.

"Look, Sonny! Over there, by the storehouse." The boy froze with fear but he saw nothing. "They were three little men," she said vaguely and then she collapsed.

"Mama!" But as he screamed he saw a great yellow dog with large brown spots jump off the other end of the porch with a click of its heavy nails and disappear into the shadows that led to the creek. The boy could hear the brush rustle and a few pebbles scatter as it went. Rey only whined uneasily and did not even look to where the creature had gone.

"What is it? What's wrong?" The two older persons had come quickly onto the porch and the mother bent immediately to help her daughter.

"Oh, Shirley! George! Help me. Oh gosh! She's burning up. Sonny, put back the covers of the big bed. Quick now!"

They were inside now and the boy spoke.

"She saw dwarfs," he said solemnly and the mother looked at George Hulegy. "And there was a big yellow dog that Rey didn't even see."

"Oh, no, no," the mother wailed and leaned over Shirley, who had begun to writhe and moan. "Hush, baby, hush. Mama's here. Hush, baby, your Mama's here." She began to sing softly a very old song while George Hulegy took a lantern from behind the stove.

"I'm going to the creek and get some pebbles where the water still runs," he said. "I have to hurry." He closed the screen quietly behind him and the boy watched him as he disappeared with the swinging lantern through the brush and trees, down into the darkness to the ford. Behind him the mother still sang softly as Shirley's voice began to rise, high and thin like a very small child's. The boy shivered in the heat and sat down in the corner to wait helplessly as he tried not to look at the dark space of the window. He grew stiff and tired trying to control his trembling muscles as they began to jump.

Then George Hulegy came in with some pebbles that still were dripping and they left little wet spots of dark on the floor as he placed them above all the doors and windows throughout the house. Finally he placed three round ones at the foot of the bed where Shirley lay twisting and crying with pain and fever.

The mother had managed to start a small fire in the kitchen stove and told the boy to go out and bring in a few pieces of cook wood from the woodpile. He looked at her and couldn't move. He stood stiff and alert and heard George Hulegy, who was bending close over Shirley, muttering some words that he could not understand. He looked at the door but the sagging screen only reflected the yellow lamplight so that he couldn't see through into the darkness; he froze even tighter.

"Hurry, son!"

He looked at Shirley lying on the bed and moving from side to side.

"Sonny, I have to make Shirley some medicine!" His body shook from a spasm. The mother saw and turned to the door.

"I'll get them," she said.

"Mama!"

She stopped and he barged through the door and found the darkness envelop him. As he fixed his wide-open gaze on the woodpile that faintly reflected the starlight and that of the moon, which had risen above the trees, he couldn't look to either side nor could he run. When he reached for the first piece of wood, the hysteria that was building inside him hardened into an aching bitter core. He squeezed the rough cool wood to his chest and felt the fibers press into his bare arms as he staggered toward the house and the two rectangles of light. The closer he came the higher the tension inside him

stretched until he could scarcely breathe. Then he was inside
again and he sat limply in the corner, light and drained of any
support. He could feel nothing except that Shirley was lying
in the big feather bed across the room, wailing with hurt and
a scalding fever.

His mother was hurrying from the kitchen with a tin cup of
grass tea when Shirley began to scream, louder and louder
until the boy thought that he would never hear another sound
as he stood straight and hard, not leaning at all.

She stopped.

In the silence he saw his mother standing above and behind
the lamp, casting a shadow on the ceiling, stopped with fear
as they heard the other sound. The little girls had come into
the room from their bedroom and were standing whimpering
in their nightgowns by the door. The mother signaled and they
became still and quiet, their mouths slightly open and their
eyes wide. They heard nothing.

Then like a great, beating heart the sound rose steadily until
they could smell the heat of a monstrous flesh, raw and hot.
Steadily it grew to a gagging, stifling crescendo—then
stopped. They heard the click of dog's nails on the porch's
wooden planks, and afterwards, nothing. In the complete
silence the air became cold for an instant and Shirley was
quiet.

It was three days now since Shirley had begun to die and
everyone knew now and had given up any hope. Even the
white doctor could find nothing wrong and all the old Indians
nodded their solemn heads when he went away saying that
Shirley would be up in a few days, for now, to them, her
manner of death was confirmed. He said to send for him if
there was any "real" change. No need to move her—there was
nothing wrong—nothing physically wrong, he had said. He
could not even feel her raging fever. To him Shirley was only
sleeping.

Everyone had accepted that Shirley was going to die and
they were all afraid to go near her. "There is evil around her,"

they said. They even convinced the mother to put her in the back room and close off all light and only open it after three days. She would not die until the third day's night, nor would she live to see the fourth day's dawn. This they could know. A very old woman spoke these words to the mother and she could not disbelieve.

On this third day the boy sat and watched the flies as they crawled over the dirty floor, over the specks and splotches, the dust and crumbs. They buzzed and droned about some drops of water, rubbing their legs against themselves, nibbling, strutting, until the drops dried into meaningless little rings while the hot wind blew softly through the open window, stirring particles of dust from the torn screen. A droplet of sweat broke away from above his eyebrow and ran a crooked rivulet down his temple until he wiped it away. In his emptiness the boy did not want his sister to die.

"Mama?"

"What is it, son?"

"Is Shirley going to die?"

"Yes, son."

He watched her as she stood with her back to him. She moved the heavy skillet away from the direct heat and turned the damper so that the flames would begin to die. She moved automatically, as if faster movement would cause her to breathe in too much of the stifling heat. And as she moved the floor groaned under the shift in weight and her feet made whispering sounds against the sagging boards. The flies still flitted about, mindless and nasty, as the boy looked away from them to his mother.

"Does she have to, Mama?"

"Shirley is dying, son."

Again he saw how the flies went about, unaware of the heat, himself, his mother across the room or that Shirley lay in her silence in the back room. He splashed some more water from his glass and they knew he was there but immediately forgot and settled back to their patternless walking about. And even though the table was clean they walked jerkily among the dishes and inspected his tableware. The boy had lived all his life among these creatures, but now he could not stand their nature.

"Darn flies!"

"Well, we won't have to worry when cold weather gets here," she said. "Now go call the kids and eat. I want to get some sewing done this afternoon."

He said nothing and watched her as she went into the other room. He went to the door and leaned out to call the small children. Then he slipped quietly into the back room and closed the door behind him, fastening the latch in the dark. The heat was almost choking and he blinked away the saltiness that stung his eyes. He stood by the door until he could see a little better. High above his head a crack in the shingles filtered down a star of daylight and he stepped to the bed that stood low against the rough planks of the wall. There were no flies in this room and there was no sound.

The boy sat down on a crate and watched the face of his sister emerge from the gloom where she lay. Straining his eyes, he finally saw the rough army blanket rise and fall, but so slight was the movement that when his eyes lost their focus he could not see it and he quickly put out his hand, but stopped. Air caught in his throat and he stifled a cough, still letting his hand hover over the motionless face. Then he touched the smooth forehead and jerked his hand away as if he had been burned.

He sat and watched his sister's well-formed profile and saw how the skin of the nose and forehead had become taut and dry and now gleamed pale and smooth like old ivory in the semidarkness. A smell like that of hot wood filled the room, but underneath it the boy could smell the odor of something raw, something evil—something that was making Shirley die.

The boy sat on the empty crate in the darkness through the late afternoon and did not answer when his mother called him. He knew that she would not even try the door to this room. He waited patiently for his thoughts to come together, not moving in the lifeless heat, and let the sweat flow from his body. He smelled the raw smell, and when it became too strong he touched the smooth, round pebbles that had come from the creek where it still flowed, and the smell receded.

For many hours he sat, and then he got up and took down the heavy blanket that had covered the single window and let the moonlight fall across the face of his sister through the opening. He began to force his thoughts to remember, to relive every living moment of his life and every part that Shirley had lived in it with him. And then he spoke softly, saying what they had done, and how they would do again what they had done because he had not given up, for he was alive, and she was alive, and they had lived and would *still* live. And so he prayed to his will and forced his will out through his thoughts and spoke softly his words and was not afraid to look out through the window into the darkness through which came the coolness of the summer night. He smelled its scents and let them touch his flesh and come to rest around the "only sleeping" face of his sister. He stood, watching, listening, living.

Then they came, silently, dark-bellied clouds drifting up from the south, and the wind, increasing, swept in the heavy scent of the approaching storm. Lightning flashed over the low, distant hills and the clouds closed quietly around the moon as the thunder rumbled and the heavy drops began to fall, slowly at first, then irregularly, then increasing to a rhythmic rush of noise as the gusts of wind forced the rain in vertical waves across the shingled roof.

Much later, when the rain had moved ahead and the room became chilly when the water began to drip from the roof and the countless leaves, the boy slipped out of his worn denim pants and took off his shirt and lay down beside his sister. She felt him and woke up.

"You just now gettin' to bed?" she asked. "It's pretty late for that, ain't it?"

"No, Shirley," he said. "Go on back to sleep. It'll be morning pretty soon, and when it gets light again we'll go see how high the water's risen in the creek."

He pulled the cover over him and drew his bare arms beneath the blanket and pulled it over their shoulders as he turned onto his side. Lying thus, he could see in the darkness the even darker shapes of the trees and the storehouse his father had built.

Judgment Day

●●◉◉

ARTURO ISLAS

They took him to the cemetery for three years before Miguel
Chico understood what it was. At first, he was held closely by
his nursemaid, Maria, or his uncle Felix. Later, he walked
alongside his mother and godmother, Nina, or sometimes,
when Miguel Grande was not working, with his father, holding
onto their hands or standing behind them as they knelt on the
ground before the stones. No grass grew in the poor peoples'
cemetery, and the trees were too far apart to give much shade.
The desert wind tore the leaves from them and Miguel Chico
asked if anyone ever watered these trees. His elders laughed
and patted him on the head to be still.

Mama Chona never accompanied them to the cemetery.
"Campo Santo" she called it, and for a long time Miguel Chico
thought it was a place for the saints to go camping. His grandmother taught him and his cousins that they must respect the
dead, especially on the Day of the Dead when they wandered

about the earth until they were remembered by the living. Telling the family that the dead she cared about were buried too far away for her to visit their graves, Mama Chona shut herself up in her bedroom on the last day of October and the first day of November every year for as long as she lived. Alone, she said in that high-pitched tone of voice she used for all important statements, she would pray for their souls and for herself that she might soon escape from this world of brutes and fools and join them. In that time her favorite word was *brute,* and in conversation, when she forgot the point she wanted to make, she would close her eyes, fold her hands in prayer, and say, "Oh, dear God, I am becoming like the brutes."

At the cemetery, Miguel Chico encountered no saints but saw only stones set in the sand with names and numbers on them. The grown-ups told him that people who loved him were there. He knew that many people loved him and that he was related to everyone, living and dead. When his parents, Miguel Grande and Juanita, were married, his godmother, Nina, told him, all the people in the Church, but especially her, became his mothers and fathers and would take care of him if his parents died. Miguel Chico did not want them to die if it meant they would become stones in the desert.

They bought flowers that smelled sour like Mama Chona and her sister, his great-aunt Cuca, to put in front of the stones. Sometimes they cried, and he did not understand that they wept for the dead in the sand.

"Why are you crying?" he asked.

"Because she was my sister" or "because she was my mother" or "because he was my father," they answered. He looked at the stones and tried to see these people. He wanted to cry too, but was able to make only funny faces. His heart was not in it. He wanted to ask them what the people looked like but was afraid they would become angry with him. He was five years old.

There were other people walking and standing and kneeling and weeping quietly in front of the stones. Most of them were old like his parents, some of them were as old as Mama Chona, a few were his own age. They bought the yellow and white flowers from a dark, toothless old man who set them out in pails in front of a wagon. Miguel shied away when the ugly little man tried to give him some flowers.

"Take them Mickie," said his godmother, "the nice man is giving them to you."

"I don't want them." He felt like crying and running away, but his father had told him to be a man and protect his mother from the dead. They did not scare him as much as the flower man did.

A year later, he found out about the dead. His friend Leonardo, who was eight years old and lived in the corner house across the street, tied a belt around his neck. He put one end of the belt on a hook in the back porch, stood on a chair, and knocked it over. Nardo's sister thought he was playing one of his games on her and walked back into the house.

The next morning Miguel's mother asked if he wanted to go to the mortuary and see Leonardo. He knew his friend was dead because all the neighborhood was talking about it, about whether or not the boy had done it on purpose. But he did not know what a mortuary was and he wanted to find out.

When they arrived there, Miguel saw that everything was white, black, or brown. The flowers, like the kind they bought from the old man only much bigger and set up in pretty ways, were mostly white. The place was cold and all the people wore dark, heavy clothes. They were saying the rosary in a large room that was like the inside of the church but not so big. It was brightly lit and had no altar, but there were a few statues, which Miguel recognized. A long, shiny metal box stood at the end of the room. It was open, but Miguel was not able to see inside because it was too far away and he was too small to see over people's heads, even though they were kneeling.

Maria and his mother said that he must be quiet and pray like the others in the room. He became bored and sleepy and felt a great longing to look into the box. After the praying was over, they stood in line and moved slowly toward the box. At last he would be able to see. When the people in front of them got out of the way, he saw himself, his mother, and Maria reflected in the brightly polished metal. They told him it was all right to stand so that his head was level with theirs as they knelt. The three of them looked in.

Leonardo was sleeping, but he was a funny color and he was very still. "Touch him," his mother said, "it's all right. Don't be afraid." Maria took his hand and guided it to Nardo's face. It was cold and waxy. Miguel looked at the candles and flowers behind the box as he touched the face. He was not afraid. He felt something but did not know what it was.

"He looks just like he did when he was alive, doesn't he, Mickie?" his mother said solemnly.

"Yes," he nodded, but he did not mean it. The feeling was circling around his heart and it had to do with the stillness of the flowers and the color of Nardo's face.

"Look at him one more time before we go," Maria said to him in Spanish. "He's dead now and you will not see him again until Judgment Day."

That was very impressive and Miguel Chico looked very hard at his friend and wondered where he was going. As they drove home, he asked what they were going to do with Leonardo.

His mother, surprised, looked at Maria before she answered. "They are going to bury him in the cemetery. He's dead, Mickie. We'll visit him on the Day of the Dead. *Pobrecito, el inocente*," she said, and Maria repeated the words after her. The feeling was now in his stomach and he felt that he wanted to be sick. He was very quiet.

"Are you sad, Mickie?" his mother asked before saying goodnight to him.

"No."

"Is anything wrong? Don't you feel well?" She put her hand on his forehead. Miguelito thought of his hand on Nardo's face.

"I'm scared," he said, but that was not what he wanted to say.

"Don't be afraid of the dead," his mother said. "They can't hurt you."

"I'm not afraid of the dead." He saw the sand and stones for what they were now.

"What are you afraid of, then?"

The feeling and the words came in a rush like the wind tearing the leaves from the trees. "Of what's going to happen tomorrow," he said.

The next day, Miguel Chico watched Maria comb her long beautiful black and white hair in the sun. She had just washed it, and the two of them sat on the backstairs in the early morning light, his head in her lap. Her face was wide, with skin the color and texture of dark parchment, and her eyes, which he could not see because as he looked up her cheekbones were in the way, he knew were small and the color of blond raisins. When he was very young, Maria made him laugh by putting her eyes very close to his face and saying in her uneducated Spanish, "Do you want to eat my raisin eyes?" He pretended to take bites out of her eyelids. She drew back and said, "Now it's my turn. I like your chocolate eyes. They look very tasty and I'm going to eat them!" She licked the lashes of his deeply set eyes and Miguel Chico screamed with pleasure.

Maria was one of hundreds of Mexican women from across the border who worked illegally as servants and nursemaids for families on the American side. Of all ages, even as young as thirteen or fourteen, they supported their own families and helped to rear the children of strangers with the care and devotion they would have given their own relatives had they been able to live with them. One saw these women standing at the bus stops on Monday mornings and late Saturday nights. Sunday was their only day off and most of them returned to spend it on the other side of the river. In addition to giving her half of her weekly salary of twenty-five dollars, Juanita helped Maria pack leftover food, used clothing, old newspapers—anything Maria would not let her throw away—into paper bags that Maria would take to her own family. Years later, wandering the streets of New York, his own bag glued to his side, Miguel Chico saw Maria in all the old bag ladies waiting on street corners in Chelsea or walking crookedly through the Village, stopping to pick through garbage, unable to bear the waste of the more privileged.

"Now, Maria," Juanita said, "if the immigration officials ask you where you got these things, tell them you went to bargain stores."

"Sí, señora."

"And if they ask you where you have been staying during the week, tell them you've been visiting friends and relatives. Only in emergencies are you to use our name and we'll come to help you no matter what it is."

"Sí, señora."

The conversation was a weekly ritual and unnecessary because Miguel Grande through his police duties was known by immigration officials, who, when it came to these domestics, looked the other way or forgot to stamp cards properly. Only during political campaigns on both sides of the river were immigration laws strictly enforced. Then Maria and all women like her took involuntary vacations without pay.

Mama Chona did not approve of any of the Mexican women her sons and daughters hired to care for her grandchildren. They were ill educated and she thought them very bad influences, particularly when they were allowed to spend much time with her favorites. Mama Chona wanted Miguel Chico to be brought up in the best traditions of the Angel family. Juanita scoffed at those traditions. "They've eaten beans all their lives. They're no better than anyone else," she said to her sister Nina. "I'm not going to let my kids grow up to be snobs. The Angels! If they're so great, why do I have to work to help take care of them?"

Miguel Chico could not remember a time when Maria was not part of his family, and even though Mama Chona disapproved of the way she spoke Spanish, she was happy to know that Maria was a devout Roman Catholic. She remained so the first six years of his life, taking him to daily mass and holding him in her arms throughout the services until he was four. After mass during the week and before he was old enough to be instructed by Mama Chona, Maria took him to the five-and-ten stores downtown. If she had saved money from the allowance Juanita gave her, she would buy him paper doll books. He and Maria spent long afternoons cutting out dolls and dressing them. When he got home from the police station, Miguel Grande would scold Maria for allowing his son to play with dolls. "I don't want my son brought up like a girl," he said to Juanita in Maria's presence. He did not like to speak directly to the Mexican women Juanita and his sisters took on to help them with the household chores. Miguel Chico's aunts Jesus Maria and Eduviges left notes for the "domestics" (the Spanish word *criadas* is harsher) and spoke to them only when they had not done their chores properly. Mama Chona had taught all her children that the Angels were better than the illiterate riff-raff from across the river.

"Maria does more good for people than all of them put together," Juanita complained to her sister and to her favorite brother-in-law Felix, who shared her opinion of his sisters. "They're so holier than thou. Just because they can read and write doesn't make them saints. I'd like to see them do half the work Maria does." Juanita knew that Jesus Maria and Eduviges considered Felix's wife an illiterate and not worthy of their brother, who, after all, was an Angel.

"Apologize to your father for playing with dolls," Juanita said to Miguel Chico. He did but did not understand why he needed to say he was sorry. When his father was not there, his mother permitted him to play with them. She even laughed when Maria made him a skirt and they watched him dance to the jitterbug music on the radio. "Yitty-bog," Maria called it. Miguel Grande had caught them at that once and made a terrible scene. Again, Miguel Chico was asked to apologize and to promise that he would never do it again. His father said nothing to him but looked at Juanita and accused her of turning their son into a *joto*. Miguel Chico did not find out until much later that the word meant "queer." Maria remained silent throughout these scenes; she knew enough not to interfere.

After Miguel Chico's birthday, several months after his friend Leonardo "accidentally" hanged himself, Maria stopped taking him to mass. Instead, she spent the afternoons when he got home from school talking to him about God and reading to him from the Bible, always with the stipulation that he not tell his parents or Mama Chona. She especially liked to talk to him about Adam and Eve and the loss of paradise. He loved hearing about Satan's pride and rebelliousness and secretly admired him. Before he was expelled from the heavenly kingdom, Maria told him, Satan was an angel, the most favored of God's creatures, and his name was *Bella Luz*.

"Why did he turn bad, Maria?"

"Out of pride. He wanted to be God."

"Did God make pride?"

Miguel Chico learned that when he asked Maria a difficult question she would remain silent, then choose a biblical passage that illustrated the terrible power of God the Father's wrath. She loved to talk to him about the end of the world.

Maria began braiding her hair and tying it up in a knot that lay flat on her neck. It gave her a severe look he did not like, and he missed those mornings when she let her hair hang loosely to her waist and brushed or dried it in the sun, with his head on her lap. She did not allow him into her room any more and asked him to leave if he opened the door and caught her with her hair still unbraided. The word *vice* occurred frequently now in her talks with him; everything, it seemed, was becoming a vice to Maria. She had become a Seventh Day Adventist.

His mother and Maria got involved in long, loud, and tearful arguments about the nature of God and about the Catholic church as opposed to Maria's new religion. They excluded him from these discussions and refused to let him into the kitchen where they wrangled with each other and reached no conclusions. Miguel Chico hid in his mother's closet in order not to hear their shouting.

"The Pope is the Antichrist!" Maria said loudly, hoping he would hear. And before Juanita could object, Maria cited a passage from the Bible as irrefutable proof.

"It's not true," Juanita said just as strongly, but she was not at ease with the holy book, and there was no priest at hand to back her up. She wept out of frustration and tried to remember what she had learned by rote in her First Communion classes.

In the closet, Miguel Chico hugged his mother's clothes in terror. The familiar odors in the darkness kept him company and faintly reassured him. In the distance, the strident voices arguing about God continued. What would happen if he told his mother and father that Maria was sneaking him off to the Seventh Day Adventist services while they were away at work or having a good time? His father had said to his mother that he would kill Maria if she did that.

The services—which were not so frightening as his father's threats and the arguments between his mother and Maria—were held in a place that did not seem like a church at all it was so brightly lit up, even in the middle of the day. There were no statues and the air did not smell of incense and burning candles. The singing was in Spanish, not Latin, and it was not the sort he enjoyed because it reminded him of the music played in the newsreels about the war. The people at these services were very friendly and looked at him as if they all shared a wonderful secret. "You are saved," they would say to him happily. He did not know what they meant, but he sensed that to be saved was to be special. The more he smiled, the more they smiled back; they spent most of the time smiling, though they talked about things that scared him a great deal, such as the end of the world and how sinful the flesh was. He could not rid himself of the guilt he felt for being there, as no matter how much they smiled, he knew he was betraying his mother and father and Mama Chona in some deep, incomprehensible way.

The voices of the women he loved were farther away now, which meant they were almost finished for the time being and would soon resume their household chores. His mother had just given birth to a second son and was staying home from work to nurse him. They named him Gabriel, and Miguel Chico was extremely jealous of him.

Opening the closet door after the voices had stopped altogether, Miguelito stumbled over the clothes hamper and some of his mother's things spilled out into the light. He saw an undergarment with a bloody stain on it. Quickly, he threw the clothes back into the basket and shoved it into the closet. He was careful not to touch the garment. Its scent held him captive.

Maria swept him up from behind, forcing him to laugh out of surprise, and trotted him into the kitchen. Together they stood looking out into the backyard through the screen door. It was a hot day and the sun made the screen shimmer. Miguel saw his mother bending over the verbena and snapdragons that she and Maria took great pains to make grow out of the desert. The flowers were at their peak, and already he knew that the verbena, bright red, small, and close to the ground, would outlast the more exotic snapdragons he liked better. The canna lilies, which formed the border behind them, were colorful, but they had no fragrance and were interesting only when an occasional hummingbird dipped its beak into their red-orange cups. In the corner of that bed grew a small peach tree that he had planted at Maria's suggestion from a pit he had licked clean two summers earlier. It was now a foot high and had branched. His mother was approaching it. Leaning over him and with her hand on his face directing his gaze toward the tree, Maria whispered hypnotically. "Look at the little tree," she said very softly in Spanish so that his mother could not hear. "When it blooms and bears fruit that means that the end of the world is near. Now look at your mother. You must respect and love her because she is going to die." In front of him, in the gauzy brightness of the screen, the red of the flowers merged with the red stain he had seen a few moments before. He believed Maria. In that instant, smelling her hair and feeling her voice of truth moist on his ear, love and death came together for Miguel Chico, and he was not from then on able to think of one apart from the other.

Two years later, in a fit of terror because he knew the world was going to end soon, he told his parents that Maria had been taking him to her church. His father threw her out of the house but allowed her to return a few weeks later, on the condition that she say nothing about her religion to anyone while she lived in his house. The arguments stopped, and she no longer read to him from the Bible.

Maria treated him nicely, but she hardly spoke to him and spent more time caring for his brother. Once or twice Miguel Chico caught her looking at him sadly and shaking her head as if he were lost to her forever. One day after school, when he was feeling bold, he said, "If God knew that Satan and Adam and Eve were going to commit a sin, why did He create them?"

"You must not ask me such things," she replied, "I'm not allowed to talk to you about them."

It was a lame answer, and he knew that in some important way, he had defeated her. He hated her now and hoped that she would leave them soon and return to Mexico. When, several months later, she did go away, he stayed at Mama Chona's house all day and did not say good-bye to her. Juanita was upset with him when he got home.

"Maria wanted to tell you good-bye. Why didn't you come home before she left?"

"I don't like her any more," he said. "I'm glad she's gone." But later that night he felt an awful loneliness when he thought about her hair and eyes.

The Floating World

●●◉◎

CYNTHIA KADOHATA

Nobody talked at all. I couldn't tell what my parents were thinking, or feeling. Sometimes I spent hours trying to figure them out, trying to make order of the random facts. My mother's body shook once, and I couldn't tell whether she was still crying or just had a chill.

My mother was thirty, tall, with a smooth face except for two furrows between her brows. She had a quiet, throaty voice I loved to listen to. Often my mother gave me advice I couldn't yet fathom. I remembered how, when I was seven, we passed a plot of opened morning glories. She pointed at them. "That's the way you'll feel inside the first time a boy you love touches you." Later we passed the same flowers, closed into tight little twists. "And that," she said, "is how you'll feel inside the first time a boy you don't love touches you."

The only grandparent I knew well was Obāsan. My father's

parents had left the United States when he was a teenager. They'd joined a religion based in Kyoto. The leader of the religion had been an eleven-year-old girl who said she spoke with God. When she got old and died, her younger brother and sister both said they now spoke with God, and they took over the religion.

I was born in Fresno, where my mother lived. My father, or the man I have always thought of as my father, lived in Oregon before he married my mother. I was not that much smaller than he. He was five feet three, and his name was Charles Osaka—Charlie-O to everyone except my mother, who called him Charles when she didn't like him and Chuck when she did, just as she called me Olivia or Livvie, depending on my behavior. Charlie-O was almost always cheerful, and he had a childlike joie de vivre that would not quite have fit a larger man. Obāsan forced my mother to marry him, though I wasn't supposed to know that. I'd picked it up over the years.

I don't know exactly how my grandmother found Charlie-O, but I later heard she'd first brought him to Fresno to meet my mother when she was seven months pregnant with me. My father used to keep a picture on his bureau of my mother on prom night, when she was seventeen, and sometimes I wonder whether that was the picture Obāsan first sent him to get him to Fresno. He married my mother when she was eight months pregnant, and in time they had my three brothers. I knew that Charlie-O loved me, though once in a while I worried that he loved me because I was what had brought him together with my mother. My real father visited me several times, but he was married and had two children, and we never became close. So I was devoted to Charlie-O and had followed him everywhere when I was quite young—he even took me to his poker games —and sometimes I brought him to Parents' Day at school, where, starting the past year, he was shorter than a couple of my classmates. But I was already beginning not to care about poker games and Parents' Days, and Charlie-O and I were growing apart. That hurt him. My allegiances were shifting to my mother. She was moody, but also graceful and pensive and intellectual, things I wanted to be when I grew up but already knew I never would be. Charlie-O was loud, undignified.

We'd lived in Florence, Oregon, for the past few months, and I think for a while my parents wanted to settle down. Charlie-O loved it there. He was an amateur painter, and sometimes, when my brothers or my grandmother and I went for walks not long after first light, Charlie-O would already be outside, painting on the beach. But when his friend offered him half a garage for a small down payment, he couldn't resist. Most of the Japanese where we were moving in Arkansas were chicken sexers, and I think my father sort of liked the idea of going there as a business owner. "Of course, I won't let it go to my head," he said. He told me that in Arkansas his friend sometimes met people who hadn't known that any Japanese lived in the state, although all the Japanese knew of one another.

In any case, in the car after the accident, my mother was the first to break the silence. She declared in her throaty voice that she had just decided she wanted to find Obāsan's second husband—her own second father. She hadn't seen him for nearly twenty years. I could tell that my mother felt obsessive about finding him. She was like that now and then—obsessive. But my dad didn't want to take the time. He didn't even want to stop off in Los Angeles to visit anymore. He was getting more and more excited about the garage, and we were already behind schedule.

My mother had sent her second father—Bill—a telegram about the funeral. He hadn't shown up or responded, though she thought he still lived in the same place where she'd live with him—central California, about fifty miles from Wilcox. He was twenty years older than my grandmother, which would have made him ninety-six at the time of her death. As my mother talked about finding him, my father caught my eye in the rearview mirror, and I knew he thought Bill was probably dead. My mother read his mind. "Don't even think it," she said.

My mother talked about her fathers. When her first father died, she'd just turned seven, but she didn't remember a great deal about him, except that the last thing he'd said to her was "Be good." Her third father died, of old age, after a long marriage to her mother. But my mother hadn't liked him, and he hadn't liked her. In between, Bill had been her father. I thought it was great fun to hear all this.

After a short silence, my mother told us that Obāsan hadn't loved Bill, but she herself had. "Drop me off somewhere. I'm going to take a bus and find him. Honey, can you stop the car?" she said to Charlie-O. She jiggled the door handle. I looked into the bushes on either side of the car.

"You can't get out here," said my father. "And where will you stay when you get to this town?"

"At a motel?" she said. "At a motel." She sat up very straight, what she always did when she was ready to fight for something.

I didn't know a lot, but I knew that ladies did not stay in motels alone. My father sat up straight, too—he wasn't going to change *his* mind, either. My mother slumped a little. "It's always nice when we start out somewhere, then it's less nice when we're almost there," she said.

It was raining very hard. Walker pulled my ear down to his mouth and whispered. I tapped my father's shoulder. "Walker says we've lost the Shibatas."

Charlie-O pulled over in a few minutes and made three announcements: first, he believed we were somewhere in Ventura County; second, he believed we were lost; and third, we were about to run out of gas.

"How do you know we're in Ventura County if we're lost?" I said.

"Don't worry, honey-dog. You look worried." He smiled, but his eyes didn't look happy in the rearview mirror. His eyes looked uncertain and seemed to be asking me something— nothing specific; just asking.

I got out a map. "Where's the highway?" I said.

He didn't know. The rain formed rivers down the windshield, and the raindrops made the windows look like textured glass. Charlie-O got out, and I pressed my nose against the backseat window and watched him squint into the darkness as the rain splashed on his face. He was looking down the road, but I didn't see why he couldn't look from inside the dry car. It was as if he were under a spell. I lowered the window. The air was warmer than I'd expected.

"Dad, what are you doing?"

"Just seeing what's what," he said. "I'm gonna walk down a ways and try to get us some gas." As he set off, he appeared as sturdy as always but even smaller than usual. I rolled up the window and ran after him, almost slipping in the mud as I hurried. Charlie-O walked on surefootedly.

"Why am I doing this?" I said. "I should just wait in the car."

We went a long way but never thought of turning back. We were both very stubborn. We'd always been alike that way. There was nothing but bush around us, and sometimes—maybe it was the play of sky light off the rain—I would think I saw lights in the leaves. Charlie-O didn't look either right or left as he walked, and I thought how much more scared I would be without him. He stopped, and I bumped into him. He was looking at three huge, beautiful signs hanging in the darkness beyond a hill. The signs were bright reds and blues and yellows: Standard, Shell, Motor Inn.

My father bought gas and suggested I wait at the station while he took the long walk back to the car. I stood under the awning while the attendant talked on the phone inside. Lightning kept illuminating the area beyond this enclave of two gas stations and a motel. When it flashed, the surrounding area looked not quite there, like a photographic negative. It seemed to take forever for my family to come.

Ben cringed from me when I got in the car. "You're all wet," he said, as if my wetness were a contagious disease.

"Just a little water," boomed Charlie-O. "Ain't nothing to have a cow about."

Usually when his voice sounded loud and happy that way, it was because he really felt loud and happy. But he was wet and tired, and though he was the one who'd decided we should leave Oregon, I thought about how much he'd liked it there, and how important it must be to him to have a success in Arkansas.

We drove across to the motel. I'd heard my parents say the day before that they would take two rooms tonight—one for my brothers and me, and one for themselves. I knew it was so they could make love. Only a couple of years earlier, I wouldn't have understood completely why it was so important for them to get their own room, as they sometimes did.

A tired-looking man with rollers in his hair registered us at the motel. When I watched my parents at the counter, they seemed to be the same person. Maybe it was just that they lived in the same world, used the same shampoo, ate the same foods. In any case, they matched. Yet I knew that sometimes my mother felt lonely and my father felt alone. And though my mother was several years younger than Charlie-O, she always struck me as womanly, whereas my father was boyish.

"One room?" said the man.

"Yes, plus cots, if you have any," said my mother.

The man got a cot. "Only have one. I won't charge you. We usually charge a dollar, but I understand. I've got seven of my own." A cry came from a back room. "There's one now," the man said with a sigh. He yawned and shook his head, and a loose roller jiggled.

Charlie-O turned and winked at me, and when we got outside he said, "Remember—you can always trust a man with seven children and the nerve to wear rollers in his hair." Charlie-O carried the cot to the room. Then he and I went to a coffee shop, where he got coffee and I stole packets of sugar and containers of ersatz cream to give my brothers. They were too young to be out so late.

When we got to our room, my mother was pensive, and I knew she was thinking again about finding her second father.

Walker, Ben, and I played cards on the floor. Walker always beat Ben and me at poker, because he wouldn't change expressions, even when he had a good hand.

This time my father seemed to read my mother's mind. "We need to get to Arkansas. We've got to get them settled." I looked up. "Them" meant us—the kids.

My father leaned back against a bureau, smoking. His left forearm rested across his ribs, his right elbow sat on the back of his hand. To draw on his cigarette, he moved his right wrist downward to inhale and flipped it back up when he finished his drag. His elbow and head never moved. Then he tossed his hair back, as if waking himself, and became alert, interested. "Driving's okay sometimes, you know. You get a chance to think."

"What do you like to think about?" said my mother.

"About you," he said.

Cool, moist air wafted through the screen door. Outside, the reflections from the motel lights made flashing ribbons of color on the wet parking lot ground. A traveler entered the motel office, and in a few minutes he came out, keys jangling, and walked across the ribbons. The NO lit up in the vacancy sign.

My father was the most tired, from driving, and he, Walker, and Ben went to sleep. Peter stayed up. My mother and I leafed through a book called *Man of Steel*. To sustain my reading ability when we were moving, my mother always picked up what books she could find. While other children were reading *Lassie Come Home* and *The Call of the Wild*, I was reading *Reptiles and Amphibians: Nature's Throwbacks* or *Innards: How to Cook Variety Meats*. Actually, I gained a lot of knowledge. But I knew I didn't read as well as most people my age, and maybe I never would. I read out loud now: "Andrew Carnegie was a man with ideas." When my mother thought of it, she made me read twenty pages at a time, but I would see she wasn't listening tonight. I closed the book. "Do you think we'll like Arkansas?" I said. I thought she might want to talk.

She smiled, just barely, and shook her head yes. "What do you think?"

"Well." I wanted to sound wise. "If we don't, we can always leave."

She went to bed. Peter was quiet but wide awake. I took him out with me and sat on the curb. The wind blew hard against the lone tree in the distance. It was very dark, but you could see the roads crisscrossing over the fields. When cars went by, far away, the beams were so bright they seemed to be ropes of light pulling the cars behind.

My mother wanted badly to go and find Bill; my father wanted to get to Arkansas. I wished we didn't have to do anything. I wanted to stay where we were—where I didn't know anyone and no one knew me, and where it seemed to me a long time ago that my grandmother had died.

Back in the room, the lights were off, and everyone was asleep—my parents on the bed and my brothers wrapped like cocoons on the floor. You couldn't see their breathing movements; occasional twitches indicated that the moths inside might be emerging in a few hours or days. I had taught my brothers to wrap themselves up that way. We each used to have our own blanket, which we would fold in half before tucking in every inch under our bodies, including our heads. So long as you didn't thrash in your dreams, you could stay warm, even if it got quite cool during the night. I laid Peter between Ben and Walker. I wondered why my mother had decided to take just one room. Did it mean my parents weren't getting along, in ways I couldn't see? Everything changed so quickly and without my noticing.

I thought I remembered a time when my parents had been unable to keep their hands off each other, always walking arm in arm or stopping to kiss lightly. But the memory was there and then not there. One night on the way down from Oregon we'd taken only one motel room, but my parents had made love anyway—quietly—probably after they thought we were all asleep. I thought they'd *had* to make love or they wouldn't have—not with me and my brothers in the room. They'd never made love in the past when we'd taken only one room. Something about their lovemaking that night, about the sound of it, seemed somehow hopeless. I'd had to go to the bathroom badly, but by the time they finally fell asleep and I could get up, I'd decided that if necessary I would wet my bed before letting them know I was awake. It was not the sex I thought I ought not to have heard but the hopelessness.

I was on the cot, and my eyes were closed. I heard my mother and Charlie-O begin speaking, though I couldn't hear what they were saying. Finally she said something, and my father didn't answer. I heard the sheets rustle. I thought they were going to make love, but they didn't. Then they did. I opened my eyes and saw their bodies moving beneath the sheets. I felt guilty for watching, so I closed my eyes again and averted my face. But I couldn't help listening closely; they were almost as silent as when they slept.

Afterward, my mother said, "It doesn't make any sense," and my father concurred. I had no idea *what* didn't make any sense. I'm not even sure they knew, yet it seemed like the right thing to say. Sometimes I worried that my parents were disappointed with their lives, and I wondered how much of that might be due to my brothers and me—maybe we weren't the kind of children they'd hoped for. But I thought I would rather they be unhappy with me than with each other. Of course, that wasn't the case—despite our faults, my parents couldn't have been happier with my brothers and me.

My parents fell asleep. The cot squeaked softly as I shook my feet up and down, back and forth. I lay still and realized Walker wasn't breathing evenly—he was awake. The others were asleep. Walker had probably heard our parents making love. I wished he hadn't. It seemed to me a burden to have heard, and I didn't want him to have that burden.

"Walk?" I said.

"Huh."

"Good night."

He didn't answer, but I knew he felt comforted not to be

be alone, and soon he fell asleep. So did I. Maybe I felt comforted, too.

The next day we headed back north. I first knew what we were doing shortly after my father drew out the map and placed it on the car hood. My mother studied the map over his shoulder, then suddenly said, "You know it's okay if you all don't come," and my father replied by making a ceremony of folding up the map and getting into the car.

We arrived in Bill's town that evening. The town had a miniature mall on the main street. My mother said there used to be several separate shops on the street, but now the shops were housed in adjoining buildings, all with the same white-and-blue facades. When we reached Bill's road, a detour blocked the way. "It's not far—ten or fifteen minutes' walking," my mother said. She was very excited. "If you want, you can let me out and pick me up later." But my father turned off the ignition and got out, and we set off.

The houses were spread out, almost as in farm country. At one time, my mother said, there had been no houses except hers in this area.

"Did I used to live here?" said Ben. He gestured hugely at the fields around us.

"No. Mom lived here a long time ago," I said.

"Will you give me a piggyback ride?"

"You're getting kind of big."

He sighed. "I know."

The lights from the downtown shops, beyond a hill, shone at the horizon, making the ground seem to glow. When we reached my mother's old address, the house was dark, and my mother hesitated, then peeked into a window on the door. The door opened as she was peeking, and she took a step back. An old woman stood at the threshold. This would be Bill's wife. My mother, beautiful, smiled her most charming smile, and the woman's suspicious face softened, but only a little. "I sent a telegram" was all my mother said.

"Yes," said the woman. The suspicion returned. She and my

mother stood, waiting. "You see, he has been dead for quite a while."

I think she expected us to say good-bye then, but my mother just stood there, and after a pause the woman let us in. It was cool outside but even cooler inside, as if the blinds had not been raised all day, and I had the feeling that the house had few visitors. The woman turned on a light. The living room was oppressively orange: the carpet was orange, the couch had orange-and-brown flowers, and the curtains were pasty orange. Probably the woman thought orange was a cheerful color; therefore, the more orange the better. The house smelled of ginger—a mix of fresh ginger and stale.

When the woman showed us around, my mother saw a pair of children's shoes sitting in a sewing room. "Oh, those are mine!" she said.

The woman looked as if she'd been accused. "Did you want them back?" She looked doubtfully at my mother's feet, then at mine, which were big.

Back in the living room, my mother found something else she thought belonged to her—an enameled box of the kind her mother used to make. She thought it was the same one her mother had given her for her tenth birthday. The woman seemed offended and said Bill had given it to her, but she was sure he'd bought it. When she left to get refreshments, my mother said, "I know that's my box. I loved that box. I always wondered what happened to it."

I piped up. "It sure looks like the other ones she used to make." Sometimes my mouth opened even when I didn't want it to.

My father said, "Let's not stay long."

When the woman returned, she talked mainly to my brothers and me. She told us how, when she first came to this country from Japan, she'd been a farmworker and picked tomatoes. The tomato plants smelled like marigolds, and now she couldn't stand that smell. I loved the scent of marigolds, and I couldn't imagine things happening in my life that would make me hate it. But I couldn't be sure.

While the woman talked I saw something strange. My mother, with that familiar obsessive look on her face, was trying to get the enameled box into her handbag, but Charlie-O had hold of her wrist, and his face was just as determined as hers. I looked at my brothers, but they hadn't noticed anything.

The woman continued to talk, and I asked her question after question while out of the corner of my eye I watched my parents struggle. They were so intent I doubt they would have noticed if we'd all turned to watch. I half expected to see them fall to the floor, wrestling. My father, of course, won. But my mother's face caved in, and I could see that a part of Charlie-O wanted to let her have the box.

Later, when everyone else was saying good-bye, I surprised myself by meandering over and slipping the box into my jacket pocket. I think I had an idea that giving it to my mother would please both my parents—my mother because she would get the box and not have to tell my father, and my father because my mother would be content, though he wouldn't know why.

When we left and the woman closed the door, the lights went off almost immediately. The woman seemed to have come to life just for us. My mother called me over to a window, and we peeked in. "What do you see?" she said.

I stared. I squinted. I tried to imagine. Finally I said, "Nothing."

She nodded sagely. "That's what I see." I thought she was still a little crazy from her mother dying.

All around I could hear the noise of dry grass riffling like paper. My father was standing right behind us, waiting, but my mother kept her face pressed to the window. "Your father's mad because he had to come all the way out here," she said. "But he didn't have to come."

I didn't answer. Though she said "your father," she was really talking to him.

"I wanted to come," he said. "I'm not mad." He shouted to Ben and Walker, "Get back here now!" Ben and Walker had been running across the road. "Watch them," he said to me.

I turned to look at them play in the empty road, then turned back to my parents. My father leaned against the house and closed his eyes and opened them again, as if he thought the world would have changed when he reopened his eyes. I peeked back inside. Maybe what my mother saw in there was something like what I would see, years from then, when I looked back on that night. I heard my brothers playing and laughing behind me but didn't hear a sound from my parents. Peter was quiet but wide-eyed in my mother's arms.

"What do you want?" said Charlie-O, very quietly.

"I don't want anything," my mother said.

"You don't understand—I want you to want something."

"I just don't want you to be mad," my mother said to the window. A small steam circle formed on the glass where she was talking. I felt very old suddenly, because I knew she'd only said that for him. What she'd said first was closer to the truth: she didn't want anything he could give her.

"I'm not mad," Charlie-O said. "Maybe we can find a sitter or something. Maybe we should go get plastered or something."

We left, my parents walking hand in hand. I didn't look back at the house, but I thought I felt the woman's eyes on my back. She was going to run out any second and reclaim her enameled box. I already knew I would never give it to my mother, she would be disappointed that I'd taken it. One of these days I was going to try to be good for a whole week.

I could see now that no gain or lack of a box was going to change my mother's life any. She'd probably already forgotten about it. I ran back to the house and placed the box carefully on the doorstep, then ran back to catch up with my family. My mother was walking ahead now. No one even asked me why I'd run back. It was getting so you could do any nutty thing and no one else would even notice.

"Why is Mom walking ahead?" said Walker to my father.

"She's thinking. It's okay."

"What's she thinking about?"

"Walker is practically having a conversation," said Ben. "He never talks."

"She's thinking about things."

"What things?"

"I can see the car," said Ben. "Livvie, I'll race you." But then he ran to a fence to look at a rabbit he thought he'd spotted.

"But is she happy up there? Is she lonely or happy? And is she thinking about Obāsan?" said Walker.

"About your grandmother, and maybe other things," Charlie-O said. "She's lonely but also happy."

"How come both?"

My father hesitated, figuring. "She's lonely because she had too many fathers, and happy because that's never going to happen to you. I didn't come all the way out here to be mad."

The lights from downtown had all been turned off, and the ground no longer seemed to glow. Darkness intensified every noise—our footsteps, our voices. I thought of how a couple of months earlier my mother had told my brothers and me about our "stars"—the word she used for the personality traits she thought would make our lives easier. One night, as she and I were sitting looking over a grove of plum trees, she lowered her voice, as if she had a great secret, and said she had finally figured out what my star was, what I had that would ease my way through the future. It wasn't Peter's alertness, or Walker's concentration, or Ben's self-assurance. But I had a happy heart —my birthright, she said. I sat leaning my head against her shoulder, hoping that someday my happy heart would take me to the right places, get me the right jobs, let me love the right man. Then I wondered whether her mother had ever told her that she had a happy heart, and I asked her the same question I asked my father now: "Did you just make a wish, or a promise?"

AFFAIRS OF
THE HEART

Yes, Young Daddy

●◉◉◉

FRANK CHIN

Hi Dirigible,

Guess hoo! Ya man, It's me, you know hoo-ooo! That fat lazy thing that lives somwere across the bay. Well, I thought I'd drop a few lines or two 'cause I's got nothing to do with myself. Seriously though, I thought it would be fun to write to you; and I know 24 hours a day isn't enough for you, you know college and drawing and all your girlfriends, but if you do get a tiney second; I would love to hear from you.

Do you know what I'm doing this summer? Well to put it flatly "NOTHING"! The most I would do is go to the movies (with the kids of course since mommy's never home). The rest of the time I'd go to the church, clean house, stay home and look at TV. Oh, yes, if you do come to the city once in a while for pleasure, I'm always free. That is if you don't mind my company. Your the only boy I think mommy will let come up, since she don't like strangers to see how a mess we live in, and she says I can't go out until I'm 18!

You know what, I got my school ring today and it's "Beautiful" (That's what I think anyway?) I know what your thinking. How come I have my ring now? You see, I don't want to pay $22.52 for the ring now? and just wear it for my last term in school. I believe it's a waste of money; so this way I can wear it through my junior and senior years.

Brother! Am I ever glad tomorrow will be the last day for my finals. Oh! It's driving me nuttie. To top off this week my English teacher hands back our term paper outlines just yesterday and said to hand in the finished term paper and he want it at least five pages long. He said we had to do a book report too, on TEST even! The termpaper and the book report is due tomorrow. What makes me so mad is that he has NO HEART, he doesn't care if you have tests in other classes or not!; and he's so last minuted. Oh, he makes me want to jump into the bay for all the other things I'd have to do plus those.

Well that's enough about my troubles, how've everything with you? Find of course. I bet you have a nice time there living so independent in your own apartment and everything. Well goodbye for now I've got to clean up the house.

Hope you'll always be very successful in what ever you do.

Lena

Dirigible waited two days to answer. He opened Lena's letter and shook it, trying to shake the smell of unimaginable dead flowers out of the paper. Finally he wrote.

Dear Lena,

Your loneliness must be very profound, indeed, to send me, your cousin, a perfumed letter. It's still smelling up my whole apartment, and soon, I'll have to hang it out the window. Really, I appreciate your letter and your *cousinly* affection. I don't have as many girlfriends as you say, and I do have a "tiny second" to write you.

Your spelling and grammar are miserable (this is cousinly concern now). "Find" is a verb meaning to discover. "Fine" is an adjective meaning, in colloquial English, "well." "I find you feel fine." Also you have your "your's" mixed up. "Your" is not "you're," okay? Now, I'm going to talk like father would talk, only in a cousinly way. You might show this to your mother if you like. I think it's time for you to start dating. I know you think about it. I know boys ask you out. You've told me, remember? And I know how your mother carried on when she found you and me and ma dancing to those old records at my house a couple of years ago, and it's not right. Why don't you work out a plan of going out every other week-end with some nice Chinese boy that your mother likes and promise to come home by midnight? If you don't go out this summer some time, a girl of your vitality might start sneaking out and meet up with the wrong kind of guy, you know the kind of guy that has "one thing on his mind" and steals cars, reads poetry and drinks, gambles, hates his mother and George Washington, calls San Francisco "Frisco" and rolls drunks . . . the kind of guy my mother thinks I am. But honestly I know that's the way a girl could go . . . don't ask me how I know, I know, okay? . . . And maybe, when I have time, a friend and his sister (about your age) and me and you can go to the zoo or Playland or something in the daytime, okay? No promises, just maybe. Practice your grammar, don't disparage school, be a good girl, give little Boo Boo a haircut . . . you're not fat.

Your eldest and outcast cousin,
Dirigible (*Dirge* for you)

He began by crossing out "Dirge for you." Time to break the habit of answering to that nickname. Let the old Chinamans and his relatives get his name right. The letter was right, he thought, a vocabulary that would make her use a dictionary, plenty of commas and semicolons; it was the right tone, he was sure, concerned without giving anything away. "Some nice Chinese boy," he read aloud from his letter. Well, he thought, Lena and some nice Chinese boy would go good together. She's not ambitious, and she's young . . . maybe smarter'n I think, and if she listens to her cousin's advice, tempers it with what she sees? He stopped planning his cousin's life, mailed the letter and forgot it.

Her next letter was not perfumed.

Dear, young Daddy;

All my girlfriends at the church call you that now, how 'bout that? I showed the letter to them and they finded it real fine. Why don't you come back and help build the church and get some of Buddha's *gum hay*? Whatever that is in English nobody has heard, right? The church is really needing help with it. Mommy is out in Los Angeles getting people to donate stuff for it (she's so pretty in her Chinese dress!) and you know what that means ME AND THE KIDS. Say! Howcome you made me look up all those funny words in the dictionary? You think I'm a brain or something?

Mommy lets some of the girls from the church come over to the apartment (what a mess it's) and we lock ourself in the bathroom and make ourself up with lipstick and stuff we buy. But that's girlses business and shuld not tell boys. But your a man, I'd forgot. Boy! do we look funny in the mirro sometimes. You should see us. Why don't you come over and watch TV with us? They all want to see you. They think your so hand-some? They all remember you at the church and think you was "cute" and oh, so tall! And your smart too.

Oh! Don't get mad now. I forgot to show your letter to mommy. She was talking so much about Detroit and some girdles she got them to donate to build the church and stuff; but I's going to do it soon's she gets back from L.A. Ok? I am too fat! Boo Boo wants you to cut his hair. It's so LONG!

So long "Young Daddy."
Lena

Just one x

Enclosed in the letter was a photograph of Lena in a miniature bridesmaid gown. Dirigible remembered the photograph;
it had been his grandmother's favorite. He put in his steel
ammunition box where he kept his letters and social security
stub and wrote.

Lena,

You have to stop this "young daddy" jazz. People will think
you have an Oedipus complex and are crazy. And I wish you'd
stop showing your friends my letters. I'll write to them (I won't
really) if they're so interested in my prose style . . . though I
am flattered . . . a little. I'm sorry to be so curt with you (I
know you'll understand) but I'm having a time with a poem
I'm working on. I'm trying to figure out whether or not dawn
really looks like the sound of a thousand muted pops of champagne corks or not, and if it does, what is a good word that
rhymes with "corks"? . . . this is just a short note, dear cousin.
Don't worry about your looking fat or thinking you're fat;
you're not. No matter your mother came back from Detroit
with girdles instead of girders. Actually I think girdles are what
the church needs more than structural steel. Me. I'm skinny,
and I don't worry about girdles or girders. Put ribbons on Boo
Boo and tell him he's a girl. Show the first letter to your
mother. Your spelling is not much better . . . but better.

As ever,
Dirigible

I concede ½ an x

Dear Dirigible;

I know how really busy you're now, writing poems and
drawings. By the way! I finded a bunch of words that "rhyme"
with corks. There're porks storks forks and works and torque

and bork (I heared that one on the radio.) Anyways why don't you come over sometime when your not busy with your girlfriends or nothing? I'm always free I told you, and mommy is gone for awhile. I losed three WHOLE POUNDS, man! And I can't do nothing with the kids here.

What are you doing these days? Busy, I know.

Your friend,
Lena

P.S. You can see my new ring if your coming xxx

Dirigible felt the same sour embarrassment, pity, and disgust that he felt after seeing a cripple wearing trousers too long for his legs, selling colored carnations in front of a theater. Lena had such a happy way of writing her loneliness, he thought, like the cripple, bent and ugly, half dancing in front of the crowd and shouting, "Flowers! Quarter! Half a dollar!" Sentimentalist! Dirigible thought to himself. But he always had a quarter, the flowers he never kept. He knew he would visit his plump cousin. He opened his ammunition box and put her note inside. The smell of perfume was all through the papers inside and bloomed into his face as he lifted the lid. He wished suddenly that Lena was not his cousin, that he never knew her. And he was ashamed when he thought that she might remember them at his grandmother's house, bouncing on the cold sheets of the bed with a flashlight that made the skin look like soap. Ashamed wasn't it. He was still afraid she would, after all these years, tell on him. Perhaps if her name wasn't Lena, he thought, as if her name were to blame, then kicked the box under his desk where it belonged.

She lived in an apartment house owned and lived in by her dead father's family. Everybody in every one of the apartments here belonged to the same family and the same Buddhist church. The apartment house was far enough above Chinatown to have a hedge and a few flowers planted around it. A boy was doing a Chinese battle dance, using a broom for a sword in the front hall. He stopped and opened the door before Dirigible could press the buzzer. "Are you Boo Boo?" Dirigible asked.

"No. He lib up da stair," the boy said. He stabbed toward the stairs.

"You're not bad with that kung fu fighting," Dirigible said. "Where do you study?" toward the stairs.

"I go see lod a Chinese moobies!" the boy shouted after him.

The vague familiarity, not all that forgotten, not all that grabbing, short of nostalgia and déjà vu he found in the apartment house, the shadows in the corners, the worn rug with the pattern more walked out of it, made Dirigible realize the long time he had been away. At one time he had known everybody in the house, had lived here on weekends and gone down to help build the Buddhist church with them. But he did not regret leaving, for like the boy downstairs who was like all the boys in this house, everything was the same. The same and familiar beyond recognition, stagnant. That was why he had left and forgotten his cousin, all this part of the family, except for his glittering aunt, his mother's glamorous sister, Lena's mother. No, he thought, reaching the second flight of stairs, it's not comfortable at all to be back, even to be nice.

Lena opened the door, "Hello, Dirge, how're you?" She could write his name but still couldn't get it out of her Chinatown mouth. None of his relatives could. What a great name his mother had given him. No one else in the family could pronounce it. "Well, come on inside stranger." Her face was made up as if she had been practicing a long time, and she wore a pair of her mother's earrings. And she did not trip on her high heels when she stepped backward, making room for Dirigible's first step inside. Dirigible blushed, then turned his head to stifle a laugh. He had never seen his cousin with breasts before. Nice breasts.

"Chiyaaaaah! Hite!" they heard shouted from deep downstairs.

Lena smiled at Dirigible and still held the door. "I guess he killed a dragon or something," he said, nodding toward the stairs.

The walls of the apartment were covered with child-high crayon drawings, of trains, gardens, and battles that had been half washed off. A doorknob was missing from one of the doors, but the apartment was neat in a logical, if not attractive, sort of way, like a war surplus store. "Same old place," Dirigible said.

"It's a mess. I'm sorry."

"Oh no. It's fine. You should see my place if you want to see a real mess." Dirigible laughed.

"When?"

"When what?"

"When can I see your messy apartment?"

"Oh, some time." He spoke quickly, looking over Lena's head. He shoved his fists into his pockets and nodded as he laughed. It was difficult trying to find the right tone, the right slouch with which to assuage his cousin's loneliness. Diplomacy. Psychology. Dirigible wished he had not come, or at least that he had dressed to match his cousin. "I didn't know you were going to dress up," he said and it didn't sound right. He sounded like a kid with his voice changing, and cleared his throat.

"Well, that's all right." She stood in front of him and he looked at her chest. "I like to dress up for . . . oh, company," she said. She closed the door with one hand, not moving from her stand in Dirigible's stare. He looked down and watched the muscles of her calves bulge as her body leaned slightly after her arm, throwing the door shut. "Where are the kids?" Dirigible asked.

"Downstairs with auntie. They're gonna be there all night."

"Oh," Dirigible said. "The first auntie, Foon Foon's mother?"

"No, she died."

"Oh, I'm sorry," Dirigible said, looking quickly about him for something to make a joke about.

"Don't be sad! Are you? She died a long time ago." Lena grabbed the swell of Dirigible's forearm, near the elbow. Her hands stopped and held tightly. Dirigible patted the back of her hand and smiled. "No, I'm fine. I should've sent flowers."

"That reminds me," Lena said quickly. "Look!" She gripped her arm and squeezed, clenching her teeth in a savage smile. "You can see all the veins and blue blood. I never knowed there was so many before! Ever! Remember when we used to did that?"

"Yeah," Dirigible stepped a step back from Lena, who was squeezing her own arm white.

"Let's see yours." She grabbed Dirigible's arm and squeezed with both hands, her body coming close to Dirigible's chest. She put her head next to Dirigible's face. She smelled like her letter, only the smell was louder in his head. "All I can feel is muscle, all your muscle," Lena said, impressed.

"Can we sit down? My legs kind of hurt."

"Where?"

"In the . . ." He looked into what had been the living room and saw a chest of drawers and a bed with a violin case on it. "Wherever the living room is."

"Where does your leg hurt? I can rub linaments on them?"

"Oh . . ." He looked up and down his cousin's short body. She was wearing one of her mother's silk *cheongsams* slit half-way up the thighs. And she began looking very new with her young body to Dirigible. He looked again. Her wrists and ankles were too thick for her small hands and feet, and again, he had never seen her with lipstick before. "No . . ." he said finally, "I think I'll just sit down somewhere. Though it's a charming idea." He made a laugh.

"Then I'll do it! Okay? I used to do it with daddy before. I know how to rub linaments."

"No, really, Lena. I'd just like to sit down. I'm tired of standing in the hallway. I feel stupid standing in the hallway." He laughed again. Too loud.

"You don't want me to?"

"Nope . . ."

"You think I'm fat and ugly and stupid and don't know how to do anything!"

"No, I don't. I never said that. Now, come on and tell young daddy how you've been and quit acting like a little girl, huh?"

"I am a li'l girl. You're older'n me. I want to do just that . . . Nobody lets me do nothing no more. Just stay home! All the time!"

Dirigible made a face with his eyes wide and stared at her. Her logic sounded simple and sound to him, and safe enough, perhaps because he wanted it so. And he did. "Okay," he said, shrugging. And she clapped her hands and was down the hall toward the bathroom and telling him to go to the bedroom and slip into one of her daddy's bathrobes. "Okay."

He lay down on Lena's mother's bed, on his stomach, and piled his hands under his cheek and closed his eyes to the light. A small belch burst up into his throat before a long groan into relaxation at the sudden first slap of Lena's hands. Whap! Both hands. Now her hands were kneading the muscles of his calves, her hands gripped and slid slowly upwards, now at the soft spot behind the knees. Her hands were small and he enjoyed her fingers twisting the muscles over his bones. He felt the tightness drain out of his legs, and his legs felt softer, more relaxed than the rest of him.

As she beat him into a half-sleep she talked about her mother and her friends from the church, and her mother's new dresses, and taking care of Boo Boo and Cindy and her youngest brother whose name she took a long time to remember. Dirigible barely listened to her, felt only her hands rubbing the insides of his legs now. He imagined her bent over him, pushing with her shoulders and body as she rubbed and kneaded; he wondered if her breasts were trembling. "What's that?" she asked, and touched the soft spot behind his knee with her fingertips. She kissed it quickly then tapped it again. "There it'll be weller now."

"What'd you do that for?"

"You had a sore thing there."

"How can I have a sore there?" He raised himself to his elbows and twisted to see behind his back. He lifted his leg back by his ankle and looked behind his knee. "Yeah, I do, don't I?" He said and put the skirts of the bathrobe over his legs. He shook his head and sat up. He was awake now. He looked at his cousin sitting on the edge of the bed, the silk of her *cheongsam* shining where she swelled, but silk and sequins and lipstick could not change her eyes. After all these years they were the same eyes of the same little cousin she had always been to him, just like the photograph. They were young eyes, seeming younger surrounded by powder and rouge, and they were shallow-colored and so open. He did not know whether he liked them or not. He said, "I think you'd better stop or I'll forget you're my cousin and . . ." He shrugged and found a new ending for his sentence, "be sorry. . . ."

"Really?" She grinned and edged closer toward him, her rump sitting lightly against his bare calf. Does she know what she's doing, doing that? he wondered. He did not move. He felt his pulse climb up the sides of his neck into his ears. What a dumb time to blush, he thought. Couldn't I just keep this thing to a hero worship or something? Too late.

He leaned toward her, then stopped. A slight lowering of her shoulders and a quick blink of her eyes showed him what she wanted. He looked away quickly and shoved a finger up in the air and shouted, "Aha!" as if to throw his disgusting desire out of himself with a jerk. He slapped his thighs and laughed to noise the flower petals out of the air.

"What's wrong?"

"You . . ."

"You're laughing at me." She put her small hands along her hips, then quickly pulled off her mother's earrings.

"No," Dirigible laughed. "Do you know what you're doing?" He felt a chill up the outside of his legs and put the skirt of the bathrobe tighter around them.

"I didn't know I's doing nothing. Was I doin' something wrong?"

"Listen, oh, Lena." He sighed and looked at her. "You were trying to . . . I didn't think that you . . ." He stopped and jabbed at her with his fist. "I'm your cousin. God!"

"Well, gee whiz. What you want me to do? I can't help it if I like you!"

He sounded stupid to himself saying, "You're too young!"

Stupid and hypocritical. "I mean, young. You don't know if you like me. I mean, I like you too. I have to, we're relatives."

"I don't mean that kind of 'like.' I mean 'like' like liking."

"What do you have to be so honest for? Why can't you be evasive like nurses or sorority girls or high school teachers?"

"Because I don't know how!" she shouted. "I don't even know what you're talking about." He knew this was true, and it was funny in a sour, slimy sort of way. She began to cry.

"Don't cry," he said. "I'm not mad. See?" He touched her shoulder.

"Well, I am!" she said between gulps.

"Come on," he said. He took both of her shoulders and she leaned against him, her long hair against her cheek and lips and the side of his nose. "Sooner or later you'll . . . well, you'll know better."

"You think I'm a baby. I don't want to know better. I do know better now. Better'n you!"

"Well, you don't know better than to try to be like your mother yet."

"What're you talking?" She looked at herself and cried. "You're dumb."

Dirigible looked down the length of his body to her. He leaned and touched her shoulder. "Lena?"

"Don't touch me. Get out. You think I'm a joke!"

"No . . . I . . . ." Dirigible sat back and closed his eyes. It would be awkward for him to leave now, yet he could not stay.

The front door slammed and Lena's mother stepped into the room. "So dis is what goes on behind my back, huh?" Lena's mother said. She hiked her *cheongsam* up her thighs and walked quickly over to the bed and looked down at Dirigible, dressed in her dead husband's bathrobe. "And you! You should know better! Don't you know how old she is? She's your little cousin! What kind of dirty mind you got anyway?" Old makeup fell in small chips from her hairline as she spoke. Flesh shook on her arms like bread dough.

"You have the dirty mind here, Aunt Dee. I didn't do nothing."

He suddenly realized that what he was wearing didn't make sense of his righteous huff and puff. "She only put linament on my legs, because they were sore!"

"Boy, you wait till I tell your mother! What do you mean only put linament on your legs? That's what I do! Did! I'm going to take her to Dr. Jim downstairs tomorrow, man. And if . . ."

Dirigible glanced at Lena. She was sitting trying to hide herself behind her arms and crying. "And where'd you leab the kids? Can't I trust you with nothing?" Lena stood and said that she'd get them and left. Her game of Pretend was over, Dirigible thought, and she was, really was, prettier than her mother was now. Years ago they'd been under the sheets together with a flashlight and seen and touched each other in cookie-sized illuminations and never been caught, and never forgotten it, if that would be any consolation to her; it bothered him, as he left. It wasn't déjà vu, but he'd been here before. It was better when he'd been eight years old.

The trouble with his mother, he knew he could survive; he was always superlogical and composed when he was with her, but he was worried about Lena. But not anymore, he decided. No more worrying about anybody but number one for me! he thought, all to himself, not looking back to the house as he left, walking down the hill toward the lights of Chinatown and the nearest bus home.

Dirigible:

I founded your address from Lena. You're lucky this time. They said that you'd be like you're now when you left the church, remember? It's not too late to come back, you know. It would be nice if you'd work here and give your hours to your grandma. You know what me and Lena did? We earned up a hundred hours and gave them to Grandma, and now she has a million more years in heaven. So you see? The church ain't so bad after all.

I talked to your mother. I told her to be kind this time. Lucky for you. Lena and I go for Chicago next week. Think about what I told you.

Your loving aunt,
Deanna

Dear Dirigible, Hi;

It's me again, man! Ya! I'm find, really. You was right, yes, young daddy, mommy's letting me go out to town with some boys now. And I'm so happy; and I's not mad at you, ok? Boy! Next week mommy's going to Chicago for the church to talk to some magazinebook about a story for the church, and she says she's going to take me for one whole WEEK! The kids're going to stay at your mommy's hous.

I'll write you if you promise to write me, okay? Deal!

This is just a tiny letter, but I got to go down to the church now.

May you be successful in whatever you endeavor.

Yours truly,
Lena

Dear Lena,

To be brief, our roles have reversed, almost. I'm the wrong man for your "young daddy." So long.

Dirigible

Dirigible reread his note; it was brief, a pleasant tone. She would believe it, he thought. *So even the hero is gone.* He opened up his ammunition box. Her perfumed letters had gassed everything. That smell would be there forever. He took out all of Lena's letters and a piece of paper with typewriting on it. He read:

Dawn came up looking like the sound of a
thousand pops of champagne corks
And the sun with it, full of daylight and
tines of forks.

It was bad, he decided, terrible. He threw the whole bundle into the wastebag. He slapped his hands against his thighs after knotting the bag and then stepped on it.

Going to School

●●●●

D'ARCY McNICKLE

Dawn had come but it was still dark. The lights from the houses shone almost as brightly as they would have in the middle of night. A stiff wind came up at intervals and the sky over the eastern mountains was unmistakably growing lighter every minute. Roosters were crowing and occasionally a door opened and a man came out to spit and look at the sky.

A young boy stood by the dirt road and peered toward the fringe of timber that lay a quarter of a mile eastward from the town. He could see or hear nothing and was munching on an apple. In one hand he carried a lunch bucket.

Suddenly he heard horses snorting and blowing in the cold air. And then he could hear buggy wheels rattling over the frozen ground. He finished his apple in several large bites and tossed the core aside. He wiped his mouth with the sleeve of his coat and put his mitten on the hand that had held the apple. A moment later a team of horses and a buggy materialized out of the mist and gloom and a voice called out sharply:

"Whoa, there, cayuses!"

A girl's voice followed immediately after: "Good morning, Joey! Are we late?"

"Naw, you're not late. I just came from the house." He put his lunch pail in the back of the rig and climbed onto the seat.

"Put these blankets around you good. It's terribly cold." The girl helped to wrap the blankets around his legs.

"That's good enough," he said before she had finished.

The scraggy team of mares was put at a trot and the buggy was on its way again. It was precarious footing, however, and though they picked their feet up quickly and made a motion of trotting they couldn't manage anything better than a fast walk.

The sky had turned a shade lighter and the town could be made out more distinctly. It was a forlorn place clinging to the edge of the timber. Not a house was painted; they were all shanties.

On the left the mountains were still black and heavy mist hid their wide bases. High up among the peaks a ray of light gleamed now and then on a snow bank. Off to the right was the rolling prairie land and clumps of trees could be seen along some creek banks. There was a mist over the prairie, too, and it seemed dull and dead out that way. A chill breeze cut into the faces of the three travelers in the buggy and made them keep their heads pulled low on their shoulders.

Gene, the driver, was a thin-faced youth whose eyes watered constantly in the cold wind. His jaws stood out rigidly and his skin was smooth, for he hadn't yet put a razor to his face. He didn't talk as much as the others; he sat and brooded and wore a long face.

Ada sat in the middle and her blue eyes were always twinkling. She had a clear, healthy complexion and the stinging wind made her cheeks glow warmly. She was eighteen at most, yet she looked older.

Joe, who had waited at the roadside, knew of nothing better

in the world than to be sitting where he was, beside Ada. The buggy seat was narrow and he was pressed closely against her; he could feel her warmth up and down his right side. Joe was younger than the others, four years younger than Ada, but he never thought of that.

When they came to the bridge at the end of the first mile the team slowed down and looked cautiously from one side to the other as they went up the approach. The bridge planks were white with frost and after the buggy had passed over, two neat tracks were left behind. When the bridge was crossed, the horses picked up their shambling trot again. The breath came out of their nostrils in white clouds and formed a coating of frost on the hair of their necks. They were an unkempt team of little mares with their long winter's hair; bits of straw and their night's bedding still clung to their sides. Gene forgot to curry them most of the time.

A serious conversation was being carried on in the buggy. Joe had said: "My folks had a fight last night and we may be moving away one of these days."

"No! You don't meant right away—before school is out?" Ada asked.

"Well, no, not that soon."

"What was they fighting about?" Gene asked.

"Why, ma thinks that we made a bad move when we bought lots during the boom. She says we might as well have thrown the money in the river. But pa laughs about it. 'Money's no good if you don't use it,' he says. 'You just as well take a gambling chance once in a while; all you have is a gambling chance; and even then you're bound to lose,' he says."

"Were they angry?" Ada wanted to know.

"Oh yes, I suppose all the neighbors heard them."

"Well," Gene said, "your ma's right. Nobody's going to make any money out of that town!"

"You don't know anything about it! You've heard dad say that," his sister reminded him.

"We could have made a little money last fall. We were offered three hundred dollars more for the shop than it cost us. But ma said it wasn't enough. She got mad last night when we reminded her of it."

Gene went off on a tangent.

"Your folks don't fight any more than ours," he said. "There's a wrangle at home every day."

"We have dad to thank for that. If it was mother alone it would be different."

But Gene couldn't agree with that.

"It takes two to make a quarrel and she nags as much as he does. She doesn't do it outright, that's the difference. She goes around complaining until somebody has to get mad."

"She has something to complain about, I think! Not one of you kids ever help her and she's had ten of us to take care of."

"Well," said Gene, "I'll tell you one thing, Joe, don't get married! A poor man's got to work his fingers to the bone as it is, but if he gets married, he's sunk!"

But Joe disagreed. No. It wasn't that bad! It depended on yourself—and, of course, on whom you married.

"Do you think married people are never happy? Sure, lots of them are! But you've got to be in love. I don't think my folks were ever in love; they don't act like it, and that's why they row."

"You talk like a calf! What's love? I ain't seen any yet," Gene said.

What, no love! And Joe sat there burning with it! He knew no unhappiness. It was true that his father and mother made things unpleasant with their misunderstandings and unchari-table accusations. His sister was half an idiot and sat at home laughing and crying by turns and trying to draw pictures on the windowpane with her pencil. There was no money in the home most of the time though his father ran a butcher shop.

Joe lived in the midst of many things that might have been thought unpleasant, yet he went through them unscathed. When he sat beside Ada he was content. He thought of finer things; it might even be imagined that he saw them dancing by like the fence posts on either side that went flying past in an endless chain. For seven months, ever since school opened in September, he had been riding with the Silverthorns, and ever since Christmas when Ada kissed him at the School Entertainment he had been engulfed in a great world of mist and warm dew.

The sun had burst over the mountains and the gloom that had lurked in the hollows and over against the timber all disappeared. The few scattered banks of snow that lay in the nearby fields sparkled and looked whiter. The frost disappeared from the horses' necks and they got over the road with a freer gait.

On and on the road led in a straight line down the valley. The mountains were always parallel and as one traveled along one could see ever new angles to the peaks and canyons.

Gene sat on the driver's side in his peculiar hunched-over fashion and he held the lines with listless hands. He hissed at the horses and cursed them soundly when they slowed to catch a breath or when one of them slipped on a patch of ice. He seemed to dream, perhaps of the dreary round of chores that awaited him when he returned at night, perhaps of his father with his savage temper, or perhaps he dreamed of freedom from these things.

Ada, as she sat there, wore a half smile and an eager expression as if she expected every moment to come upon some marvellous discovery. No one could think of calling her a girl, exactly; she held her head with the studied grace of a woman; in a few years she would be a little too fleshy and then she would be a woman indeed.

For Joe there could be no accounting for her charm. He never relaxed in the seat beside her; he was in a continual flux of emotions. Something happened almost every day that brought him more deeply under her spell. It wasn't much, a mere nothing, but he came to regard each new day with wistful expectation. Anything might happen! In these past few months he had suddenly begun to feel like a matured young man. He looked backward from the pinnacle of his fourteen years and he saw his childhood lying somewhere in the indeterminate past.

The conversation had gone to other things.

"I've made up my mind to study law when I get to college," Joe said.

"Do you really plan to go to college, then?" Ada asked him.

"Yes. Ma always wanted me to be a lawyer. When she got her divorce they made her say a lot of things that weren't true but she couldn't help herself. So she's always wanted me to study law and make up for it, though I don't see what can be done now."

"That will be fine! When I come to get my divorce I'll see you the first thing. I'll say: 'Joey, my husband's mean to me. Please get me a divorce right away!' And then what will you do?"

Joe's tongue failed him and he couldn't think of a witty reply. He said: "I'll go and kick the seat of his pants up between his shoulders!"

Ada was surprised and didn't know whether to laugh or not, but Gene roared aloud and the horses threw up their heads and trotted faster.

Now they were approaching town. The seven-mile ride was ending. The sun was an hour above the mountains and the frostiness had almost gone from the air. The sky was completely free from cloud and mist and a golden effulgence poured down upon the land.

The school was the first building on the left as they entered town. It stood by itself in the center of a large yard. There were tall poles standing upright with crossbars over the top; these were the swings where the children played.

The school building was long and narrow and built in two stories. The lower half was covered with shingles and painted brown; white clapboards covered the upper half. From all directions one could see pupils coming toward the school in vehicles of all descriptions—some were on horseback, some had single-horse rigs, while others drove as a team; and now a green and white school-wagon came lumbering down the lane.

When Gene stopped his team of brown mares before the entrance gate, there were fully a half-hundred youngsters jumping around; they laughed and shouted and banged one another with their dinner pails. Something as fluid as electricity and as startling took possession of the three in the buggy. They looked at each other, at the crowd of pupils, and began to laugh. This was school! There was nothing else like it!

Joe got down and helped Ada from the buggy; then he drove with Gene to the stable to unhitch the horses.

It was a strange business, this going to school. Out at home things went their humdrum way; the father would be stamping around the fields to see how near the frost was to leaving the ground or he would be in the granary fanning his seed wheat; the mother would be in the kitchen mixing her bread or else out in the yard feeding the chickens. But in school it was different; they read about the capital of one state and the area of another; they learned about Nigeria and Liberia and Abyssinia and Lake Titicaca high in the mountains; they used words like *hypotenuse* and *congruent* in geometry; they found out that there had been a French Revolution and a War of the Spanish Succession and that Shakespeare had written many plays and was no doubt the greatest man in the world. But when they went home they kept their discoveries under their hats. It would never do to let the old folks feel that they didn't know everything; they would have only one way to answer such a charge, and that was with the stick.

Joe knew well enough how it was. He sat in his classroom and swallowed everything greedily. His head was full of things that had happened thousands of miles away and hundreds of years ago. But he knew better than to talk about them when he got home. There was no sense in being laughed at.

"Wipe your nose!" his father would say if Joe should tell him that Rome had been a great empire ruled over by Julius Caesar, who talked Latin.

The morning's ride had been a pleasant event in its way, and the school hours were themselves filled with moments of ecstasy; but the pleasantest time of all was when they drove home at night.

The air was warm then, so warm that coats were left unbuttoned and one could crane one's neck around and have a look at the scenery; and there were heavy shadows lying across the land. At the big cattle ranch along the foothills it was feeding time and the steers could be heard blowing and bellowing. The feeding wouldn't last much longer; soon there would be a coating of green over the hills and prairie and the stockman could leave off measuring his haystacks with his eye.

But there was no green grass yet. Indeed, the frost had by no means left the ground. The first few inches were free and soft with mud but down below there was something hard. And when morning came around everything would be stiff with frost again.

Everyone felt the glory of those first spring afternoons. Even Gene's shabby mares held their heads with a certain pride and they took to the long road with renewed energy as they swung around the corner and left the school house behind. And Gene himself was not the same. Whatever sparkle of humor his system could muster then came on the surface and played about for a moment like faint blue lightning on the horizon. But he wasn't at home when it came to playing with wit; he would stumble around for a while and before long take to cursing something or other as a more effective way of getting over what he wanted to say. No, Gene didn't fit into this world of youthful thoughts and feelings. He had shrivelled already. He had been broken to the plow when he was too young a colt and now he could never enjoy running wild.

Ada was touched by the same searing process. If she escaped at all it was something to marvel at. She was the eldest in the family of ten and she had borne the brunt of it all; she had mothered nine of the ten children; but it hadn't proved too heavy a task for her. She was charming and sprightly for an elderly woman of eighteen!

The family of ten was gradually becoming valuable as time went on. Over half of them were working now and if the first ones had been put at it a little too early it was easier for the latecomers.

Ada had kissed Joe at Christmastime and here it was March

and he hadn't awakened from the spell yet! He hadn't enjoyed it at the time, it is true. He had been too ashamed and confused to know just what had happened. Besides, the room had been full of people. Since then the event had revealed its proper significance. He would know how to act the next time.

His father and mother spent all their time making life unpleasant for each other. Every night when Joe came home they were at it. He lived his life on the road to school; the night was only spent in waiting for another day. Sometimes he couldn't avoid being drawn into a family melee; he went about looking so dreamy and absent-minded that his parents must turn and attack him occasionally. And he became more pointedly aware of the two worlds he was attempting to straddle. But on the road to school much was left behind and he dreamed astounding dreams. In fact, it would be hard to say which of Joe's thoughts were real and which were but the froth and mist of some dream pot bubbling over. And on this very day one dream, at least, was to put on a cloak of reality and meet Joe face to face.

For over seven months the two brown mares had performed their task in the most irreproachable manner possible. They had trotted mile after mile without complaint—though it is true that a fast-legged man could have kept abreast of them at any time; and as they went they looked neither on one side nor the other but with bowed heads kept the middle of the road. Viewing them critically, they were commonplace and shabby and a whip lash falling on their scrawny backs brought no protest. Yet on this day they did a most unexpected and unreasonable thing.

They had been trotting along with their eyes glued to the road and the three young people in the buggy behind them had been engaged in a methodical discussion of the day's events. The mares were shedding heavily and it was really difficult to talk as one had to stop at every other word and spit out a horse hair. Gene sat with the lines held loosely in his hands and he seemed to be pondering things in his uninspired way.

And then three pigs appeared suddenly.

They had escaped their pen and were in the lane, looking for the feast of green grass they had scented on the wind, no doubt. They had been hidden from view behind a pile of last years's tumbleweeds and just as the buggy came abreast of them they ran into the road to sniff the air and decide which way to run. They grunted and squealed and one old sow grew confused and tried to run between the legs of Tricksey, the mare on the rear side.

Tricksey was patient enough but she couldn't be expected to allow a pig to run between her legs. She sat back on her haunches for just a second and then she shot ahead like a cannon ball and it was a wonder that the tug straps didn't snap like cotton twine. Tricksey's mate caught the panic too and it took only a moment to get their legs and harness untangled and then they were off!

The buggy swayed from side to side; it dashed into the gutter and balanced for a moment on two wheels, then it straightened itself and lurched to the other side of the road. All the loose bolts and rods and wheel spokes were rattling as they never had rattled before.

It was strange to see what happened inside the buggy. At the first unexpected move Gene straightened himself in the seat. When the horses took the bits into their teeth and began their mad gallop straight for destruction—he lost no time in contemplation. With one movement he thrust the lines into Ada's hands and with a second motion he had vaulted out of the buggy and clear of the wheels. He landed in a lump on the roadside.

Joe sat there in a daze. If he had tried to talk he would have stuttered. The buggy swayed perilously, the slightest obstruction sent the wheels bounding into the air. He probably would have continued to sit in a trance until they had smashed against a fence or telephone post if he hadn't thrown his hand out involuntarily to balance himself. In doing so he grasped the lines. The next moment he had braced his feet against the dashboard and was pulling for all he was worth. He was thoroughly frightened by now and he had the strength of desperation.

Joe stopped the mares by running them into a sand bank at the corner of the lane where the road had been cut through a low hill. The moment they stopped he scrambled out and took them by the bridles. He was trembling. He led them around into the road again before they tried to climb the hill. He kept saying over and over:

"You damn mutts! You damn mutts! Hold up now!"

Gene didn't overtake them for half an hour. He came up the road with a limp in one leg.

Ada looked at him with amazement and contempt. "Why on earth did you jump?" she asked.

He didn't answer until he had examined the buggy and harness to see that nothing was broken. He climbed wearily onto the seat and he looked like quite an old man.

"Why did I jump? What do you suppose! Am I going to risk my neck for a team of scrub cayuses? Not much! I'll die soon enough as it is!"

Ada scorned such premature wisdom. "Look at little Joe!" she said. "He isn't thinking of himself all the time! He acts like a little man!—Why Joe!" She turned to him ecstatically. "You're so brave!"

With a swift movement she grasped his coat and pulled him close and kissed him, once on the cheek and once on the mouth. Then she laughed gently and let him go.

Joe had anticipated her action. He braced himself to meet it—to no avail. His courage gave way and he turned red; after the second kiss he actually put up his hands to protect himself! And immediately afterwards he felt miserable. He pushed his shoulders up and drew in his head to hide his confusion.

"You girls make me sick!" Gene said. "Always kissing people!"

"We don't kiss everybody, do we, Joe?"

What could Joe say!

They started down the road again. The mares had spent themselves and were content to go at an ordinary pace though they threw their heads from side to side and blew through their nostrils with the pride of their deed.

Darkness was coming now and there was coolness in the air. After the buggy had disappeared in the shadows and mist that arose from the cooling earth, the wheels could still be heard rattling over the graveled road. One more day of school was ending.

A Spell of Kona Weather

●●◉◉

SYLVIA WATANABE

For a couple of months after my sister Lulu ran Henry Hanabusa's '49 DeSoto into the tree at the bottom of Dead Man's Slide, she had to go to Doc McAllister's once a week to get the glass picked out of her face. Every Saturday morning, after she came home from the hospital, I walked her to his surgery in the big white house across the road, and then stood with my eyes shut, squeezing her hand, as he picked the slivers out with a pair of pointed stainless steel tweezers.

The accident had happened in April, the night she found out that Henry's son Jimmy had been killed in Vietnam. Jimmy and she had been going together since their senior year in high school, and his mother had always had about as much use for Lulu as our grandmother had for him. At any rate, Lulu didn't get the news of his death till nearly a week later when she overheard a couple of customers gossiping during her shift at Grandmother's store. That night, after she'd finished work, she stole over to the Hanabusa house and hot-wired Jimmy's father's DeSoto. She told me later that she and Jimmy had spent almost every minute of his last R and R working on that damn thing, and according to her calculations of time put in, it was more hers than anyone else's. After she got it started, she drove to the top of Dead Man's Slide, turned off the ignition, and let out the brake. For a couple of seconds, she said, she had the highest high she'd ever had.

On the day when Lulu's bandages came off, Grandmother locked up the grocery and accompanied us to Doc's for the first and last time. Dressed all in black, with her black-dyed hair pulled tightly into a bun, she looked like she was going to someone's funeral. When my sister emerged from the examining room, the old lady took in the damage with that measuring gaze of hers. Lulu had never been a beauty, but she had had a kind of vividness that almost made you think she was—with her brown skin, and black hair, and large dark eyes. Now, much of her face was still badly bruised. There were small gashes all over her cheeks and lips, and a row of stitches extended along one side of her jaw to her chin.

"Lucky nothing was broken. Just give it time," Doc said, putting the bandages aside and gently smoothing Lulu's rumpled hair, still as long and glossy as ever—so strangely untouched.

Grandmother got to her feet, then said. "There's nothing to be done. It's too broken to fix."

With that assessment, she abandoned years of trying to put my sister right. Once, when I asked the old lady exactly what she thought was wrong with Lulu, she'd said, "If you were a perfect stranger, would you ever guess that that girl was a granddaughter of mine?" I have always considered it my bad luck that no one could mistake me for anything else. Lulu gets her looks from our father, on the Amalu side of the family. I take after the tight-lipped, narrow-eyed Koyamas. When we were going to school, Lulu was called fast, and it wasn't for her brain. I was a plodder who got good grades. She is "wild" like our mama was. My middle name is Caution.

The one advantage I ever got from all this was that Grandmother left me alone the whole time she was sending my sister off to learn kimono wearing, or tea pouring, or pigeon-toed walking at the deportment classes sponsored by the Buddhist Mission's Ladies' Auxiliary. If this reform program worked, Grandmother had believed, she could eventually hook Lulu up with some Nice Young Man, like Clyde Sakamoto, who had recently inherited his father's hardware business, or Mrs. Kobayashi's cousin's friend's son, who was opening a dermatology practice in the resort town nearby. According to Grandmother's standards, Jimmy did not qualify as a Nice Young Man. He belonged to another category called Bad Influences. I never had anything against him, though. It seemed Lulu had found something in him that she'd always been looking for.

Before Lulu met Jimmy, she used to drive me crazy with her talk about finding our mama. Sometimes, when she got fed up with Grandmother's meddling, she'd do more than talk, she'd run away, then Grandmother would call in the authorities to haul her back. Once, to teach Lulu a lesson, the old lady even had her put in the Girls' Detention Home over at the county seat. For a while, all that stopped when my sister was with Jimmy.

Personally, I can't say I ever understood Lulu's obsession with Mama, especially since I can't remember a thing. Papa died when I was just a few years old, and our mother took off for California not long after. As the old saying goes, out of sight, out of mind; that's pretty much how it's been with me.

Lulu is only two years older than I am and can't claim much more of a memory. Still, while we were growing up, she tried to convince me that grief had driven Mama away, and that she'd send for us once she was feeling herself again. But when our mother went off, she left everything, except the five thousand dollars from our father's insurance policy, behind with our grandmother—a sure sign, I'd decided when I was old enough to figure things out, that she'd never intended to return. Besides, if someone ups and leaves for sixteen years and you don't hear anything from them except an occasional store-bought greeting with no return address, you figure they're trying to tell you something, and it isn't Dying to See You, Please Come Soon. For the last five years or so, we haven't heard a single word.

With Jimmy's death and then the accident, I was afraid that the old craziness would start up again. But Lulu seemed to have left all that behind. After her visits to Doc's had ended, and her face had started returning to normal, she began going for long swims out in the bay. Though she hadn't gotten her old looks back, she wasn't exactly at a loss. Several times, I saw her with a white guy. I saw him running after her on the sand, catching her, brushing back her hair with his hands. You could tell by the way he moved that he was older than the surfers who usually hang out at the beach, and there was something familiar about him, though I'd never gotten close enough to find out what.

Then, a couple of weeks ago, Lulu asked me to go with her. There's almost nothing I hate worse than ocean swimming— with the sting of salt in your eyes and the live feel of the water. But I know that Lulu knows that about me, so I make it a point never to refuse her invitations. That day, I followed her into the surf where it broke high up on the beach and swirled around our legs, pulling us deeper and deeper until the ocean bottom suddenly dropped off into nothing. Beneath the surface, I felt the current pulling at me, and fear tightened my chest. We swam out to the raft about a hundred yards from shore and stayed there talking awhile before turning back.

She told me about the man I'd seen her with. "It isn't like it was with Jimmy," she said. "But after his divorce, we'll move to the West Coast, and maybe I can even get one of those plastic surgeons there to fix my face."

I said, "You mean he's *married*? How do you know he's going to leave his wife?"

"I just know," she answered, and smiled dreamily.

"But did he actually come out and say so?" I demanded.

She snapped, "Not in so many words. You've got to read

between the lines." She sat up and put her legs in the water. "Annie, do you know what your problem is? You've got no imagination."

"And maybe you have too much of one," I said. But she was already swimming back toward shore.

After that day, she didn't bring up the subject again, though I continued to go with her on her swims. Each time we swam farther and farther, until one afternoon we reached the buoy at the center of the bay. The currents were stronger there, and ran deeper, and if you fitted yourself into the wrong channel by mistake, or if you went out between tides, you could be swept into the open sea. As I stroked out toward the buoy, I fought down the voice in my head screaming to turn back.

Then, a couple of days ago, she did not turn around. I stopped and clung to the buoy as it bobbed up and down, and I watched her moving, strong and smooth, away from me. When I could hardly see her anymore, I turned and headed for the beach, now more afraid of the ocean than of Lulu.

She took a long time swimming back, and stumbled out of the surf, nearly falling. When she saw me watching her, she broke into a run. She gasped, "Annie, you chicken. I turned to look for you, and you weren't there."

As she sat catching her breath, I asked, "You been seeing that guy?"

Lulu laughed. "Sure have. He's crazy about me." She looked out over the water. "But not crazy enough to ditch his wife."

Around us, in the gathering dark, the afternoon had turned to lead. The sky and the sea had become the same dull shade of gray, and you couldn't tell where one began and the other ended.

"So, aren't you going to say, 'I told you so'?" she finally said. I looked down and began digging at the sand with a stick. She tossed back her hair. "Who needs him anyway?" She gave me a sly, triumphant look. "This morning I got a letter from Mama. She's moved to Oregon, and she wants me to join her."

I began to protest, but I looked at her face just then and

stopped. Instead, I said, "What are you going to do for a plane ticket?"

She gave me a pitying look. "Poor Annie," she said. "Always the businesswoman."

Yesterday morning, when Lulu was supposed to be working at the store, she emptied the cash register. Grandmother put Sheriff Kanoi on her, and he found her a few hours later, full of vodka and 7-Up, at the La Hula Rhumba Bar and Grill. After he'd brought her back and I'd put her to bed upstairs, the old lady and I sat outside on the front steps with sodas.

Grandmother swallowed the last of her root beer and set down the bottle. "If that girl doesn't get hold of herself, she's going to end up in a crazy house, just like your mama."

When she said that, she caught me off balance the way she and Lulu are always so good at; and, for a second, I couldn't believe I'd heard what I did. "What're you talking about?" I finally said. "Mama's in Oregon."

She stood and started up the steps. "That's just another of your sister's stories."

I knew it was, but I wasn't admitting anything. "What about California?" I cried. "She sent us birthday cards. That wasn't a story."

Grandmother turned back toward me, then said, "No, she was in California all right. Still is. But what do you suppose she's doing there? She went nuts after your father died; that man had such a hold on her, I never understood it." She sighed. "From what I've heard, they shot her brain full of electricity a few years back, and she hasn't done much letter writing since."

I was so stunned, at first, I couldn't move. Then I threw my soda at her. She ducked as it went past, and the bottle crashed against the wall and broke, spewing root beer across the porch.

Grandmother stepped around the puddles of soda and broken glass. "You be sure and clean up that mess," she called over her shoulder as she pushed open the door to the grocery and went inside.

Upstairs, the screen door slammed, and there was the sound of footsteps on the stairs. I knew that Lulu must have heard.

"Lulu!" I called as she headed down the road to the beach. "Where're you headed?" She began walking even faster in the direction of the water. I could see the old lady at the back of the store, closing up the register, but I didn't say anything, and took off after my sister.

When I got to the beach, it was deserted, and the tide was going out. "Lulu!" I shouted again, but she ignored me. I was still feeling tired from the previous day's swim, and shouting only used up breath.

The sand pulled at my legs. My chest burned. I stumbled and nearly fell, but I was gaining on her. She was so close— just ahead, at the edge of the water. Oh, please, I thought, please let me reach her before we have to start swimming. The waves fanned out across the sand, pulling at my ankles. Lulu was about ten feet away. Then, suddenly, she seemed to drop off the edge of the world. I saw her head bobbing above the water, and I knew I had to go in too. I waded in, feeling sand under my feet, and sand, and sand, then nothing. The ocean was unbearably alive around me, the pull of the current strong. I swam toward Lulu, closed on her, reached, and missed. The movement disrupted the rhythm of our strokes. We flailed around for a little, trying to pick it up again.

"Go back," she gasped. I reached for her, and she repeated, "Go back."

I reached a third time and got her. She struggled. We both went under. She stopped fighting. We were almost at the raft; then we were there. We pulled ourselves onto it and lay, panting, with our heads on our arms. For a long time we were too spent to talk. When we'd recovered a little, she said she'd return with me; maybe she knew I wouldn't make it if I had to pull her in.

We swam across the current to get back to shore and crawled out onto the beach. As we rested, side by side, I kept remembering how it was when we were kids—the way she'd marched straight into things, while I tagged along. "Are you sure, Lulu? Is it safe?" But I'd followed, afraid of what lay ahead—the top branch of the mango tree in the graveyard, Dead Man's Slide in the dark, the deep water out beyond the buoy—but more afraid to be left behind.

I reached over and touched her face with my fingers. I could still feel the hard lumps under her skin where the fragments of glass sometimes came poking through. She opened her eyes and smiled. "I bet I could have made it clear to the other side," she said.

During the night the wind shifted to the southeast, and the Kona weather moved in. Now the wet, still air presses close, heavy with the threat of rain. My sister has stayed upstairs and slept all day. Whenever I look at my grandmother's face or hear her voice, I think of the pistols I saw once in a glass cabinet at the Sakamoto Hardware, and I imagine picking one of them up in my hand, and feeling the weight of it, and slowly easing the trigger back.

"It's better if Lulu goes away for a little while," Grandmother says from across the store. Her angular shape pokes out from behind the cash register—her black dress, blacker than the shadows around her. "Doc McAllister's told me he knows a place where they will give her proper care."

You mean, like they did to Mama? I want to say. Instead, I pick up a rag and begin dusting the jars of colored puffed rice, preserved plums, and dried cuttlefish lined up on tiers across from where she's sitting. Beads of moisture drop from my forehead onto the heavy glass lids.

Grandmother finishes counting out the cash in the register, and slips it into a bank bag. "There's nothing more to be done," she says.

Upstairs, Lulu has wakened and is moving around. It is the sound I have been listening for. "You finished counting the money?" I ask, a little too loudly. The screen door bangs softly, as if a breeze is pushing at it, but there is no breeze. There is the sound of footsteps on the stairs.

Grandmother is halfway to the door, then turns. "You saw

me," she says. "Do you need glasses?" The footsteps move across the drive and out into the road.

I say, "You're right. I forgot. Shall I close up now?"

"There's no need to shout." The old lady waves impatiently, muttering, "Do what you like," and lets herself out.

When she is gone, I switch off the lights and sit for a while, listening.

What Means Switch

●●●●

GISH JEN

There we are, nice Chinese family—father, mother, two born-here girls. Where should we live next? My parents slide the question back and forth like a cup of ginseng neither one wants to drink. Until finally it comes to them, what they really want is a milkshake (chocolate) and to go with it a house in Scarsdale. What else? The broker tries to hint: the neighborhood, she says. Moneyed. Many delis. Meaning rich and Jewish. But someone has sent my parents a list of the top ten schools nationwide (based on the opinion of selected educators and others), and so, *many-deli* or not we nestle into a Dutch colonial on the Bronx River Parkway. The road's windy where we are, very charming; drivers miss their turns, plough up our flower beds, then want to use our telephone. "Of course," my mom tells them, like it's no big deal, we can replant. We're the type to adjust. You know—the lady drivers weep, my mom gets out the Kleenex for them. We're a bit down the hill from the private-plane set, in other words. Only in our dreams do our jacket zippers jam, what with all the lift tickets we have stapled to them, Killington on top of Sugar-bush on top of Stowe, and we don't even know where the Virgin Islands are—although certain of us do know that virgins are like priests and nuns, which there were a lot more of in Yonkers, where we just moved from, than there are here.

This is my first understanding of class. In our old neighbor-hood everybody knew everything about virgins and non-virgins, not to say the technicalities of staying in-between. Or almost everybody, I should say; in Yonkers I was the laugh-along type. Here I'm an expert.

"You mean the man . . . ?" Pig-tailed Barbara Gugelstein spits a mouthful of coke back into her can. "That is *so* gross!"

Pretty soon I'm getting popular for a new girl, the only problem is Danielle Meyers, who wears blue mascara and has gone steady with two boys. "How do *you* know," she starts to ask, proceeding to edify us all with how she French-kissed one boyfriend and just regular-kissed another. ("Because, you know, he had braces.") We hear about his rubber bands, how once one popped right into her mouth. I begin to realize I need to find somebody to kiss too. But how?

Luckily, I just about then happen to tell Barbara Gugelstein I know karate. I don't know why I tell her this. My sister Callie's the liar in the family; ask anybody. I'm the one who doesn't see why we should have to hold our heads up. But for some reason I tell Barbara Gugelstein I can make my hands like steel by thinking hard. "I'm not supposed to tell anyone," I say.

The way she backs away, blinking, I could be the burning bush.

"I can't do bricks," I say—a bit of expectation management. "But I can do your arm if you want." I set my hand in chop position.

"Uhh, it's okay," she says. "I know you can, I saw it on TV last night."

That's when I recall that I too saw it on TV last night—in fact, at her house. I rush on to tell her I know how to get pregnant with tea.

"With *tea?*"

"That's how they do it in China."

She agrees that China is an ancient and great civilization that ought to be known for more than spaghetti and gunpowder. I tell her I know Chinese. "*Be-yeh fa-foon,*" I say. "*Shee-veh. Ji nu.*" Meaning, "Stop acting crazy. Rice gruel. Soy sauce." She's impressed. At lunch the next day, Danielle Meyers and Amy Weinstein and Barbara's crush, Andy Kaplan, are all impressed too. Scarsdale is a liberal town, not like Yonkers, where the Whitman Road Gang used to throw crabapple mash at my sister Callie and me and tell us it would make our eyes stick shut. Here we're like permanent exchange students. In another ten years, there'll be so many Orientals we'll turn into Asians; a Japanese grocery will buy out that one deli too many. But for now, the mid-sixties, what with civil rights on TV, we're not so much accepted as embraced. Especially by the Jewish part of town—which, it turns out, is not all of town at all. That's just an idea people have, Callie says, and lots of them could take us or leave us same as the Christians, who are nice too; I shouldn't generalize. So let me not generalize except to say that pretty soon I've been to so many bar and bas mitzvahs, I can almost say myself whether the kid chants like an angel or like a train conductor, maybe they could use him on the commuter line. At seder I know to forget the bricks, get a good pile of that mortar. Also I know what is schmaltz. I know that I am a goy. This is not why people like me, though. People like me because I do not need to use deodorant, as I demonstrate in the locker room before and after gym. Also, I can explain to them, for example, what is tofu (*der-voo,* we say at home). Their mothers invite me to taste-test their Chinese cooking.

"Very authentic." I try to be reassuring. After all, they're nice people, I like them. "De-lish." I have seconds. On the question of what we eat, though, I have to admit, "Well, no, it's different than that." I have thirds. "What my mom makes is home style, it's not in the cookbooks."

Not in the cookbooks! Everyone's jealous. Meanwhile, the big deal at home is when we have turkey pot pie. My sister Callie's the one who introduced them—Mrs. Wilder's, they come in this green-and-brown box—and when we have them, we both get suddenly interested in helping out in the kitchen. You know, we stand in front of the oven and help them bake. Twenty-five minutes. She and I have a deal, though, to keep it secret from school, as everybody else thinks they're gross. We think they're a big improvement over authentic Chinese home cooking. Ox-tail soup—now that's gross. Stir-fried beef with tomatoes. One day I say, "You know Ma, I have never seen a stir-fried tomato in any Chinese restaurant we have ever been in, ever."

"In China," she says, real lofty, "we consider tomatoes are a delicacy."

"Ma," I say. "Tomatoes are *Italian*."

"No respect for elders." She wags her finger at me, but I can tell it's just to try and shame me into believing her. "I'm tell you, tomatoes *invented* in China."

"*Ma*."

"Is true. Like noodles. Invented in China."

"That's not what they said in *school*."

"In *China*," my mother counters, "we also eat tomatoes un-cooked, like apple. And in summertime we slice them, and put some sugar on top."

"Are you sure?"

My mom says of course she's sure, and in the end I give in, even though she once told me that China was such a long time ago, a lot of things she can hardly remember. She said sometimes she has trouble remembering her characters, that sometimes she'll be writing a letter, just writing along, and all of a sudden she won't be sure if she should put four dots or three.

"So what do you do then?"

"Oh, I just make a little sloppy."

"You mean you *fudge?*"

She laughed then, but another time, when she was showing me how to write my name, and I said, just kidding, "Are you sure that's the right number of dots now?" she was hurt.

"I mean, of course you know," I said. "I mean, *oy.*"

Meanwhile, what *I* know is that in the eighth grade, what people want to hear does not include how Chinese people eat sliced tomatoes with sugar on top. For a gross fact, it just isn't gross enough. On the other hand, the fact that somewhere in China somebody eats or has eaten or once ate living monkey brains—now that's conversation.

"They have these special tables," I say, "kind of like a giant collar. With a hole in the middle, for the monkey's neck. They put the monkey in the collar, and then they cut off the top of its head."

"Whadda they use for cutting?"

I think. "Scalpels."

"*Scalpels?*" says Andy Kaplan.

"Kaplan, don't be dense," Barbara Gugelstein says. "The Chinese *invented* scalpels."

Once a friend said to me, "You know, everybody is valued for something." She explained how some people resented being valued for their looks; others resented being valued for their money. Wasn't it still better to be beautiful and rich than ugly and poor, though? You should be just glad, she said, that you have something people value. It's like having a special talent, like being good at ice skating, or opera singing. She said you could probably make a career out of it.

Here's the irony: I am.

Anyway. I am ad-libbing my way through eighth grade, as I've described. Until one bloomy spring day, I come in late to homeroom, and to my chagrin discover there's a new kid in class.

Chinese.

So what should I do, pretend to have to go to the girls'

room, like Barbara Gugelstein the day Andy Kaplan took his ID back? I sit down; I am so cool I remind myself of Paul Newman. First thing I realize, though, is that no one looking at me is thinking of Paul Newman. The notes fly:

"*I* think he's cute."

"Who?" I write back. (I am still at an age, understand, when I believe a person can be saved by aplomb.)

"I don't think he talks English too good. Writes it either."

"Who?"

"They might have to put him behind a grade, so don't worry."

"He has a crush on you already, you could tell as soon as you walked in, he turned kind of orangish."

I hope I'm not turning orangish as I deal with my mail, I could use a secretary. The second round starts:

"What do you mean who? Don't be weird. Didn't you *see* him??? Straight back over your right shoulder!!!!"

I have to look; what else can I do? I think of certain tips I learned in Girl Scouts about poise. I cross my ankles. I hold a pen in my hand. I sit up as though I have a crown on my head. I swivel my head slowly, repeating to myself, *I* could be Miss America.

"Miss Mona Chang."

Horror raises its hoary head.

"Notes, please."

Mrs. Mandeville's policy is to read all notes aloud.

I try to consider what Miss America would do, and see myself, back straight, knees together, crying. Some inspiration. Cool Hand Luke, on the other hand, would, quick, eat the evidence. And why not? I should yawn as I stand up, and boom, the notes are gone. All that's left is to explain that it's an old Chinese reflex.

I shuffle up to the front of the room.

"One minute please," Mrs. Mandeville says.

I wait, noticing how large and plastic her mouth is.

She unfolds a piece of paper.

And I, Miss Mona Chang, who got almost straight A's her

whole life except in math and conduct, am about to start
crying in front of everyone.

I am delivered out of hot Egypt by the bell. General pandemo-
nium. Mrs. Mandeville still has her hand clamped on my
shoulder, though. And the next thing I know, I'm holding the
new boy's schedule. He's standing next to me like a big blank
piece of paper. "This is Sherman," Mrs. Mandeville says.

"Hello," I say.

"Non how a," I say.

I'm glad Barbara Gugelstein isn't there to see my Chinese in
action.

"Ji nu," I say. *"Shee veh."*

Later I find out that his mother asked if there were any
other Orientals in our grade. She had him put in my class on
purpose. For now, though, he looks at me as though I'm much
stranger than anything else he's seen so far. Is this because he
understands I'm saying "soy sauce rice gruel" to him or because he doesn't?

"Sher-man," he says finally.

I look at his schedule card. Sherman Matsumoto. What kind
of name is that for a nice Chinese boy?

(Later on, people ask me how I can tell Chinese from Japanese.
I shrug. You just kind of know, I say. *Oy!*)

Sherman's got the sort of looks I think of as pretty-boy. Monsi-
gnor-black hair (not monk brown like mine), bouncy. Crayola
eyebrows, one with a round bald spot in the middle of it, like
a golf hole. I don't know how anybody can think of him as
orangish; his skin looks white to me, with pink triangles hanging down the front of his cheeks like flags. Kind of delicate
looking, but the only truly uncool thing about him is that his
spiral notebook has a picture of a kitty cat on it. A big white
fluffy one, with a blue ribbon above each perky little ear. I get
much opportunity to view this, as all the poor kid understands
about life in junior high school is that he should follow me

everywhere. It's embarrassing. On the other hand, he's obviously even more miserable than I am, so I try not to say anything. Give him a chance to adjust. We communicate by sign language, and by drawing pictures, which he's better at than I am; he puts in every last detail, even if it takes forever. I try to be patient.

A week of this. Finally I enlighten him. "You should get a new notebook."

His cheeks turn a shade of pink you mostly only see in hyacinths.

"Notebook." I point to his. I show him mine, which is psychedelic, with big purple and yellow stick-on flowers. I try to explain he should have one like this, only without the flowers. He nods enigmatically, and the next day brings me a notebook just like his, except that this cat sports pink bows instead of blue.

"Pret-ty," he says. "You."

He speaks English! I'm dumbfounded. Has he spoken it all this time? I consider: Pretty. You. What does that mean? Plus actually, he's said *plit-ty*, much as my parents would; I'm assuming he means pretty, but maybe he means pity. Pity. You.

"Jeez," I say finally.

"You are wel-come," he says.

I decorate the back of the notebook with stick-on flowers and hold it so that these show when I walk through the halls. In class I mostly keep my book open. After all, the kid's so new; I think I really ought to have a heart. And for a livelong day nobody notices.

Then Barbara Gugelstein sidles up. "Matching notebooks, huh?"

I'm speechless.

"First comes love, then comes marriage, and then come chappies in a baby carriage."

"Barbara!"

"Get it?" she says. "Chinese Japs."

"Bar-*bra*," I say to get even.

"Just make sure he doesn't give you any *tea*," she says.

Are Sherman and I in love? Three days later, I hazard that we are. My thinking proceeds this way: I think he's cute, and I think he thinks I'm cute. On the other hand, we don't kiss and we don't exactly have fantastic conversations. Our talks *are* getting better, though. We started out, "This is a book." "Book." "This is a chair." "Chair." Advancing to, "What is this?" "This is a book." Now, for fun, he tests me.

"What is this?" he says.

"This is a book," I say, as if I'm the one who has to learn how to talk.

He claps. "Good!"

Meanwhile, people ask me all about him, I could be his press agent.

"No, he doesn't eat raw fish."

"No, his father wasn't a kamikaze pilot."

"No, he can't do karate."

"Are you sure?" somebody asks.

Indeed he doesn't know karate, but judo he does. I am hurt I'm not the one to find this out; the guys know from gym class. They line up to be flipped, he flips them all onto the floor, and after that he doesn't eat lunch at the girls' table with me anymore. I'm more or less glad. Meaning, when he was there, I never knew what to say. Now that he's gone, though, I seem to be stuck at the "This is a chair" level of conversation. Ancient Chinese eating habits have lost their cachet; all I get are more and more questions about me and Sherman. "I dunno," I'm saying all the time. *Are* we going out? We do stuff, it's true. For example, I take him to department stores, explain to him who shops in Alexander's, who shops in Saks. I tell him my family's the type that shops in Alexander's. He says he's sorry. In Saks he gets lost; either that, or else I'm the lost one. (It's true I find him calmly waiting at the front door, hands behind his back, like a guard.) I take him to the candy store. I take him to the bagel store. Sherman is crazy about bagels. I explain to him that Lender's is gross, he should get his bagels from the bagel store. He says thank you.

"Are you going steady?" people want to know.

How can we go steady when he doesn't have an ID bracelet? On the other hand, he brings me more presents than I think any girl's ever gotten before. Oranges. Flowers. A little bag of bagels. But what do they mean? Do they mean, Thank you, I enjoyed our trip; do they mean, I like you; do they mean, I decided I liked the Lender's better even if they are gross, you can have these? Sometimes I think he's acting on his mother's instructions. Also I know at least a couple of the presents were supposed to go to our teachers. He told me that once and turned red. I figured it still might mean something that he didn't throw them out.

More and more now, we joke. Like, instead of "I'm thinking," he always says, "I'm sinking," which we both think is so funny that all either one of us has to do is pretend to be drowning and the other one cracks up. And he tells me things —for example, that there are electric lights everywhere in Tokyo now.

"You mean you didn't have them before?"

"Everywhere now!" He's amazed too. "Since Olympics!"

"Olympics?"

"1960," he says proudly, and as proof, hums for me the Olympic theme song. "You know?"

"Sure," I say, and hum with him happily. We could be a picture on a UNICEF poster. The only problem is that I don't really understand what the Olympics have to do with the modernization of Japan, any more than I get this other story he tells me, about that hole in his left eyebrow, which is from some time his father accidentally hit him with a lit cigarette. When Sherman was a baby. His father was drunk, having been out carousing; his mother was very mad but didn't say anything, just cleaned the whole house. Then his father was so ashamed he bowed to ask her forgiveness.

"Your mother cleaned the house?"

Sherman nods solemnly.

"And your father *bowed*?" I find this more astounding than

anything I ever thought to make up. "That is so weird," I tell him.

"Weird," he agrees. "This I no forget, forever. *Father* bow to *mother!*"

We shake our heads.

As for the thing he asks me, they're not topics I ever discussed before. Do I like it here? "Of course I like it here, I was born here," I say. Am I Jewish? Jewish! I laugh. *Oy!* Am I American? "Sure I'm American," I say. "Everybody who's born here is American, and also some people who convert from what they were before. You could become American." But he says no, he could never. "Sure you could," I say. "You only have to learn some rules and speeches."

"But I Japanese," he says.

"You could become American anyway," I say. "Like I *could* become Jewish, if I wanted to. I'd just have to switch, that's all."

"But you Catholic," he says.

I think maybe he doesn't get what means switch.

I introduce him to Mrs. Wilder's turkey pot pies. "Gross?" he asks. I say they are, but we like them anyway. "Don't tell anybody." He promises. We bake them, eat them. While we're eating, he's drawing me pictures.

"This American," he says, and he draws something that looks like John Wayne. "This Jewish," he says, and draws something that looks like the Wicked Witch of the West, only male.

"I don't think so," I say.

He's undeterred. "This is Japanese," he says, and draws a fair rendition of himself. "This Chinese," he says, and draws what looks to be another fair rendition of himself.

"How can you tell them apart?"

"This way," he says, and he puts the picture of the Chinese so that it is looking at the pictures of the American and the Jew. The Japanese faces the wall. Then he draws another picture, of a Japanese flag, so that the Japanese has that to contemplate. "Chinese lost in department store," he says. "Japanese know how go." For fun, he then takes the Japanese flag and fastens it to the refrigerator door with magnets. "In school, in ceremony, we this way," he explains, and bows to the picture.

When my mother comes in, her face is so red that with the white wall behind her she looks a bit like the Japanese flag herself. Yet I get the feeling I better not say so. First she doesn't move. Then she snatches the flag off the refrigerator, so fast the magnets go flying. Two of them land on the stove. She crumples up the paper. She hisses at Sherman, "*This is the U. S. of A., do you hear me!*"

Sherman hears her.

"You call your mother right now, tell her come pick you up."

He understands perfectly. *I*, on the other hand, am stymied. How can two people who don't really speak English understand each other better than I can understand them? "But Ma," I say.

"Don't *Ma* me," she says.

Later on she explains that World War II was in China, too. "Hitler," I say. "Nazis. Volkswagens." I know the Japanese were on the wrong side, because they bombed Pearl Harbor. My mother explains about before that. The Napkin Massacre. "*Nan*-king," she corrects me.

"Are you sure?" I say. "In school, they said the war was about putting the Jews in ovens."

"Also about ovens."

"About both?"

"Both."

"That's not what they said in school."

"*Just forget about school.*"

Forget about school? "I thought we moved here for the schools."

"We moved here," she says, "for your education."

Sometimes I have no idea what she's talking about.

"I like Sherman," I say after a while.

"He's nice boy," she agrees.

Meaning what? I would ask, except that my dad's just come home, which means it's time to start talking about whether we should build a brick wall across the front of the lawn. Recently a car made it almost into our living room, which was so scary, the driver fainted and an ambulance had to come. "We should have discussion," my dad said after that. And so for about a week, every night we do.

"Are you just friends, or more than just friends?" Barbara Gugelstein is giving me the cross-ex.

"Maybe," I say.

"Come on," she says, "I told you *everything* about me and Andy."

I actually *am* trying to tell Barbara everything about Sherman, but everything turns out to be nothing. Meaning, I can't locate the conversation in what I have to say. Sherman and I go places, we talk, one time my mother threw him out of the house because of World War II.

"I think we're just friends," I say.

"You think or you're sure?"

Now that I do less of the talking at lunch, I notice more what other people talk about—cheerleading, who likes who, this place in White Plains to get earrings. On none of these topics am I an expert. Of course, I'm still friends with Barbara Gugelstein, but I notice Danielle Meyers has spun away to other groups.

Barbara's analysis goes this way: To be popular, you have to have big boobs, a note from your mother that lets you use her Lord and Taylor credit card, and a boyfriend. On the other hand, what's so wrong with being unpopular? "We'll get them in the end," she says. It's what her dad tells her. "Like they'll turn out too dumb to do their own investing, and then they'll get killed in fees, and then they'll have to move to towns where the schools stink. And my dad should know," she winds up. "He's a broker."

"I guess," I say.

But the next thing I know, I have a true crush on Sherman

Matsumoto. *Mister* Judo, the guys call him now, with real respect; and the more they call him that, the more I don't care that he carries a notebook with a cat on it.

I sigh. "Sherman."

"I thought you were just friends," says Barbara Gugelstein.

"We were," I say mysteriously. This, I've noticed, is how Danielle Meyers talks; everything's secret, she only lets out so much. It's like she didn't grow up with everybody telling her she had to share.

And here's the funny thing: the more I intimate that Sherman and I are more than just friends, the more it seems we actually are. It's the old imagination giving reality a nudge. When I start to blush, he starts to blush; we reach a point where we can hardly talk at all.

"Well, there's first base with tongue, and first base without," I tell Barbara Gugelstein.

In fact, Sherman and I have brushed shoulders, which was equivalent to first base I was sure, maybe even second. I felt as though I'd turned into one huge shoulder; that's all I was, one huge shoulder. We not only didn't talk, we didn't breathe. But how can I tell Barbara Gugelstein that? So instead I say, "Well there's second base and second base."

Danielle Meyers is my friend again. She says, "I know exactly what you mean," just to make Barbara Gugelstein feel bad.

"Like *what* do I mean?" I say.

Danielle Meyers can't answer.

"You know what I think?" I tell Barbara the next day. "I think Danielle's giving us a line."

Barbara pulls thoughtfully on one of her pigtails.

●

If Sherman Matsumoto is never going to give me an ID to wear, he should at least get up the nerve to hold my hand. I don't think he sees this. I think of the story he told me about his parents, and in a synaptic firestorm realize we don't see the same things at all.

So one day, when we happen to brush shoulders again, I

don't move away. He doesn't move away either. There we are. Like a pair of bleachers, pushed together but not quite matched up. After a while, I have to breathe, I can't help it. I breathe in such a way that our elbows start to touch too. We are in a crowd, waiting for a bus. I crane my neck to look at the sign that says where the bus is going; now our wrists are touching. Then it happens: He links his pinky around mine.

Is that holding hands? Later, in bed, I wonder all night. One finger, and not even the biggest one.

Sherman is leaving in a month. Already! I think, well, I suppose he will leave and we'll never even kiss. I guess that's all right. Just when I've resigned myself to it, though, we hold hands—all five fingers. Once when we are at the bagel shop, then again in my parents' kitchen. Then, when we are at the playground, he kisses the back of my hand.

He does it again not too long after that, in White Plains.

I invest in a bottle of mouthwash.

Instead of moving on, though, he kisses the back of my hand again. And again. I try raising my hand, hoping he'll make the jump from my hand to my cheek. It's like trying to wheedle an inchworm out the window. You know, *This way, this way.*

All over the world, people have their own cultures. That's what we learned in social studies.

If we never kiss, I'm not going to take it personally.

It is the end of the school year. We've had parties. We've turned in our textbooks. Hooray! Outside the asphalt already steams if you spit on it. Sherman isn't leaving for another couple of days, though, and he comes to visit every morning, staying until the afternoon, when Callie comes home from her big-deal job as a bank teller. We drink Kool-Aid in the back-yard and hold hands until they are sweaty and make smacking noises coming apart. He tells me how busy his parents are, getting ready for the move. His mother, particularly, is very tired. Mostly we are mournful.

The very last day we hold hands and do not let go. Our palms fill up with water like a blister. We do not care. We talk more than usual. How much airmail is to Japan, that kind of thing. Then suddenly he asks, will I marry him?

I'm only thirteen.

But when old? Sixteen?

If you come back to get me.

I come. Or you can come to Japan, be Japanese.

How can I be Japanese?

Like you become American. Switch.

He kisses me on the cheek, again and again and again.

His mother calls to say she's coming to get him. I cry. I tell him how I've saved every present he's ever given me—the ruler, the pencils, the bags from the bagels, all the flower petals. I even have the orange peels from the oranges.

All?

I put them in a jar.

I'd show him, except that we're not allowed to go upstairs to my room. Anyway, something about the orange peels seems to choke him up too. Mister Judo, but I've gotten him in a soft spot. We are going together to the bathroom to get some toilet paper to wipe our eyes when poor tired Mrs. Matsumoto, driving a shiny new station wagon, skids up onto our lawn.

"Very sorry!"

We race outside.

"Very sorry!"

Mrs. Matsumoto is so short that about all we can see of her is a green cotton sun hat, with a big brim. It's tied on. The brim is trembling.

I hope my mom's not going to start yelling about World War II.

"Is all right, no trouble," she says, materializing on the steps behind me and Sherman. She's propped the screen door wide open; when I turn I see she's waving. "No trouble, no trouble!"

"No trouble, no trouble!" I echo, twirling a few times with relief.

Mrs. Matsumoto keeps apologizing; my mom keeps in-

sisting she shouldn't feel bad, it was only some grass and a
small tree. Crossing the lawn, she insists Mrs. Matsumoto get
out of the car, even though it means trampling some lilies-of-
the-valley. She insists that Mrs. Matsumoto come in for a cup
of tea. Then she will not talk about anything unless Mrs. Matsumoto sits down, and unless she lets my mom prepare her a
small snack. The coming in and the tea and the sitting down
are settled pretty quickly, but they negotiate ferociously over
the small snack, which Mrs. Matsumoto will not eat unless she
can call Mr. Matsumoto. She makes the mistake of linking Mr.
Matsumoto with a reparation of some sort, which my mom
will not hear of.

"Please!"

"No no no no."

Back and forth it goes: "No no no no." "No no no no." "No
no no no." What kind of conversation is that? I look at Sherman, who shrugs. Finally Mr. Matsumoto calls on his own,
wondering where his wife is. He comes over in a taxi. He's a
heavy-browed businessman, friendly but brisk—not at all a
type you could imagine bowing to a lady with a taste for tie-
on sun hats. My mom invites him in as if it's an idea she just
this moment thought of. And would he maybe have some tea
and a small snack?

Sherman and I sneak back outside for another farewell, by
the side of the house, behind the forsythia bushes. We hold
hands. He kisses me on the cheek again, and then—just when
I think he's finally going to kiss me on the lips—he kisses me
on the neck.

Is this first base?

He does it more. Up and down, up and down. First it
tickles, and then it doesn't. He has his eyes closed. I close my
eyes too. He's hugging me. Up and down. Then down.

He's at my collarbone.

Still at my collarbone. Now his hand's on my ribs. So much
for first base. More ribs. The idea of second base would probably make me nervous if he weren't on his way back to Japan
and if I really thought we were going to get there. As it is,

though, I'm not in much danger of wrecking my life on the shoals of passion; his unmoving hand feels more like a growth than a boyfriend. He has his whole face pressed to my neck skin so I can't tell his mouth from his nose. I think he may be licking me.

From indoors, a burst of adult laughter. My eyelids flutter. I start to try and wiggle such that his hand will maybe budge upward.

Do I mean for my top blouse button to come accidentally undone?

He clenches his jaw, and when he opens his eyes, they're fixed on that button like it's a gnat that's been bothering him for far too long. He mutters in Japanese. If later in life he were to describe this as a pivotal moment in his youth, I would not be surprised. Holding the material as far from my body as possible, he buttons the button. Somehow we've landed up too close to the bushes.

●

What to tell Barbara Gugelstein? She says, "Tell me what were his last words. He must have said something last."

"I don't want to talk about it."

"Maybe he said, 'Good-bye'?" she suggests. " 'Sayonara'?" She means well.

"I don't want to talk about it."

"Aw, come on, I told you everything about . . ."

I say, "Because it's private, excuse me."

She stops, squints at me as though at a far-off face she's trying to make out. Then she nods and very lightly places her hand on my forearm.

●

The forsythia seemed to be stabbing us in the eyes. Sherman said, more or less, *You will need to study how to switch.*

And I said, *I think you should switch. The way you do everything is weird.*

And he said, *You just want to tell everything to your friends. You just want to have boyfriend to become popular.*

Then he flipped me. Two swift moves, and I went sprawling

through the air, a flailing confusion of soft human parts such
as had no idea where the ground was.

It is the fall and I am in high school, and still he hasn't written,
so finally I write him.

I still have all your gifts, I write. *I don't talk so much as I used
to. Although I am not exactly a mouse either. I don't care about
being popular any more. I swear. Are you happy to be back in
Japan? I know I ruined everything. I was just trying to be entertain-
ing. I miss you with all my heart, and hope I didn't ruin everything.*

He writes back, *You will never be Japanese.*

I throw all the orange peels out that day. Some of them, it
turns out, were moldy anyway. I tell my mother I want to
move to Chinatown.

"Chinatown!" she says.

I don't know why I suggested it.

"What's the matter?" she says. "Still boy-crazy? That Sherman?"

"No."

"Too much homework?"

I don't answer.

"Forget about school."

Later she tells me if I don't like school, I don't have to go
everyday. Some days I can stay home.

"Stay home?" In Yonkers, Callie and I used to stay home all
the time, but that was because the schools there were a *waste
of time.*

"No good for a girl be too smart anyway."

For a long time I think about Sherman. But after a while I
don't think about him so much as I just keep seeing myself
flipped onto the ground, lying there shocked as the Matsu-
motos get ready to leave. My head has hit a rock; my brain
aches as though it's been shoved to some new place in my
skull. Otherwise I am okay. I see the forsythia, all those
whippy branches, and can't believe how many leaves there are
on a bush—every one green and perky and durably itself. And

past them, real sky. I try to remember about why the sky's blue, even though this one's gone the kind of indescribable gray you associate with the insides of old shoes. I smell grass. Probably I have grass stains all over my back. I hear my mother calling through the back door, "Mon-a! Everyone leaving now," and "Not coming to say good-bye?" I hear Mr. and Mrs. Matsumoto bowing as they leave—or at least I hear the embarrassment in my mother's voice as they bow. I hear their car start. I hear Mrs. Matsumoto directing Mr. Matsumoto how to back off the lawn so as not to rip any more of it up. I feel the back of my head for blood—just a little. I hear their chug-chug grow fainter and fainter, until it has faded into the whuzz-whuzz of all the other cars. I hear my mom singing, "Mon-a! Mon-a!" until my dad comes home. Doors open and shut. I see myself standing up, brushing myself off so I'll have less explaining to do if she comes out to look for me. Grass stains—just like I thought. I see myself walking around the house, going over to have a look at our churned-up yard. It looks pretty sad, two big brown tracks, right through the irises and the lilies-of-the-valley, and that was a new dogwood we'd just planted. Lying there like that. I hear myself thinking about my father, having to go dig it up all over again. Adjusting. I think how we probably ought to put up that brick wall. And sure enough, when I go inside, no one's thinking about me, or that little bit of blood at the back of my head, or the grass stains. That's what they're talking about—that wall. Again. My mom doesn't think it'll do any good, but my dad thinks we should give it a try. Should we or shouldn't we? How high? How thick? What will the neighbors say? I plop myself down on a hard chair. And all I can think is, we are the complete only family that has to worry about this. If I could, I'd switch everything to be different. But since I can't, I might as well sit here at the table for a while, discussing what I know how to discuss. I nod and listen to the rest.

CRISIS

FROM

This Boy's Life

 ●◉◓◔

TOBIAS WOLFF

Chuck got drunk almost every night. Some nights he was jolly. Other nights he went into silent rages in which his face would redden and swell, and his lips move to the words he was shouting inside his head. At the peak of his fury he threw himself against unyielding objects. He would ram his shoulder into a wall, then back up and do it again. Sometimes he just stood there, saying nothing, and pummeled the wall with his fists. In the morning he would ask me what he'd done the night before. I didn't really believe that he had forgotten, but I played along and told him how wiped out he'd been, how totally out of control. He shook his head at the behavior of this strange other person.

I could not keep up with him and I stopped trying. He never said anything, but I knew he was disappointed in me.

Chuck's father had run a dairy before he became a store-keeper and preacher. The family still owned the farm, though now they leased the pastures and barn to a neighbor. Mr. and Mrs. Bolger and their two young daughters lived in the main house. Chuck and I were off by ourselves in a converted storage shed a couple of hundred feet away. Mr. Bolger had the idea that a good dose of trust would rouse us to some adult conception of ourselves. It should have. It didn't.

The Bolgers went to bed at nine-thirty sharp. Around ten, if Chuck wasn't already in the bag, we pushed his car down the drive a ways, then cranked it up and drove over to Veronica's house. Arch and Psycho were usually there, sometimes Huff. They drank and played poker. I had no money, so I sat on the floor and watched the late show with Veronica. Veronica ruined the movies by telling me all about the stars. She had the inside track on Hollywood. She knew which actor, supposedly dead, was actually a drooling vegetable, and which actress could not be satisfied except by entire football teams. She was especially hard on the men. According to Veronica they were all a bunch of homos, and she proved it by pointing out the little signals and gestures by which they advertised their persuasion. The lighting of a cigarette, the position of a handkerchief in a breast pocket, the way an actor glanced at his watch or angled his hat—everything was evidence to Veronica. Even when she wasn't talking I could feel her watching the men on the screen, ready to pounce.

On the way home Chuck scared me by weaving all over the road and giving sermons about damnation. He meant these sermons to be parodies of his father's, but they were all his own. Mr. Bolger did not preach like this. Chuck could catch his father's inflections and rhythms, but not his music. What came out instead was his own fear of being condemned.

I wasn't used to people who took religion seriously. My mother never had, and Dwight was an atheist of the Popular Science orthodoxy. (Jesus hadn't really died, he had taken a drug that made him look dead so he could fake a resurrection later. The parting of the Red Sea was caused by a comet passing overhead. Manna was just the ancient word for potato.) There was an Episcopalian minister, Father Karl, who drove up to

Chinook every couple of weeks and was entirely serious, but the possibilities Father Karl made me feel when I listened to him did not stay with me after he left.

Mr. Bolger was careful never to pressure me, but I understood that he was a fisher of men and that I was fair game. Not a prize catch, maybe, but legal. The danger wasn't that he would force me into anything but that I would force myself in order to get on his good side. Mr. Bolger was tall and dignified. He had a long face and brooding eyes. When I talked to him, he looked at me in so direct a way that I sometimes forgot what I was saying. I had the feeling that he could see into me. He treated me with courtesy, though without affection; always he seemed to be holding something back. I wanted him to think well of me.

That was one danger. The other was the music. At Mr. Bolger's church the music was passionate, not like the menopausal Catholic hymns I'd learned in Salt Lake. People got carried away singing these songs. They wept and clapped their hands, they cried out, they swayed up the aisle to the Amen Corner. I felt like doing it myself sometimes but I held back. Chuck was always beside me, silent as a stone. He moved his lips without singing. He had never been to the Amen Corner, and I was afraid he would ridicule me if I went. So I hung back even though I wanted, out of musical sentimentality and eagerness to please, to go forward. And after church I was always glad I hadn't done it, because I knew that Mr. Bolger would see through me and be disgusted.

Chuck never turned on me. In his drunkest, darkest rages he hurt only himself. That was my good luck. Chuck was bullishly built, thickset and chesty. I wouldn't have stood a chance against him. Other boys left him in peace and he left them in peace, which he was inclined to do anyway. Except with himself he was gentle—not as his father was, with that least suggestion of effort dignified men give to their gentleness, but as his mother was. He looked like her, too. Milky skin with a wintry spot of red on each cheek. Yellow hair that turned white in sunshine. Wide forehead. He also had his mother's pale blue eyes and her way of narrowing them when she listened, looking down at the floor and nodding in agreement with whatever you said.

Everyone liked Chuck. Sober, he was friendly and calm and openhanded. When I admired a sweater of his he gave it to me, and later he gave me a Buddy Holly album we used to sing along with. Chuck liked to sing when he wasn't in church. It was hard to believe, seeing him in the light of day, that he had spent the previous night throwing himself against a tree. That was why the Bolgers had so much trouble coming to terms with his wildness. They saw nothing of it. He lingered over meals at the main house, talked with his father about the store, helped his mother with the dishes. His little sisters fawned on him like spaniels. Chuck seemed for all the world a boy at home with himself, and at these times he was. It wasn't an act. So when the other Chuck, the bad Chuck, did something, it always caught the Bolgers on their blind side and knocked them flat.

One night Psycho and Huff came over to play cards. They were as broke as I was, so I joined the game. We drank and played for matchsticks until we got bored. Then we decided that it would be a great idea to drive over to Bellingham and back. Chuck didn't have enough gas for the trip but said he knew where we could get some. He collected a couple of five-gallon cans and a length of hose, and the four of us set off across the fields.

It had rained heavily that day. A fine spray still fell through the mist around us. The ground, just ploughed for sowing, was boggy. It pulled at our shoes, then let them go with a rich mucky gasp. Psycho was wearing loafers, and he kept coming out of them. Finally he gave up and turned back. The rest of us pushed on. Every few steps we could hear Psycho shout with rage behind us.

We walked a good half mile before we got to the Welch farm. We loitered by the outbuildings for a while, then crossed the yard to Mr. Welch's truck. Chuck siphoned gas out of the

tank while Huff and I watched the house. I had never been
here before, but I knew the Welch boys from school. There
were three of them, all sad, shabbily dressed, and quiet to the
point of muteness. One of the boys, Jack, was in my class. He
was forlorn and stale-smelling, like an old man who has lost
his pride. Because we had the same first name it amused Mr.
Mitchell to match us up as sparring partners during PE. Then
the other boys would circle us and shout, "Go, Jack! Get him,
Jack! Kill him, Jack!" But Jack Welch had no stomach for it.
He held his gloves up dubiously, as if he thought they might
turn on him, and gave me a look of apology whenever Mr.
Mitchell goaded him into taking a swing. It was strange to
think of him in that dark house, his unhappy eyes closed in
sleep, while I kept watch outside. Huff grunted as he scraped
at his shoes with a stick. The air smelled of gasoline.

Chuck filled the cans and we started back. The going was
harder than the coming. We were headed uphill now. We took
turns carrying the cans, swinging them forward and stumbling
after them. Their weight drove us into the mud and threw us
off balance, making us flounder and fall. By the time we got
back we were caked with mud. I had torn my shirt on some
barbed wire. My good arm was dead from the pull of the cans,
the other arm pulsing with pain where I had brushed my
finger against a post. I was dead tired and so were the others.
Nobody said a thing about Bellingham. While Chuck drove
Huff and Psycho home, I cleaned myself off and fell into bed.

Mr. Bolger woke us late the next morning. He only put his
head in the door and said, "Get up," but something in his
voice snapped me upright, wide awake. Chuck too. We looked
at each other and got out of the bed without a word. Mr.
Bolger waited by the door. Once we were dressed he said,
"Come on," and set off toward the main house. He walked in
long pushing strides, head bent forward as if under a weight,
and never once turned to see if we were behind him. When I
glanced over at Chuck his eyes were on his father's back. His
face was blank.

We followed Mr. Bolger into the kitchen. Mrs. Bolger was

sitting at the breakfast table, crying into a napkin. Her eyes
were red and a blue vein stood out on her pale forehead. "Sit
down," Mr. Bolger said. I sat down across from Mrs. Bolger
and looked at the tablecloth. Mr. Bolger said that Mr. Welch
had just been by, for reasons we would have no trouble figuring out. I kept quiet. So did Chuck. Mr. Bolger waited, but we
still said nothing. Then, to spare himself the stupidity of a
denial, he told us we'd left a trail anyone could follow. You
didn't even have to follow it—you could see it all the way
from here.

"How could you do such a thing?" Mrs. Bolger asked. "To
the Welches, of all people?"

I looked up and saw that Mr. Bolger was studying me. We
both looked away when our eyes met.

Mrs. Bolger shook with sobs. Mr. Bolger put his hand on
her shoulder. "What's your excuse?" he said to Chuck.

Chuck said there wasn't any excuse.

"Jack?"

"No excuse, sir."

He looked at each of us. "Were you drinking?"

We both admitted we'd been drinking.

Mr. Bolger nodded, and I understood that this was in our
favor, so great was his faith in the power of alcohol to transform a person. It also worked to our advantage that we ourselves had not suggested drink as a defense but confessed it as
a further wrong. That left Mr. Bolger free to make our excuses
for us.

Chuck and I were ritually abashed, Mr. Bolger ritually
angry, but the worst was over and we all knew it. We spent
the rest of the morning at the kitchen table, working out a
plan of reparation. Chuck and I would return the gasoline,
which we had been too tired to pour into his tank. We would
apologize to Mr. Welch, and we would give our word not to
drink again. No mention was made of the promises we had
already broken. We agreed to all of Mr. Bolger's conditions but
one—we would not tell him who had been with us. He harried
us for their names, but it was plain to me that this was part of

the ceremony, and that he was glad to find us capable at least of loyalty. Anyway, he must have known who the others were.

We stood up and shook hands. Mr. Bolger made it clear that he did not want to lord this over us. He wanted to put the whole thing behind him, the sooner the better. Mrs. Bolger did not get up. I could see that she was still feeling the wrong of what we had done, though I did not feel it myself.

Chuck and I loaded up the cans and drove them over to the Welch farm. It wasn't that far through the fields, but to get there by car we had to drive up to the main road and then turn off on a winding, unpaved track still muddy from yesterday's rain. Chuck went fast so we wouldn't get stuck. The mud pounded against the floor of the car. We passed through scrub pine that opened up here and there to show a house or a clearing with some cows in it. Chuck swore a blue streak the whole way.

We pulled into the Welches' drive and sat there a moment, silent, before we got out.

I had worked on several farms during my summer vacations picking and haying. These farms were in the upper valley near Marblemount, close but not too close to the river, with good drainage and rich soil. The owners prospered. They had up-to-date equipment, and kept their houses and barns painted. Their yards were grassy, trimmed with flower beds and decorated with birdbaths and wagon wheels and big ceramic squirrels.

The Welch farmyard was all mud, a wallow without hogs. Nothing grew there. And nothing moved, no cats, no chickens, no mutts running out to challenge us. The house was small, ash gray, and decrepit. Moss grew thickly on the shingle roof. There was no porch, but a tarpaulin had been stretched from one wall to give shelter to a washtub with a mangle and a clothesline that dropped with dull flannel shirts of different sizes, and dismal sheets.

Smoke rose from a stovepipe. It was surprising to look up and see that the sky was blue and fresh.

Chuck knocked. A woman opened the door and stood in the doorway, a little girl behind her. Both of them were red-haired and thin. The little girl smiled at Chuck. Chuck smiled sadly back at her.

"I was surprised," the woman said. "I have to say I was surprised."

"I'm sorry," Chuck said. He made the abashed face he'd been wearing in the kitchen that morning.

"I wouldn't have never thought it of you," she said. She looked at me, then turned back to Chuck. "You say you're sorry. Well, so am I. So is Mr. Welch. It's just not what we ever expected."

Mrs. Welch told us where to find her husband. As we slogged through the mud, the fuel cans swinging at our sides, Chuck said, "Shit, shit, shit . . ."

Mr. Welch was sitting on a pile of wood, watching Jack and one of the other Welch boys. They were a little ways off, taking turns digging with a post-holer. Mr. Welch was bareheaded. His wispy brown hair floated in the breeze. He had on a new pair of overalls, dark blue and stiff-looking and coated with mud around the ankles. We came up to him and set the cans down. He looked at them, then looked back at his sons. They kept an eye on us as they worked, not with any menace, but just to see what was going to happen. I could hear the post-holer slurping up the mud with the same sound our shoes had made the night before. Chuck waved at them and they both nodded.

We looked at them for a time. Then Chuck went to Mr. Welch's side and began to talk in a low voice, telling him how sorry he was for what we had done. He offered no explanations and did not mention that we had been drinking. His manner was weightily sincere, almost tragical.

Mr. Welch watched his sons. He did not speak. When Chuck was through, Mr. Welch turned and looked at us, and I could see from the slow and effortful way he moved that the idea of looking at us was misery to him. His cheeks were stubbled and sunken in. He had spots of mud on his face. His brown eyes were blurred, as if he'd been crying or was about to cry.

I didn't need to see the tears in Mr. Welch's eyes to know that I had brought shame on myself. I knew it when we first drove into the farmyard and I saw the place in the light of day. Everything I saw thereafter forced the knowledge in deeper. These people weren't making it. They were near the edge, and I had nudged them that much farther along. Not much, but enough to take away some of their margin. Returning the gas didn't change that. The real harm was in their knowing that someone could come upon them in this state, and pause to do them injury. It had to make them feel small and alone, knowing this—that was the harm we had done. I understood some of this and felt the rest.

The Welch farm seemed familiar to me. It wasn't just the resemblance between their house and the house where I'd lived in Seattle, it was the whole vision, the house, the mud, the stillness, the boys lifting and dropping the post-holer. I recognized it from some idea of failure that had found its perfect enactment here.

Why were Jack and his brother digging post holes? A fence there would run parallel to the one that already enclosed the farmyard. The Welches had no animals to keep in or out—a fence there could serve no purpose. Their work was pointless. Years later, while I was waiting for a boat to take me across a river, I watched two Vietnamese women methodically hitting a discarded truck tire with sticks. They did it for a good long while, and were still doing it when I crossed the river. They were part of the dream from which I recognized the Welches, my defeat-dream, my damnation-dream, with its solemn choreography of earnest, useless acts.

It takes a childish or corrupt imagination to make symbols of other people. I didn't know the Welches. I had no right to see them this way. I had no right to feel fear or pity or disgust, no right to feel anything but sorry for what I had done. I did feel these things, though. A kind of panic came over me. I couldn't take a good breath. All I wanted was to get away.

Mr. Welch had said something to Chuck, something I could not hear, and Chuck had stepped aside. I understood that his apology had been accepted. Mr. Welch was waiting for mine, and the attitude of his waiting told me that this business was hard on him. It was time to get it over with. But I stayed where I was, watching the Welch boys pull up mud. I could not make myself move or speak. Just to stand there was all I could do. When Chuck realized I wasn't going to say anything, he murmured good-bye and shook Mr. Welch's hand. I followed him to the car without looking back.

Mr. Bolger knocked on our door when we got home. That small courtesy was full of promise, and when he came in I saw that he was eager to be forgiving. It made me sad, being so close to his pardon and knowing I couldn't have it. He nodded at us and said, "How did it go?"

Chuck didn't answer. He had not spoken to me since we left the Welch place. I knew he despised me for not apologizing, but I had no way of explaining my feelings to him, or even to myself. I believed that there was no difference between explanations and excuses, and that excuses were unmanly. So were feelings, especially complicated feelings. I didn't admit to them. I hardly knew I had them.

Chuck surrounded himself with silence. We were close to our breaking point. I couldn't keep up with him in debauchery, and now I had failed him in repentance as well.

Mr. Bolger looked at me when he got no answer from Chuck.

"Chuck apologized," I said. "I didn't."

Mr. Bolger asked Chuck to leave us alone, and sat down on the other bed when Chuck had gone. With a show of patience, he tried to understand why I had not apologized. All I was able to say was that I couldn't.

He asked for more.

"I wanted to," I said. "I just couldn't."

"You agreed that you owed the Welches an apology."

"Yes sir."

"You promised to apologize, Jack. You gave your word."

I said again that I wanted to but couldn't.

Mr. Bolger lost interest in me then. I saw it in his eyes. He told me that he and Mrs. Bolger had hoped I would be happy with them, happier than I'd apparently been with my step-father, but it didn't seem as if I was. All in all, he saw no point in my staying on. He said he would call my mother that night and make arrangements to have her come and get me. I didn't argue. I knew that his mind was made up.

So was mine. I had decided to join the army.

My mother drove down the next day. She huddled with the Bolgers for a couple of hours, then took me for a drive. At first she didn't speak. Her hands were clenched tight on the steering wheel; the muscles of her jaw were tensed. We went down the road a few miles, to a truck stop. My mother pulled into the parking lot and turned off the engine.

"I had to beg them," she said.

Then she told me what her begging had accomplished. Mr. Bolger had agreed to let me stay on after all, if I would put things right with the Welches by working on their farm after school.

I said I would rather not do that.

She ignored me. Looking over the steering wheel, she said that Mr. Bolger also wanted Father Karl to have a talk with me. Mr. Bolger hoped that Father Karl's brand of religion might reach me, being closer to the one I was raised in than his own. My mother said I had a couple of choices: I could either go along with Mr. Bolger or pack up. Today. And if I did pack up, I'd better have a plan, because I couldn't come home with her—Dwight wouldn't let me in the door. It looked like she might have a job lined up in Seattle but it would be a while until she knew for sure, and then she would need time to get started and find a place.

"Why didn't you apologize to those people?" she said.

I told her I couldn't.

She looked at me, then stared through the windshield again.

She had never been so far away. If I had robbed a bank she would have stuck by me, but not for this. She said, "So what are you going to do." She didn't sound especially interested.

I told her I would do whatever the Bolgers wanted.

She started the car and took me back. After letting me out she drove away fast.

●

Mr. Bolger was too busy that week to arrange my service with the Welches, but I did not know that. I came into the store after school each day expecting to be told to go back outside and get in the car. I came in, and hesitated, and when no one said anything I walked lightly into the back room and put my apron on and began to do my chores. Chuck and I used to work together, talking, joking around, snapping dust cloths and goosing each other with broom handles. Now we worked by ourselves, in silence. I dreamed. Sometimes I thought of the Welch farm and of myself there, drowning in mud, surrounded by accusing faces. Whenever this thought came to me I had to close my eyes and catch a breath.

Toward the end of the week Father Karl came in. He talked to Mr. Bolger in the storeroom for a few minutes, then called me outside. "Let's take a walk," he said.

We followed a footpath down to the river. Father Karl didn't say anything until we were at the riverbank. He picked up a rock and threw it into the water. I had the cynical suspicion that he was going to give me the same sermon the chaplain at Scout camp had given to every new group of boys on their first day last summer. He would walk up to the edge of the lake, casually pick up a handful of stones and toss one in. "Only a pebble," he would say musingly, as if the idea were just occurring to him, "only a pebble, but look at all the ripples it makes, and how far the ripples reach . . ." By the end of the summer we camp counselors all held him in open scorn. We called him Ripples.

But Father Karl did not give this sermon. He couldn't have. He had come by his faith the hard way, and did not speak of it with art or subtlety. His parents were Jewish. They had both been killed in concentration camps, and Father Karl himself barely survived. Sometime after the war he became a convert to Christianity, and then a minister. Some trace of Eastern Europe still clung to his speech. He had dark good looks of which he seemed unaware, and a thoughtful manner that grew sharp when he had to deal with pretense or frivolity. I had felt this sharpness before, and was about to feel it again.

He asked me who I thought I was.

I did not know how to answer this question. I didn't even try.

"Look at yourself, Jack. What are you doing? Tell me what you think you are doing."

"I guess I'm screwing up," I said, giving my head a rueful shake.

"No baloney!" he shouted. "No baloney!"

He looked about ready to hit me. I decided to keep quiet.

"If you go on like this," he said, "what will happen to you? Answer me!"

"I don't know."

"Yes you do. You know." His voice was softer. "You know." He picked up another rock and hurled it into the river. "What do you want?"

"Sorry?"

"Want! You must *want* something. What do you want?"

I knew the answer to this question, all right. But I was sure that my answer would enrage him even more, worldly as I knew it to be, and contrary to what I could imagine of his own wants. I could not imagine Father Karl wanting money, a certain array of merchandise, wanting, at any price, the world's esteem. I could not imagine him wanting anything as much as I wanted these things, or imagine him hearing my wants without contempt.

I had no words for any of this, or for my understanding that to accept Father Karl's hope of redemption I would have to give up my own. He believed in God, and I believed in the world.

I shrugged off his question. I wasn't exactly sure what I wanted, I said.

He sat down on a log. I hesitated, then sat a little ways down from him and stared across the river. He picked up a stick and prodded the ground with it, then asked me if I wanted to make my mother unhappy.

I said no.

"You don't?"

I shook my head.

"Well, that's what you're doing."

I said nothing.

"All right, then. Do you want to make her happy?"

"Sure."

"Good. That's something. That's one thing you want. Right?" When I agreed, he said, "But you're making her unhappy, aren't you?"

"I guess."

"No guessing to it, Jack. You are." He looked over at me. "So why don't you stop? Why don't you just stop?"

I didn't answer right away, for fear of seeming merely agreeable. I wanted to appear to give his questions some serious thought. "All right," I said. "I'll try."

He threw down the stick. He was still watching me, and I knew that he understood what had happened here; that he had not "reached me" at all, because I was not available to be reached. I was in hiding. I had left a dummy in my place to look sorry and make promises, but I was nowhere in the neighborhood and Father Karl knew it.

Still, we didn't leave right away. We sat gazing out across the water. The river was swollen with runoff. More brown than green, it chuckled and hissed along the bank. Farther from shore it seethed among mossy boulders and the snarled roots of trees caught between them. From under the changing surface sounds of the river came a deep steady sigh that never changed, and grew louder as you listened to it until it was the only sound you heard. Birds skimmed the water. New leaves glinted on the aspens along the bank.

It was spring. We were both caught in it for a moment, forgetful of our separate designs. We were with each other the way kindred animals are with each other. Then we stirred, and remembered ourselves. Father Karl delivered some final admonition, and I said I would do better, and we walked back to the store.

That weekend Mr. Bolger told me that he had spoken to the Welches and that they had refused my help. "They wouldn't have you," he said, and let me know by the gravity of his expression that this was the ultimate punishment, a punishment far worse than doing hard time on their farm. He actually succeeded in making me feel disappointed. But I got over it.

Eyes and Teeth

⬤◉◉◎

WANDA COLEMAN

Day shimmers aglow with our laughter. Me and my cousin Buzz run through the house, teasing and funning. It is our blackness and our blood that makes us more than kin, be that possible. Be life that deeply sweet.

They've come the long way from the Midwest. Along the old Route 66 to Los Angeles to visit Disneyland and Knott's Berry Farm. To walk the glittering avenue of the stars and point to this one and point to that one. To pick citrus wonders in orange groves. To wind and twist along the broad boulevards following outdated maps to the once glamorous homes of movie greats. To baptize themselves in that truly blue Pacific. To rave about mama's fried chicken and macaroni and cheese.

Me and Buzz get along about like always: Him gettin' the best of me even though I'm smarter. Him tickling my feet till my sides ache and I cry "uncle." Buzz and his two brothers crowded in with me and my two brothers in our tiny bedroom. And him scaring me late at night, talking about spooky creatures in the dark, especially that rat just waiting to take a healthy bite out of my big toe.

It is one summer in a cascade of summers. Visits from down home relations coming to see what the city is like, exploring the possibility of permanent uprooting. The small black farmers are disappearing, their lands swallowed up by wealthy white professionals, sold in turn to agricultural giants. It is this movement/flow that brings Buzz and his family west to test the climate and get a fix on the lay of urban turf.

Our fathers sit out back most days talking sports and the progress of humankind. His mother and my mother gab hours on end, catching up on old schoolmates, old flames, and old times.

"Remember that ornery old sow we used to tease till one day she up and got loose and chased us cross the south field? Do you ever get over to So-and-So-ville to see Mrs. What-was-her-name, the Sunday school teacher at Such-and-Such A.M.E.?"

We only half listen, more concerned with bossing our youngers. We're both the eldest, so we eat the most, we're eager to compete, we scrap the loudest, and are first to go running when mothers call.

This summer Buzz seems to have taken on a foreign edginess. Almost a sadness, but not quite. And while we fuss and wrestle, we're older now and I sense he's beginning to regard me as the young woman I'm becoming. But there's something else eating at him. I ask him if something's wrong. He looks at me and I watch his eyes go weepy. Nothing's the matter, he says. And it takes a while, but after a couple of days I provoke him back to mischief and he's more his usual self.

In no time we're roughing and tumbling about the house. This one afternoon me and Buzz are playing hide and seek while our brothers take their naps. I tap Buzz and he's it. He counts slowly to ten as I scout out a place to hide. We've been warned to stay out of the front room, and keep our noise down or suffer a spanking. I'm bold enough to think I can hide right under mama's nose and get away with it.

I tiptoe into the living room, crawl up under the old upright piano, and wedge myself in between it and the cloth-covered bench. From where I am, I can overhear our mamas' chitchat. My mama has the ironing board up in the dining room and is pressing out a week's laundry. His mama is sitting at the table, one of her breasts out, nursin' Buzz's new baby brother. There's a crack between the piano and the adjacent armchair which allows me to watch them without being seen.

Then here comes Buzz. He tiptoes up to the bench. I can see the quick little steps of his worn sneakers. I hold my breath. Next thing I know I'm looking into his eyes and teeth. He's smiling and laughing silently at finding me so quickly. He gets down on all fours and crawls in under the piano and starts tickling the stuffings out of me, daring me to laugh out loud. I hold it in. I don't want my legs tanned with one of them peach tree limbs my mama favors.

Then suddenly something his mama and my mama are sayin' catches our ears and we listen.

"I've had my last child," his mama says. "This is it."

"He's such a pretty boy," my mama says.

"He's my favorite of the boys. He's so light-skinned and look at this good straight hair. And lookahere at them gray eyes!"

"He takes after you."

"I'm so glad the other boys didn't turn out dark. But they could stand to be a shade brighter."

My mama made a strange little laugh.

"I'm so glad this baby didn't turn out black and ugly like Buzz. I can't stand to look at nothin' that *black,* and I feel so sorry Buzz is as black as he is—tar black like his granddaddy."

Me and Buzz were staring at one another, our mouths and eyes as wide as could be. And I saw hurt, pain, and hate flood his face all at once.

I wondered what my aunt thought of me and my brothers. And my father too. We—all of us were only a couple of shades shy of Buzz, who was what we called charcoal. At the same

time I was filled with a powerful hate for the woman. She
thought she was better than us because she was high yellow
and closer to being white. My mama had raised us to believe
that that way of thinking was sick. And now I was filled with
shame. Why wasn't my mother taking her to task?

Maybe she would've if she'd seen the tears burst silently
from Buzz's eyes. She didn't see the hardness that took hold of
his heart. And she didn't see me reach out my arms, trying to
leap beyond my tomboy years to be the mother he lost in that
instant.

Buzz crawled out, went to the bathroom, and closed the
door. He stayed there a long time. I went into the room where
the others were napping and thought about it till I couldn't
think anymore. We would never speak about it. No one
seemed to notice the change in Buzz during the rest of that
visit. No one, except me, noticed how sullen, withdrawn, and
mean-tempered Buzz was becoming. I remember standing just
off the hallway, by the piano, watching them leave. His mother
reached out to touch Buzz as he was going through the door.
He jerked away and she gave him a puzzled look. I took it as
a sign. It could be our last time to see each other as children.

When his mother died twenty years later, I did not attend the
funeral. Mama went back there to visit, and came home with
all manner of family gossip, especially about Buzz. Some said
Buzz was gay. Some said he had joined up with a black para-
military group and was doing all kinds of evil, including dope.
Then Buzz showed up at the services with a beautiful young
wife, two babies, and a new car. Seems he's holding his own
among the black middle class.

"And you should see Buzz's children," Mama crowed.
"They're beautiful! And every one of them looks like their
father."

A Bag of Oranges

●●●●

SPIRO ATHANAS

The city market was crowded. The boy, Nikos Pappanoulos, bobbed and weaved among the shoppers. He held a blue cloth sack tightly; his father walking briskly ahead carried three others. Skip stepping, the ten-year-old tried to keep up with his father's long stride. Stavro Pappanoulos strode easily, cutting a smooth path through the thick crowd like a plow turning earth. Something about the set of his shoulders said, "Step aside," and people did. The boy was proud of his father's stocky strength, yet at the same time it made him uneasy.

Nikos loved the market, loved coming to shop with his father on Saturday mornings. He loved the smells and bright fall colors of apples, pears, pumpkins, of the fresh fruits and vegetables in the October morning air. The market was like a magic farm indomitably growing and prospering in the heart of the rotting slum.

The boy's father knew many of the truck farmers who displayed their colorful harvests in pyramids, bunches, or boxes in the open-air market. He was especially friendly with a gray, old Albanian who hawked strawberries.

"Lulustrouthia! Lulustrouthia!" the gaunt, hook-nosed farmer yelled. And it worked. No one could hear that cry against the other banal sounds without investigating.

"Lulustrouthia? That's Albanian for the freshest, juiciest, sweetest strawberries ever grown," was his stock reply, uttered rather condescendingly to the fat matron who stood before him. "Fifteen cents a box." She bought a box and waddled away, biting off the stems of the unwashed strawberries and popping the fruit into her mouth.

"Twenty cents for two?" The boy's father plunked down two shiny dimes next to the rows of boxes overflowing with plump strawberries.

"No, no, Stavro Pappanoulos, thirty cents for two! Two times fifteen is thirty." He said this distinctly and rocked back on his heels delighted with his arithmetic.

"Twenty-two."

"Thirty."

"Twenty-five!"

"Sold!" The old Albanian adroitly slid the dimes into his money pouch.

"Sonofabitch," his father mumbled as he flipped a nickel to the Albanian.

"Move away from the stand now, Stavro Pappanoulos, I don't want people to see how you rob me—Lulustrouthia! HEY LULUSTRRROUTHIA!"

The boy watched and listened to this dialogue, intrigued— and a little frightened. But the smile on his father's lips as they walked away reassured him.

When the sacks were at last filled and the boy held the one bag of oranges that could not be coaxed into any of them, he and his father made their weekly visit to the Greek coffeehouse across the street. To get there they had to pass through the enclosed end of the U-shaped market, the only part the boy didn't like. It was poorly lighted. The chicken house, butcher

shop, and fish market all reeked of death. The boy ran ahead
of his father, out the double door, and again into the light. He
waited at the curb for his father. Stavro took his hand and
strode into the street, defying traffic. He seemed to delight in
making cars stop to let him pass.

In the coffeehouse the boy sat on a corner of his father's
chair. Stavro unbuttoned his pin-striped suit coat and removed
his gray hat. As he sipped dark, viscous coffee, the boy ate
from the bag of peanuts given him by his uncle, Peter Pappas,
proprietor of the coffeehouse. Peter was Stavro's brother, but
had shortened his name "for business purposes."

The boy, dark and quiet and shy, watched the men at the
other tables playing backgammon and pinochle. The men at
Stavro's table spoke in low confiding tones.

"Michales is dying, you know." Peter clenched the stub of
his cigar between his teeth.

"It's that woman," a slight bald man chirped. The boy didn't
know him. "He's not enough man for Aphrodite."

"No one is enough man for Aphrodite, eh Stavro?" Peter
nudged his brother.

"Old ladies, all of you. Gossiping old ladies." Stavro spat
between the space in his front teeth into a cuspidor, smiling
mischievously. The talk continued. They spoke of politics and
business and gambling. Stavro sat like a rock with his legs
corralling the four brimming cloth sacks. He lit a Fatima and
put one of his hands gently on the boy's head. The boy enjoyed
the talk and sometimes felt he was being allowed to hear all
the secrets of the world, and was only mildly frustrated by the
mysteries he could not understand.

"Time to go, Nikos." Stavro ran his fingers through his own
thick, black hair and put on his hat. "I need a haircut," he
said, to no one in particular.

Nikos was glad to be in the fresh air again when they left. It
was even sweeter after being in the mustiness of his uncle's
tiny coffeehouse. And he ran ahead of his father again, this
time to the bus stop at the corner.

The bus was crowded. There were many elderly women and

young girls with bright packages returning from downtown shopping trips, but only a few men. It was midafternoon in October, and the bus was uncomfortably warm. The boy sat beside his father on the long seat at the rear.

The bus jolted over the city streets, jerking to an abrupt halt at nearly every corner, picking up and surrendering passengers. The boy was holding the oranges so lightly that when the bus lurched into motion after one of the stops, the bag was thrust forward and five oranges bounded into the aisle. Like pin balls, they careened off the brackets and poles. The boy regained control of the bag before any more could escape, and his father scampered down the aisle chasing oranges.

On his hands and knees, Stavro Pappanoulos ducked beneath a seat on which two old ladies sat, to their mild humor and fussy dismay, and emerged with three of the oranges. The two others had rolled farther down the aisle. He picked up one, and as he started for the other, a neatly dressed young man reached down from where he was sitting and took it up. Stavro quickly grabbed the young man's wrist and began squeezing. The man gasped slightly, opening his mouth in a grimace of pain and disbelief. Stavro tightened his grip and stared menacingly into the pink face. Finally the young man's grasp was loosened by the pressure and he dropped the orange. Stavro picked it up and walked back to his seat at the rear of the bus. The young man stared after him, his mouth still open, rubbing his wrist briskly.

"You know," he began, "I mean anyone could see—I wasn't about to steal your precious orange!"

A wave of laughter ran through the bus. Stavro Pappanoulos looked at the man mildly and popped the five oranges back into the boy's bag, carefully folding over the top. He settled himself in his seat again and looked satisfied. The young man shrugged his shoulders and turned around. There were a few whispers and a few more smiles.

The boy felt every whisper piercing his skin, every smile was a slap. His ears burned with embarrassment and shame. The remainder of the trip was an agony. Even the backs of the old gray heads, the light ponytails, the clean-shaven necks, seemed to mock the boy. For the first time in his life he hated his father.

At their stop, the boy and his father had to pass the young man to get to the door. The boy, mortified, walked by stiffly, staring straight ahead, his head ringing, tears in his eyes. He felt the shadow and weight of his father behind him, placid and unashamed. Oh how he hated him and his smug, foreign stupidity! Why did he have to be *his* father?

Once on the sidewalk the boy dared not look back at the bus as it coughed and whined away for fear it too would mock him. He walked behind his father now, crying silent hot tears. His father turned once and must have noticed the tears, but said nothing.

At the gate to their front yard the boy's older sister bounded out to greet them and leaped with remarkable agility onto her father's back. Viki, who was twelve, snuggled her head in Stavro's neck and kissed him affectionately. And as they both laughed, Stavro carried her up the stairs to the porch where the boy caught up with them. Viki jumped from her father's back, snatched the bag of oranges from her brother, and disappeared into the house. Stavro put his bags down for a moment and placed a hand on the boy's head. The boy sprang to him, putting his arms around his father's neck and wrapping his legs around his hard body.

In this way, they arrived at the kitchen—the boy still clinging to his amused father.

"Look at my monkey!" Stavro said to his wife. And the boy was delighted to be his father's monkey again. It was so easy and natural he could scarcely believe the emotions he experienced moments ago were real. Had he *really* thought he hated his father?

The boy's mother was looking at the oranges Viki had given her. She took a few out of the bag.

"And what happened to these, Stavro? Did you sit on them on the way home?"

"Some dropped. It is of no importance." Stavro looked at the boy.

"Well, we can't eat these, but I can use them for juice. Viki, why don't you go to the store and buy a dozen for Poppa's lunches?" Viki frowned, but she knew it was not a question. She went to her mother's purse in the hall closet, removed a dollar, and left for the store.

"And you, Nikos, be a good boy and bring in the cans from the alley. If you leave them they will get dented worse than they are."

The late afternoon sun, subdued by the October mist, hung quietly just above the horizon. It was getting dark earlier. The boy sent a flattened bottle cap skimming down the vacant alley. Then he carried in the empty, battered trash cans, one at a time. He stopped after his third and last trip to watch a lone gray pigeon gracefully circle his backyard. In a flutter of furious motion the fat bird ascended to the gutter atop the three-story house and settled gently on the edge. It flicked its nervous head from side to side. And the boy remembered the trap his father had made on the roof: kernels of corn leading to a chicken-wire box. He remembered pigeon soup. There had been the need.

He felt a sudden chill, an inner void; and he began to run. Up the brick wall and over the mound, the swelling where the roots of the gnarled oak had had their say; up the porch stairs, two, three steps at a time: the agile, plastic ten-year-old, a piece of tempered wire.

Near the top of a second flight of stairs, still trying to outrun his own insides, the boy heard the soft, familiar voices: his mother and father as they communed over coffee. He stopped running. Slowly, carefully, he walked the brown crack in the flowered linoleum down the hall to the kitchen. A sheer drop of ten thousand feet on either side.

"Did you bring in the cans?" The boy nodded and his mother smiled her approval. She wiped a loose, dark hair from her smooth brow.

The boy moved from the doorway to the table. His father sat there easily, his legs spread. And the boy remembered the coffeehouse; remembered the mischief in his father's eyes as the men spoke of "Aunt" Aphrodite; remembered the dying Michales.

"Coffee?"

"Yes, black coffee," the boy said quietly.

"So it's *black* coffee is it; a man's drink." His mother already moving toward the cupboard—petite, slender in a bright print dress. Dark smiling eyes, affectionate, maternal. She filled a hand-painted demitasse from a copper pot at the stove and brought it to the boy.

He sipped. It was bitter, the price of being a man.

"I'm going now to get a haircut. Borsch will be closed in half an hour." The boy's father finished his coffee in one long swallow and pushed himself up heavily. Thick, dark, quiet, he spoke a familiar word to his wife, a parting—and he was gone. The boy sat in the chair, in the warmth of his father's body, and watched his mother clear the table.

"Why don't you play outside now?"

"Nobody's around."

"Viki will be back soon."

He watched his mother wash the cups at the sink. And he thought of his "Aunt" Aphrodite, again. Aphrodite Skouras was not a relation, but she was a very close friend of the family. She read fortunes in the swirling patterns of coffee grounds made in empty cups. On more than one occasion the boy had sat in a corner of the kitchen and watched the cluster of women and girls clinging to her every word. He had watched, amused, amazed, and, sometimes, frightened. At last they would discover him, usually it was his mother, for she was the most skeptical and paid the least attention, and he was ushered from the room. For days afterwards he would hear talk of "Aunt" Aphrodite's predictions. Now he remembered that her last visit had caused a pall to settle over the company. The bright sarcasm and laughter of his mother seemed false in the face of the dark future Aphrodite must have forecast.

The boy's mother began to hum a particularly gay Greek tune as she worked at the sink. But somewhere, deep in the boy's mind, the song was transformed into a wail. And then it broke upon a distant reality. Suddenly the room was filled with the sound—screaming terrifically, ominously. And then, abruptly, it subsided to a low, soft moan.

"Go to the window and see." His mother, urgent, always frightened by sirens. She listened intently.

The boy rushed to a living room window, pushed aside the long hand-crocheted curtains and parted the blind. He saw nothing unusual in the street below except the autos backed up, bumper to bumper. But it was Saturday and theirs was a busy street.

Back in the kitchen he said nothing. The wailing sound was gone. His mother wiped the worn oilcloth that covered the solid oak table. She stopped midway in the arc of a smooth stroke, "Shhh."

The boy had not uttered a sound. He held his breath. His mother lifted her head and seemed to prick her ears listening to something he could not hear. She held the hand with which she sought to quiet him poised above the table—motionless. "What?" The boy said, "I don't hear anything."

"Nothing. Nothing at all." His mother finished wiping the table and went back to her work. The boy saw her knitted brow reflected in the mirror above the sink. She did not hum any more.

The boy sat in his father's chair sipping the thick coffee; both had lost their warmth. He watched his mother's efficient hands preparing mousaka at the sink for their evening meal, and thought of nothing.

The noise of the front door slamming against the wall echoed violently in the hollow stairwell. The boy had often heard it slammed shut, but this was a different, urgent sound which compelled both him and his mother to rush to the stairs. "Momma, oh Momma, Momma," it was a thin hysterical voice that came to them. They watched Viki, alert and afraid. Her mouth formed the words but she did not, could not speak.

Her body writhed and her face twisted but no sound came. Finally, "It's Poppa. Oh, Momma, Poppa!"

His mother's eyes were glazed black, wild with terror. She clasped her hands together and ran down the stairs. The boy, rooted to the spot, faced his sister. He began to shake. His neck felt stiff. Then he saw the empty bag Viki clutched to her breast as she rocked side to side. The bottom had torn out. She followed his eyes to the tear. "The oranges! I lost them. Oh Poppa!" The tears now began to flow down her flushed face, from terrified eyes.

The boy wanted to know, but he did not dare ask. He watched and waited. Viki put the bag on the dining room table and turned back to face the boy. He still could not move. "I saw his hat. The people were in a circle and there was Poppa's hat. I didn't believe it was Poppa's at first. But I knew it was. I knew it was his gray hat." She paused and sobbed and wiped the tears from her frightened face. "Then I saw Poppa. He wasn't bleeding. He looked okay. Like he was asleep. Like he was lying in the street asleep. Nikos, Nikos." She went to the motionless, terrified boy and put her hands on his shoulders. "Poppa's been hit by a car, Nikos. He couldn't talk or see, but maybe it's not bad. There wasn't any blood. He looked okay, Nikos. He's okay." She began to choke on her fear, her deep hurt.

The boy felt a drop of perspiration slip down his side. He could hear and feel his heart work faster, faster. And he broke away from his sister; running stumbling down the stairs to the front porch.

He could make nothing out of what he saw in the street. There was a car double-parked in the next block, but police and people milled about on the corner. He could not see his mother amongst them. Too late, he was confused and bewildered. He had made up his mind to run down to the corner. But he found he couldn't run. And then he knew he didn't want to run. He didn't want to reach the corner—ever. Halfway down the block he saw them; the oranges his sister had dropped. Most of them were in a little pile by the curb. But one was in the center of the sidewalk, near the corner.

Of a sudden, a man who had been part of the small crowd which seemed unable to leave the scene of the excitement, though there was nothing left to see . . . of a sudden a young man broke from the crowd and picked up the orange near the corner. He tested it in the palm of his hand, and, as if finding it acceptable, turned to walk up the street, away from the boy.

A neighbor, an old woman, noticed the boy and made a comforting gesture, a movement toward him. Seeing this, Nikos began to run, past the woman and the corner. In the middle of the next block he caught up with the young man who had picked up the orange. Without breaking stride, the boy leaped onto his back, his small fists flailing wildly. "That's my orange!" he screamed. "Give me my orange!"

How the García Girls Lost Their Accents

●●◉◉

JULIA ALVAREZ

The day the Garcías were one American year old, they had a celebration at dinner. Mami had baked a nice flan and stuck a candle in the center. "Guess what day it is today?" She looked around the table at her daughters' baffled faces. "One year ago today," Papi began orating, "we came to the shores of this great country." When he was done misquoting the poem on the Statue of Liberty, the youngest, Fifi, asked if she could blow out the candle, and Mami said only after everyone had made a wish.

What do you wish for on the first celebration of the day you lost everything? Carla wondered. Everyone else around the table had their eyes closed as if they had no trouble deciding. Carla closed her eyes too. She should make an effort and not wish for what she always wished for in her homesickness. But just this last time, she would let herself. "Dear God," she began. She could not get used to this American wish-making without bringing God into it. "Let us please go back home, please," she half prayed and half wished. It seemed a less and less likely prospect. In fact, her parents were sinking roots here. Only a month ago, they had moved out of the city to a neighborhood on Long Island so that the girls could have a yard to play in, so Mami said. The little green squares around each look-alike house seemed more like carpeting that had to be kept clean than yards to play in. The trees were no taller than little Fifi. Carla thought yearningly of the lush grasses and thick-limbed, vine-laden trees around the compound back home. Under the *amapola* tree her best-friend cousin, Lucinda, and she had told each other what each knew about how babies were made. What is Lucinda doing right this moment? Carla wondered.

Down the block the neighborhood dead-ended in abandoned farmland that Mami read in the local paper the developers were negotiating to buy. Grasses and real trees and real bushes still grew beyond the barbed-wire fence posed with a big sign: PRIVATE, NO TRESPASSING. The sign had surprised Carla since "forgive us our trespasses" was the only other context in which she had heard the word. She pointed the sign out to Mami on one of their first walks to the bus stop. "Isn't that funny, Mami? A sign that you have to be good." Her mother did not understand at first, until Carla explained about the Lord's Prayer. Mami laughed. Words sometimes meant two things in English too. This trespass meant that no one must go inside the property because it was not public like a park, but private. Carla nodded, disappointed. She would never get the hang of this new country.

Mami walked her to the bus stop for her first month at her new school over in the next parish. The first week, Mami even rode the buses with her, transferring, going and coming, twice a day, until Carla learned the way. Her sisters had all been enrolled at the neighborhood Catholic school only one block away from the house the Garcías had rented at the end of the summer. But by then, Carla's seventh grade was full. The nun who was the principal had suggested that Carla stay back a year in sixth grade, where they still had two spaces left. At twelve, though, Carla was at least a year older than most six graders, and she felt mortified at the thought of having to repeat yet another year. All four girls had been put back a year when they arrived in the country. Sure, Carla could use the practice with her English, but that also meant she would be in the same grade as her younger sister, Sandi. That she could not bear. "Please," she pleaded with her mother, "let me go to the other school!" The public school was a mere two blocks beyond the Catholic school, but Laura García would not hear of it. Public schools, she had learned from other Catholic parents, were where juvenile delinquents went and where teachers taught those new crazy ideas about how we all came from monkeys. No child of hers was going to forget her family name and think she was nothing but a kissing cousin to an orangutan.

Carla soon knew her school route *by heart*, an expression she used for weeks after she learned it. First, she walked down the block by heart, noting the infinitesimal differences between the look-alike houses: different color drapes, an azalea bush on the left side of the door instead of on the right, a mailbox or door with a doodad of some kind. Then by heart, she walked the long mile by the deserted farmland lot with the funny sign. Finally, a sharp right down the service road into the main thoroughfare, where by heart she boarded the bus. "A young lady señorita," her mother pronounced the first morning Carla set out by herself, her heart drumming in her chest. It was a long and scary trek, but she was too grateful to have escaped the embarrassment of being put back a year to complain.

And as the months went by, she neglected to complain about an even scarier development. Every day on the playground and in the halls of her new school, a gang of boys chased after her, calling her names, some of which she had heard before from the old lady neighbor in the apartment they had rented in the city. Out of sight of the nuns, the boys pelted Carla with stones, aiming them at her feet so there would be no bruises. "Go back to where you came from, you dirty spic!" One of them, standing behind her in line, pulled her blouse out of her skirt where it was tucked in and lifted it high. "No titties," he snickered. Another yanked down her socks, displaying her legs, which had begun growing soft, dark hairs. "Monkey legs!" he yelled to his pals.

"Stop!" Carla cried. "Please stop."

"Eh-stop!" they mimicked her. "Plees eh-stop."

They were disclosing her secret shame: her body was changing. The girl she had been back home in Spanish was being shed. In her place—almost as if the boys' ugly words and taunts had the power of spells—was a hairy, breast-budding grown-up no one would ever love.

Every day, Carla set out on her long journey to school with a host of confused feelings. First of all, there was this body whose daily changes she noted behind the closed bathroom door until one of her sisters knocked that Carla's turn was over. How she wished she could wrap her body up the way she'd heard Chinese girls had their feet bound so they wouldn't grow big. She would stay herself, a quick, skinny girl with brown eyes and a braid down her back, a girl she had just begun to feel could get things in this world.

But then, too, Carla felt relieved to be setting out toward her very own school in her proper grade away from the crowding that was her family of four girls too close in age. She could come home with stories of what had happened that day and not have a chorus of three naysayers to correct her. But she also felt dread. There, in the playground, they would be waiting for her—the gang of four or five boys, blond, snotty-nosed, freckle-faced. They looked bland and unknowable, the way all Americans did. Their faces betrayed no sign of human warmth. Their eyes were too clear for cleaving, intimate looks. Their pale bodies did not seem real but were like costumes they were wearing as they played the part of her persecutors.

She watched them. In the classroom, they bent over workbooks or wore scared faces when Sister Beatrice, their beefy, no-nonsense teacher, scolded them for missing their homework. Sometimes Carla spied them in the playground, looking through the chain link fence and talking about the cars parked on the sidewalk. To Carla's bafflement, those cars had names beyond the names of their color or size. All she knew of their family car, for instance, was that it was a big black car where all four sisters could ride in the back, though Fifi always made a fuss and was allowed up front. Carla could also identify Volkswagens because that had been the car (in black) of the secret police back home; every time Mami saw one she made the sign of the cross and said a prayer for Tío Mundo, who had not been allowed to leave the Island. Beyond Volkswagens and medium blue cars or big black cars, Carla could not tell one car from the other.

But the boys at the fence talked excitedly about Fords and Falcons and Corvairs and Plymouth Valiants. They argued over how fast each car could go and what models were better than others. Carla sometimes imagined herself being driven to school in a flashy red car the boys would admire. Except there was no one *to* drive her. Her immigrant father with his thick mustache and accent and three-piece suit would only bring her more ridicule. Her mother did not yet know how to drive. Even though Carla could imagine owning a very expensive car, she could not imagine her parents as different from what they were. They were, like this new body she was growing into, givens.

One day when she had been attending Sacred Heart about a month, she was followed by a car on her mile walk home from the bus stop. It was a lime-green car, sort of medium sized, and with a kind of long snout, so had it been a person, Carla would have described it as having a long nose. A long-nosed, lime-green car. It drove slowly, trailing her. Carla figured the driver was looking for an address, just as Papi drove slowly and got honked at when he was reading the signs of shops before stopping at a particular one.

A blat from the horn made Carla jump and turn to the car, now fully stopped just a little ahead of her. She could see the driver clearly, from the shoulders up, a man in a red shirt about the age of her parents—though it was hard for Carla to tell with Americans how old they were. They were like cars to her, identifiable by the color of their clothes and a general age group—a little kid younger than herself, a kid her same age, a teenager in high school, and then the vast indistinguishable group of American grown-ups.

This grown-up American man about her parents' age beckoned for her to come up to the window. Carla dreaded being asked directions since she had just moved into this area right before school started, and all she knew for sure was the route home from the bus stop. Besides, her English was still just classroom English, a foreign language. She knew the neutral bland things: how to ask for a glass of water, how to say good morning and good afternoon and good night. How to thank someone and say they were welcomed. But if a grown-up American of indeterminable age asked her for directions, invariably speaking too quickly, she merely shrugged and smiled an inane smile. "I don't speak very much English," she would say in a small voice by way of apology. She hated having to admit this since such an admission proved, no doubt, the boy gang's point that she didn't belong here.

As Carla drew closer, the driver leaned over and rolled down the passenger-door window. Carla bent down as if she were about to speak to a little kid and peeked in. The man smiled a friendly smile, but there was something wrong with it that Carla couldn't put her finger on: this smile had a bruised, sorry quality as if the man were someone who'd been picked on all his life, and so his smiles were appeasing, not friendly. He was wearing his red shirt unbuttoned, which seemed normal given the warm, Indian-summer day. In fact, if Carla's legs hadn't begun to grow hairs, she would have taken off her school-green knee socks and walked home barelegged.

The man spoke up. "Whereyagoin?" he asked, running all his words together the way the Americans always did. Carla was, as usual, not quite sure if she had heard right.

"Excuse me?" she asked politely, leaning into the car to hear the man's whispery voice better. Something caught her eye. She looked down and stared, aghast.

The man had tied his two shirt ends just above his waist and was naked from there on down. String encircled his waist, the loose ends knotted in front and then looped around his penis. As Carla watched, his big blunt-headed thing grew so that it filled and strained at the lasso it was caught in.

"Where ya' going?" His voice had slowed down when he spoke this time, so that Carla definitely understood him. Her eyes snapped back up to his eyes.

"Excuse me?" she said again dumbly.

He leaned toward the passenger door and clicked it open. "C'moninere." He nodded towards the seat beside him. "C'm'on," he moaned. He cupped his hand over his thing as if it were a flame that might blow out.

Carla clutched her book bag tighter in her hand. Her mouth hung open. Not one word, English or Spanish, occurred to her. She backed away from the big green car, all the while keeping her eyes on the man. A pained, urgent expression was deepening on his face, like a plea that Carla did not know how to answer. His arm pumped at something Carla could not see, and then after much agitation, he was still. The face relaxed into something like peacefulness. The man bowed his head as if in prayer. Carla turned and fled down the street, her book bag banging against her leg like a whip she was using to make herself go faster, faster.

Her mother called the police after piecing together the breathless, frantic story Carla told. The enormity of what she had seen was now topped by the further enormity of involving the police. Carla and her sisters feared the American police almost as much as the SIM back home. Their father, too, seemed uneasy around policemen; whenever a cop car was behind them in traffic, he kept looking at the rearview mirror and insisting on silence in the car so he could think. If officers stood on the sidewalk as he walked by, he bowed ingratiatingly at them. Back home, he had been tailed by the secret police for months and the family had only narrowly escaped capture their last day on the Island. Of course, Carla knew American policemen were "nice guys," but still she felt uneasy around them.

The doorbell rang only minutes after Carla's mother had called the station. This was a law-abiding family neighborhood, and no one wanted a creep like this on the loose among so many children, least of all the police. As her mother answered the door, Carla stayed behind in the kitchen, listening with a racing heart to her mother's explanation. Mami's voice was high and hesitant and slightly apologetic—a small, accented woman's voice among the booming, impersonal American male voices that interrogated her.

"My daughter, she was walking home—"

"Where exactly?" a male voice demanded.

"That street, you know?" Carla's mother must have pointed. "The one that comes up the avenue, I don't know the name of it."

"Must be the service road," a nicer male voice offered.

"Yes, yes, the service road." Her mother's jubilant voice seemed to conclude whatever had been the problem.

"Please go on, ma'am."

"Well, my daughter, she said this, this crazy man in this car—" Her voice lowered. Carla heard snatches: something, something "to come in the car—"

"Where's your daughter, ma'am?" the male voice with authority asked.

Carla cringed behind the kitchen door. Her mother had promised that she would not involve Carla with the police but would do all the talking herself.

"She is just a young girl," her mother excused Carla.

"Well, ma'am, if you want to file charges, we have to talk to her."

"File charges? What does that mean, file charges?"

There was a sign of exasperation. A too-patient voice with dividers between each word explained the legal procedures as if repeating a history lesson Carla's mother should have learned long before she had troubled the police or moved into this neighborhood.

"I don't want any trouble," her mother protested. "I just think this is a crazy man who should not be allowed on the streets."

"You're absolutely right, ma'am, but our hands are tied unless you, as a responsible citizen, help us out."

Oh no, Carla groaned, now she was in for it. The magic words had been uttered. The Garcías were only legal residents, not citizens, but for the police to mistake Mami for a citizen was a compliment too great to spare a child discomfort. "Carla!" her mother called from the door.

"What's the girl's name?" the officer with the voice in charge asked.

Her mother repeated Carla's full name and spelled it for the officer, then called out again in her voice of authority, "Carla Antonia!"

Slowly, sullenly, Carla wrapped herself around the kitchen door, only her head poking out and into the hallway, "¿Sí, Mami?" she answered in a polite, law-abiding voice to impress the cops.

"Come here," her mother said, motioning. "These very nice officers need for you to explain what you saw." There was an apologetic look on her face. "Come on, Cuca, don't be afraid."

"There's nothing to be afraid of," the policeman said in his gruff, scary voice.

Carla kept her head down as she approached the front door, glancing up briefly when the two officers introduced themselves. One was an embarrassingly young man with a face no older than the boys' faces at school on top of a large, muscular man's body. The other man, also big and fair-skinned, looked older because of his meaner, sharp-featured face like an animal's in a beast fable a child knows by looking at the picture not to trust. Belts were slung around both their hips, guns poking out of the holsters. Their very masculinity offended and threatened. They were so big, so strong, so male, so American.

After a few facts about her had been established, the mean-faced cop with the big voice and the pad asked her if she would answer a few questions. Not knowing she could refuse, Carla nodded meekly, on the verge of tears.

"Could you describe the vehicle the suspect was driving?"

She wasn't sure what a vehicle was or a suspect, for that matter. Her mother translated into simpler English, "What car was the man driving, Carla?"

"A big green car," Carla mumbled.

As if she hadn't answered in English, her mother repeated for the officers, "A big green car."

"What make?" the officer wanted to know.

"Make?" Carla asked.

"You know, Ford, Chrysler, Plymouth." The man ended his catalogue with a sigh. Carla and her mother were wasting his time.

"*¿Qué clase de carro?*" her mother asked in Spanish, but of course she knew Carla wouldn't know the make of a car. Carla shook her head, and her mother explained to the officer, helping her save face, "She doesn't remember."

"Can't she talk?" the gruff cop snapped. The boyish-looking one now asked Carla a question. "Carla," he began, pronouncing her name so that Carla felt herself coated all over with something warm and too sweet. "Carla," he coaxed, "can you please describe the man you saw?"

All memory of the man's face fled. She remembered only the bruised smile and a few strands of dirty blond hair laid carefully over a bald pate. But she could not remember the word for bald and so she said, "He had almost nothing on his head."

"You mean no hat?" the gentle cop suggested.

"Almost no hair," Carla explained, looking up as if she had taken a guess and wanted to know if she was wrong or right.

"Bald?" The gruff cop pointed first to a hairy stretch of wrist beyond his uniform's cuff, then to his pink, hairless palm.

"Bald, yes." Carla nodded. The sight of the man's few dark hairs had disgusted her. She thought of her own legs sprouting dark hairs, of the changes going on in secret in her body, turning her into one of these grown-up persons. No wonder the high-voiced boys with smooth, hairless cheeks hated her. They could see that her body was already betraying her.

The interrogation proceeded through a description of the man's appearance, and then the dreaded question came.

"What did you see?" the boy-faced cop asked.

Carla looked down at the cops' feet. The black tips of their shoes poked out from under their cuffs like the snouts of wily animals. "The man was naked all down here." She gestured with her hand. "And he had a string around his waist."

"A string?" The man's voice was like a hand trying to lift her chin to make her look up, which is precisely what her mother did when the man repeated, "A string?"

Carla was forced to confront the cop's face. It was indeed an adult version of the sickly white faces of the boys in the playground. This is what they would look like once they grew up. There was no meanness in this face, no kindness either. No recognition of the difficulty she was having in trying to describe what she had seen with her tiny English vocabulary. It was the face of someone in a movie Carla was watching ask her, "What was he doing with the string?"

She shrugged, tears peeping at the corners of her eyes.

Her mother intervened. "The string was holding up this man's—"

"Please, ma'am," the cop who was writing said. "Let your daughter describe what she saw."

Carla thought hard for what could be the name of a man's genitals. They had come to this country before she had reached puberty in Spanish, so a lot of the key words she would have been picking up in the last year, she had missed. Now, she was learning English in a Catholic classroom, where no nun had ever mentioned the words she was needing. "He had a string around his waist," Carla explained. By the ease with which the man was writing, she could tell she was now making perfect sense.

"And it came up to the front"—she showed on herself—

"and here it was tied in a—" She held up her fingers and made the sign for zero.

"A noose?" the gentle cop offered.

"A noose, and his thing—" Carla pointed to the policeman's crotch. The cop writing scowled. "His thing was inside that noose and it got bigger and bigger," she blurted, her voice wobbling.

The friendly cop lifted his eyebrows and pushed his cap back on his head. His big hand wiped the small beads of sweat that had accumulated on his brow.

Carla prayed without prayer that this interview would stop now. What she had begun fearing was that her picture—but who was there to take a picture?—would appear in the paper the next day and the gang of mean boys would torment her with what she had seen. She wondered if she could report them now to these young officers. "By the way," she could say, and the gruff one would begin to take notes. She would have the words to describe them: their mean, snickering faces she knew by heart. Their pale look-alike sickly bodies. Their high voices squealing with delight when Carla mispronounced some word they coaxed her to repeat.

But soon after her description of the incident, the interview ended. The cop snapped his pad closed, and each officer gave Carla and her mother a salute of farewell. They drove off in their squad car, and all down the block, drapes fell back to rest, half-opened shades closed like eyes that saw no evil.

For the next two months before Carla's mother moved her to the public school close to home for the second half of her seventh grade, she took Carla on the bus to school and was there at the end of the day to pick her up. The tauntings and chasings stopped. The boys must have thought Carla had complained, and so her mother was along to defend her. Even during class times, when her mother was not around, they now ignored her, their sharp, clear eyes roaming the classroom for another victim, someone too fat, too ugly, too poor, too different. Carla had faded into the walls.

But their faces did not fade as fast from Carla's life. They trespassed in her dreams and in her waking moments. Some-. times when she woke in the dark, they were perched at the foot of her bed, a grim chorus of urchin faces, boys without bodies, chanting without words, "'Go back! Go back!"

So as not to see them, Carla would close her eyes and wish them gone. In that dark she created by keeping her eyes shut, she would pray, beginning with the names of her own sisters, for all those she wanted God to especially care for, here and back home. The seemingly endless list of familiar names would coax her back to sleep with a feeling of safety, of a world still peopled by those who loved her.

FROM

Davita's Harp

⬤⬤⬤⬤

CHAIM POTOK

The cottage—three small bedrooms, a kitchen, a small dining room, a parlor—looked out on the sand and the sea. It had a screened-in front porch and a back lawn where grass and scrub brush grew from sandy soil. From the porch I would look eastward and see Rockaway Beach in the distance to my left, and the Atlantic Ocean, and Sandy Hook almost directly before me, and Staten Island to my right. I would come out the front door onto the porch—the front of the cottage faced the beach; the rear of the cottage faced the street—and hear the song of the door harp. Then I would come down off the porch onto the dunes, skirt the wild deutzia shrubs with their white blossoms and green leaves, and walk along the smooth clean yellow-white sand of the sloping beach to the rim of the sea. And there I would often stand for long minutes, looking at the water—at the rhythmic roll and crash of the waves, at the sparkles of sunlight on the curling crests, at the rush of foaming surf. The water was dark green near the shore and deep blue along the horizon. Ships sailed in the blue distance toward the line of sea and sky, freighters moving with such ponderous slowness they seemed fixed in the water. I watched them often that summer and wondered where they were sailing. To the Austria of Jakob Daw? To defeated Ethiopia and my Aunt Sarah? To the Spain that my father and mother and I were now reading about in newspapers and books and magazines?

My room faced the dunes and the sea. In the mornings, through the narrow line of high uncurtained clerestory windows came the pale brightness of dawn and then the fires of the new sun. What enchantment there was in the light and the warmth and the scent of the sand and the sea! I would listen to the wind in the giant poplars and the young sycamores; to the cries of gulls in the morning stillness; and to the occasional loud, ringing call of a strange bird, a call that sounded like a woman's voice: *Hoo hoo hoo hoo hoo*. I remember waking on our first morning in the cottage in that burning summer of 1936, the sense of newness sharp and pure, and hearing that bird's call, and wondering if it was the bird in Jakob Daw's story. *Hoo hoo hoo hoo*, the bird called as I lay in bed bathed in the morning sunlight. *Hoo hoo hoo hoo ha ha ha*.

Later that morning I went for a walk along the shaded streets of Sea Gate. The air was warm, the sun white in a blue sky. There was little traffic and no concern about unwanted strangers: Sea Gate was fenced and protected. I walked beneath the poplars and sycamores past the empty lots with their dwarf forests of wild grass and low bushes, past the small frame houses built in the twenties and the large, old, wealthy homes with their cupolas and dormer windows and deep wrap-around porches—the homes designed by Stanford White and William Van Allen for the very rich. Sea Gate was a small community, a few hundred homes, a few thousand people, and it contained in the summers I was there—the summers before my father went to Spain and our lives changed— the last remnants of that legendary set of upper-class Protestant pirates, along with the first of the Italians, Greeks, and Jews, as well as atheists, socialists, communists, writers, editors, theater people, and their various wives, mistresses, and children.

We were in a small world of sand and sea about ten miles from the heart of Manhattan. A trolley ran through the area to a ferry. The ferry brought you to South Street at the tip of Manhattan. My father would take the trolley and the ferry to the newspaper where he worked. Almost always by the time I woke in the morning he was gone. But he was always back in time for a swim and supper—unless he needed to go out of the city on a story. He would come home carrying three or four newspapers in addition to the one for which he worked, get into his bathing suit, and head across the beach to the water. He was a fine swimmer and would swim very far out, his arms and shoulders and face flashing in the afternoon sunlight. Sometimes my mother would swim with him and I would watch them moving together smoothly in the sea.

I loved the beach and the surf. In front of our cottage a small stone jetty came off the beach at a sharp angle and, together with the low wooden jetty that ran straight from the beach into the water, helped form along the water's edge a shallow tidal pool of gentle surf and smooth wet sand. I would wade in the pool, feeling the tugs of the surf; or I would sit for hours, building tall castles in the sand. I spent much of that summer building castles, sometimes with friends, often alone.

Sometimes in the mornings after breakfast or at night while my parents were talking quietly together, I would look at the newspapers my father brought home. At first I did not understand most of what I read. But certain words and phrases became quickly familiar to me that summer: heat, drought, dust bowl, weather bureau alarmed, rain is needed. Repeatedly I saw the names North Dakota, South Dakota, Minnesota, Montana, Illinois, Virginia. I imagined fields and meadows and hills burning beneath the relentless sun. The same sunlight that I loved to play in here was killing people out west. And the names of all those places were like the names in the stories about westering women told me by Aunt Sarah. How would those women have used their imaginations to save themselves from this cruel sun?

At the end of the first week in July the newspapers said that the temperature in the Midwest had reached 120 degrees. More than one hundred people had died of the heat. My father told us when he returned from the newspaper that day that the heat had begun to move eastward. I sat in my little pool, rebuilding the castle that had been attacked by the night tide and waiting for the heat.

The next day the heat in New York climbed to over 100 degrees. In the late afternoon I stood on the screened-in porch gazing at the beach and the sea. The air was still and hot. Gulls circled slowly overhead, calling. The surf rolled lazily in and out across the sand. There were many people on the beach and in the water. I heard my father's voice from somewhere in the cottage: he had just returned from his work in Manhattan. I heard my mother's voice return his greeting. Then I heard a third voice. I went quickly into the cottage.

"He looks awful," my father was saying to my mother. "Look at him, Annie. We've got to do something about how he looks."

"You chose such a hot day to return," my mother said. "Can I get you a cold drink?"

"The heat in Canada was unimaginable," Jakob Daw said. "To me it seemed the air was burning. Birds would not fly."

"Uncle Jakob!" I called from the kitchen doorway. They had not seen me standing there.

Jakob Daw turned, his pale face startled. They he broke into a smile. "Ilana Davita. How good to see you again. Look at your suntan! A Viking with a golden suntan!"

"Here's something cold for you, Jakob," my mother said.

Jakob Daw took the glass from my mother. He arched his gaunt body slightly forward from the waist, put the glass to his mouth, and drank thirstily. His Adam's apple moved up and down on his thin neck. His face was wet with perspiration.

"We have to sit and talk," my father said. "Tanner wants a report on Canada for Tuesday's meeting."

"There is much to talk about. Canada was—interesting."

"How long will you stay with us, Uncle Jakob?" I asked.

"I do not know."

"Will you stay a few days?"

"Oh, yes. At least a few days."

"Can I get you a real drink?" my father asked.

"No, thank you. Another iced tea would be very pleasant, Channah."

"Would you like to see the sand castle I made?"

"I will be happy to see your sand castle, Ilana Davita."

"Let Uncle Jakob sit down and relax now, Ilana," my mother said.

"Would you tell me another story later?"

He looked at me, a weary smile on his pale face. "Of course I will tell you another story. Of course."

That night he was up late with my parents. I could hear them talking quietly on the screened-in porch. The air was hot and humid. I lay in my bed, moist with heat, listening to the distant roll of the surf. Insects lurched wildly against the screens of my windows; I thought the heat must be driving them mad. I slept fitfully and had disquieting dreams, though when I woke I could not be certain what they had been about.

Jakob Daw remained inside the cottage all day. From my castle on the beach I saw him talking with my mother on the screened-in porch. My father had gone to work at his regular writing. During lunch, which my mother served us on the porch, Jakob Daw was silent and withdrawn. He ate very little. How pale and weary he looked. My mother moved about quietly. He fell asleep at the table, breathing raspingly, woke with a start, and glanced quickly around, a frightened look in his eyes. My mother put her hand on his shoulder. He slumped in his chair. A few moments later, he went to bed.

Very late that night—the second Saturday night of July—I was awakened by the sounds of a car pulling into the driveway between our cottage and the empty house across from us. I was bathed in sweat and dazed by the heat. I got out of bed and went to the side window. The shade was up, the curtain open. I peered through the window and saw a long dark car near the side door of the wood-and-brick house that adjoined the driveway. As I watched, the car lights and the engine were turned off. Two men, a woman, and a boy about my age came out of the car. The woman held a baby and went directly into the house, followed by the boy.

The two men began to move cartons and boxes from the car into the house. Lights were being turned on in some of the rooms of the house. By the small light over the side door of the house I saw dimly that one of the men was heavyset and bearded and the other was tall and thin. After a while the man climbed back into the car and drove off. The bearded man went into the house.

There was silence. The night pulsed rhythmically with the insect life of the sea's edge. Then the light on the screened-in porch across the way came on. I heard a door open and close and saw the boy come up to the front of the porch and look through the screen at the dark beach. There was a small high curving sliver of blue-white moon. The deep night was bathed in stars. The boy stood there a long time, gazing out at the darkness. He raised both his arms over his head and moved them back and forth a number of times. It was an odd sort of gesture, a pleading of some kind. He lowered his arms to his sides and stood still a moment longer. Then he turned and went back into the house. The porch light was extinguished. The ocean seemed loud and near in the darkness.

I went back to bed. The heat was stifling. Insects flew against my windows. In from the beach drifted low voices: people lay on the sand near the water, driven from their homes by the heat. I thought I heard a muffled cry, and I trembled. *Nothing!* Was it that word again? *Nothing.* And was that my mother's voice now, barely audible, soothing?

A long time later I fell into an exhausted sleep.

The sounds of a door opening and closing woke me. It was early morning. From my window I saw the man and the boy who had come during the night leave the house by the side door and walk toward the street. They work dark trousers, white shirts, and fishermen's caps. I went back to sleep.

Sunlight woke me. I found my mother in the kitchen. She looked tired. My father and Jakob Daw had gone into Manhattan, she said. What did I want for breakfast?

A letter arrived from Aunt Sarah. The kitchen was too hot and my parents and I were having breakfast on the porch. Jakob Daw was still asleep. My father read the letter aloud. Aunt Sarah was back in Maine, working in a hospital in Bangor. Ethiopia had been very, very bad. She was certain we were aware of what would soon transpire in Spain. How was Ilana Davita? "Be careful of the heat. Drink lots of water and take salt tablets." Maine was cool in the mornings and evenings and lovely even in these very hot days. If the heat of New York ever became intolerable, my parents should consider packing me off to Maine. She sent her love to all of us and a special kiss to Ilana Davita.

"Your sister keeps herself very busy," my mother said.

"She's telling us that she may go to Spain."

"Yes," my mother said. "I understood that."

Jakob Daw came out onto the porch, looking as if he had not slept.

"Good morning," he said, and coughed briefly. "The heat is terrible."

"It's terrible everywhere, Jakob," my mother said.

"Except in Maine," my father said.

"Sit down and I'll get you some breakfast," my mother said to Jakob Daw. "Did you sleep at all?"

"No. Early in the morning I fell asleep and was awakened by your neighbors. They seem to be very devout people. They go to synagogue every morning."

"How do you know where they're going?" my father asked.

"The man carries a prayer shawl."

"They're distant relatives of Annie's," my father said.

"The boy is my cousin's son," my mother said. "The man

and his wife are the brother and sister-in-law of my cousin's wife, who died recently. They are very religious people. The boy is saying Kaddish for his mother."

"What does Kaddish mean?" I asked.

"A prayer that's said in synagogue every morning and evening for about a year when someone close to you dies."

There was a brief pause.

"Did you know they were coming here to the beach?" I asked.

"Of course. I suggested it. The boy is very upset by his mother's death. His father asked if I would help keep an eye on him. From a distance, of course. What would you like for breakfast, Jakob?"

I looked out our screened-in porch at the empty porch of the adjoining house.

"Michael, are you going to the hunger march?" Jakob Daw asked. "Yes! Then I will come along."

"We can make the noon train to Philadelphia if we leave here inside half an hour."

"I will eat quickly," Jakob Daw said.

"Jakob, you're exhausted," my mother said.

"Yes," Jakob Daw said, "But I will go anyway."

My mother and I spent most of the day on the beach. We swam together for a long time—my father had taught me to swim—and then I worked on my castle. My mother sat on a chair nearby beneath a beach umbrella, reading. She wore a yellow, wide-brimmed sun hat and a dark blue bathing suit, and she looked trim and full-breasted and lovely. I saw the boy who had moved next to us walking across the beach with the bearded man. They wore white short-sleeved shirts and dark trousers rolled up almost to the knees and were barefooted. I watched them step into the edge of the surf. The boy's face broke into a smile. The man bent and embraced him. I turned my attention back to my castle.

We ate supper that evening on the porch in air so sultry it seemed weighted. During our meal we saw the boy and the man come off the porch of their house and start quickly along the driveway, talking in a language I could not understand.

I asked my mother what the word *religious* meant.

She said it came from an old word that meant to bind, to tie. "Religious people feel bound to their ideas," she said.

I asked her what language the man and the boy had been talking.

"Yiddish," she said, after a moment.

"Is that the language our neighbors use where we moved in Brooklyn?"

"Yes. I spoke it until I came to America. It was the language of my childhood."

"I never heard you speak it."

"I used to speak it sometimes where I worked. There's no need for me to speak it at home."

Later that evening I saw the man and the boy come back up the driveway. The man went into the house through the side door, and the boy climbed up the short flight of wooden stairs to the screened-in porch. The boy stood on the porch, looking thin and pale, and gazed out at the beach and the sky, his nose and mouth pressed against the screen. He raised his arms again in that strange gesture of supplication—lifting them over his head and waving them back and forth. Then he seemed to sense that someone was watching him, and he looked quickly around and saw me. He lowered his arms.

He stared at me a moment, his face pale and without expression. Then he turned and went quickly inside.

That night my mother and I slept outside on blankets on the dunes. There was no breeze and no sound of birds; birds did not fly at night, my mother had once told me. I lay still beneath the stars and listened to the surf. There were many people on the beach that night. I huddled against my mother and imagined I was the ocean. Would the westering women have done that in this heat? Imagined that they were the ocean? I was the waves and the surf, sliding smoothly back and forth, wet and cool, across the moist sand, in and out of the tidal pool where my castle stood. All that hot night, I slept with the rhythm of the surf in my ears. Once I thought I heard the sand-muffled beat of horses' hooves, but I knew that had to be a dream. When I woke it was light and gulls circled overhead, crying into the silent air. The ocean was a vast shimmering sheet of silver, and above it the hazy blue sky was piled high with masses of white luminous clouds. There was a faint humid breeze and the strong scent of brine.

My mother stirred and moved against me. She murmured in her sleep, words I did not understand but that sounded like the Yiddish she said she no longer spoke. She opened her eyes.

"Good morning," she said. "How hot it is! Did you sleep well? I had a dream about my grandfather. Did I say something before I woke? Look at the sky, Ilana. How beautiful it is!"

We had breakfast on the porch. I helped my mother with the dishes. The cottage felt large and empty without my father and Jakob Daw. They were away at the hunger march. Starving people were marching on the capital city of Pennsylvania. There was no more money to keep them on relief. About sixty thousand families. My mother had explained it to me. It was the end of capitalism, she had said. The end of a cruel and heartless system. Soon we would see the beginning of a new America, a kinder America, an America under the control of its working class, an America that cared for its poor.

I came out on the porch. Behind me the door harp played its soft melody. The sky had turned pale and there were tall whitecaps now far out on the water. Heaving waves rolled onto the beach, breaking, churning. I looked over toward my private world of tidal pool and castle. Standing near the castle and peering down at it was the thin pale boy from the house across the driveway. I went quickly out of the porch and along the dunes and the beach.

⬤

He must have seen me crossing the dunes. He straightened and turned and stood stiffly, watching me hurrying toward him.

"That's my castle," I said. "Don't touch it."

He turned his head slightly so that he was looking past me at the sea. He was about my height. He wore a fisherman's cap and a short-sleeved white shirt and dark trousers rolled up to a little below his knees. His face had a stiff, pinched look. He was barefooted.

"I wasn't going to touch it," he said. His voice was thin and quavery.

"I don't like anyone to touch it."

"But the water goes over it at night."

"No, it doesn't. It only reaches the bottom part."

"Doesn't that get broken?"

"So I build it again. I still don't like anyone to touch it."

"You built this by yourself?" he asked. All the time he talked he did not look at me directly but gazed past me at the sea. "Where do you get ideas for such a thing?"

"From books and magazines. From my—imagination."

"Such things really exist?"

"Sure they exist. In Spain. It's a castle."

"Is Spain a country?"

"Spain is a big country in Europe. Don't you know about Spain? Don't you see the newspapers?"

He looked faintly uncomfortable. "The castle looks like pictures I've seen of places in Yerusholayim. You've never heard of Yerusholayim? It's a very holy city. Jerusalem. The city of King David."

I thought I had heard of Jerusalem.

"You're my neighbor," he said. "I see you on your porch. Do you come here every summer? I don't like it here. There's nothing to do."

"You can go to Coney Island and the boardwalk. You can swim."

"I don't know how to swim. I don't like to swim."

"Why did you come to a beach if you don't like to swim?"

"Everyone said I needed a rest. I needed—air. I needed to get away. Everyone said that."

"Do you live in New York?"

"I live in Brooklyn."

"We just moved to Brooklyn. Just before we came here."

"My name is David," he said, still looking past me to the sea. "David Dinn."

"My name is—Ilana."

"Ilana," he said, then repeated it. "Ilana. That's a Jewish name."

"It was my grandmother's name."

"Are you Jewish?" he asked, turning to look directly at me. "Yes."

He seemed surprised. "I didn't think you were Jewish."

"Well, I am. Is the baby a boy or a girl?"

"The baby? Oh. A boy."

"I had a baby brother once. But he died. He got sick and he died."

"He's not my brother. He's my cousin. I'm here with my aunt and uncle. My father is too busy with his work to come to the beach. My mother is—my mother is dead." His voice broke and his eyes brimmed with tears. "My mother was a great person and now everyone says she's with the Ribbono Shel Olom, she's with God."

"What does your father do?" I asked.

"He's a lawyer. He works in a big office in Manhattan."

"My father works in Manhattan. He writes for newspapers and magazines."

"Where do your parents come from?"

"My mother is from Europe. My father is from Maine."

"Maine?"

"The state of Maine. It's a state north of—"

"Your father was born in Maine? Where were his parents born?"

"In Maine, too, I think."

"Your father is Jewish?"

"No. My mother is Jewish."

He stared at me.

There was a brief, tense silence.

"I have to go back," he said finally.

"All right," I said.

He turned and went up along the beach and across the dunes to his house.

During lunch I asked my mother if she had said Kaddish when her mother had died.

"Yes."

"And your father?"

She hesitated. "Yes."

"Did you say it when my brother died?"

"No. I didn't believe in it anymore."

We swam together a long time in the afternoon, and then I worked on my castle. I did not see David Dinn. Just before supper Jakob Daw returned, looking white and drained. He had left my father in Harrisburg and had come back alone because he felt ill. His hands trembled and his cough was loud. He was running a fever. He went to bed in the room next to mine and my mother brought him food and medication. I sat on the porch and saw David Dinn and his uncle come out of the house and go along the driveway together and turn into the street.

From the porch that night I watched flashes of lightning over the horizon. Distant thunder rolled in from the sea. The air lay heavy and still. A gust of hot wind stirred the shrubs and trees into life. Then the wind blew in hard and brought with it large, pelting drops of rain. The rain fell with dull thudding sounds on the sand and the trees and the roof of the cottage.

It rained most of the night. I lay in bed and listened to the roar of the wind-lashed surf and wondered how far up the beach it was. I thought I could hear it just before the dunes, foaming and boiling and reaching for our cottage. My mother came into my room and held me and cradled me in her lap and sang to me softly in a language I did not understand. I fell asleep inside her warmth.

In my sleep I thought I heard a man cry out and the soft and soothing voice of a woman. There was a sudden lurid flash of lightning and a booming roll of thunder and again a man's voice cried out, in a language I did not understand. I

heard my mother in the room next to mine. Then lightning
and thunder followed one upon the other for a long moment
in a blinding and deafening cascade of crackling blue-white
luminescence and pounding drumbeat noise. I sat up in my
bed and stared into the darkness, listening. Whispery sounds
came from the corners of my room. I felt again all the old
terrors of all the cold nights in the time of our winter wander-
ings. Lightning crackled and the room leaped into view. The
thunder that followed rattled the windows and my bed. I lay
in my bed and could not sleep. The whispers went on for a
long time. Sometime in the night the storm subsided and
became a dull and softly drumming rain. I fell asleep finally to
the rhythm of the rain on the cottage and the trees.

I woke early in radiant sunlight. The air was cool, the cottage very still. Somewhere nearby a bird called *Hoo hoo hoo
hoo*. I got out of bed and dressed quickly and went out to the
porch. The door harp played softly upon its taut wires.

The sky was clear and blue. Droplets of rain clung to the
trees and deutzia shrubs. On the horizon the sun glowed deep
red through a low bank of dazzling clouds. The floor of the
porch was wet. The air smelled of brine and clean wet sand.
All the world of beach and sky and sea lay fresh and clean to
the fair day. I walked across the sodden dunes and beach to
my tidal pool and my castle.

The walls and turrets had crumbled. The battlements were
gone. Towers and ramparts and casements had been reduced
to heaps of sand. The wharf and water gate had collapsed. The
moat and bridge were indiscernible. The castle which I had
built to nearly three feet in height was a flattened ruin.

I was the only one on the beach save for the wheeling gulls.
I bent over the wrecked castle and put my fingers into the wet
sand. I would build it again. I got down on my knees and
began to work the sand.

I worked a long time. The sun climbed high above the
horizon and the air grew warm. I had forgotten my dark
glasses and felt the sun stinging my eyes. I raised my head at
one point and looked across the dunes and saw David Dinn

watching me from the porch of his house. Then someone was standing over me. I glanced up and saw Jakob Daw. He wore baggy pants and a rumpled shirt and old shoes encrusted with wet sand. His face was pale and his eyes were dark and weary. He stood there squinting in the sunlight and gazing down at the castle I was trying to rebuild.

"Good morning, Ilana Davita. Your mother and I saw you from the porch. That was a terrible storm."

"It wrecked my castle."

"I see. I am very sorry."

"I have to rebuild it now."

"Your mother asks you to come to breakfast."

"Not now. Are you feeling better, Uncle Jakob?"

"Yes. The fever is gone. It will take you a long time to rebuild this castle, Ilana Davita."

"It's our protection against the Fascists on the other side of the ocean, Uncle Jakob. I have to rebuild it."

He said nothing. I felt his hooded eyes look at me.

"It's our magic protection. We'll live in it and never move from it. That's why I can't let it be wrecked."

I felt him standing there and looking at me. I worked on the sand. The ocean rolled quietly and rhythmically upon the shore.

Jakob Daw coughed and cleared his throat. Then I heard him ask in his soft and raspy voice, "Ilana Davita, may I help you?"

"Yes," I said.

He bent stiffly over the castle and put his white hands into the sand. His delicate features kneaded the sand, shaping it, smoothing it. Overhead in the enormous sky birds wheeled and screamed. A distant freighter moved ponderously toward the horizon. Jakob Daw and I worked together rebuilding my castle.

Marigolds

⬤⬤⬤⬤

EUGENIA COLLIER

When I think of the hometown of my youth, all that I seem to remember is dust—the brown, crumbly dust of late summer —arid, sterile dust that gets into the eyes and makes them water, gets into the throat and between the toes of bare brown feet. I don't know why I should remember only the dust. Surely there must have been lush green lawns and paved streets under leafy shade trees somewhere in town; but memory is an abstract painting—it does not present things as they are, but rather as they feel. And so, when I think of that time and that place, I remember only the dry September of the dirt roads and grassless yards of the shantytown where I lived. And one other thing I remember, another incongruency of memory —a brilliant splash of sunny yellow against the dust—Miss Lottie's marigolds.

Whenever the memory of those marigolds flashes across my

mind, a strange nostalgia comes with it and remains long after the picture has faded. I feel again the chaotic emotions of adolescence, illusive as smoke, yet as real as the potted geranium before me now. Joy and rage and wild animal gladness and shame become tangled together in the multicolored skein of fourteen-going-on-fifteen as I recall that devastating moment when I was suddenly more woman than child, years ago in Miss Lottie's yard. I think of those marigolds at the strangest times; I remember them vividly now as I desperately pass away the time waiting for you, who will not come.

I suppose that futile waiting was the sorrowful background music of our impoverished little community when I was young. The Depression that gripped the nation was no new thing to us, for the black workers of rural Maryland had always been depressed. I don't know what it was that we were waiting for; certainly not for the prosperity that was "just around the corner," for those were white folks' words, which we never believed. Nor did we wait for hard work and thrift to pay off in shining success as the American Dream promised, for we knew better than that, too. Perhaps we waited for a miracle, amorphous in concept but necessary if one were to have the grit to rise before dawn each day and labor in the white man's vineyard until after dark, or to wander about in the September dust offering one's sweat in return for some meager share of bread. But God was chary with miracles in those days, and so we waited—and waited.

We children, of course, were only vaguely aware of the extent of our poverty. Having no radios, few newspapers, and no magazines, we were somewhat unaware of the world outside our community. Nowadays we would be called "culturally deprived" and people would write books and hold conferences about us. In those days everybody we knew was just as hungry and ill-clad as we were. Poverty was the cage in which we all were trapped, and our hatred of it was still the vague, undirected restlessness of the zoo-bred flamingo who knows that nature created him to fly free.

As I think of those days I feel most poignantly the tag-end of summer, the bright dry times when we began to have a sense of shortening days and the imminence of the cold.

By the time I was fourteen my brother Joey and I were the only children left at our house, the older ones having left home for early marriage or the lure of the city, and the two babies having been sent to relatives who might care for them better than we. Joey was three years younger than I, and a boy, and therefore vastly inferior. Each morning our mother and father trudged wearily down the dirt road and around the bend, she to her domestic job, he to his daily unsuccessful quest for work. After our few chores around the tumbledown shanty, Joey and I were free to run wild in the sun with other children similarly situated.

For the most part, those days are ill defined in my memory, running together and combining like a fresh watercolor painting left out in the rain. I remember squatting in the road drawing a picture in the dust, a picture which Joey gleefully erased with one sweep of his dirty foot. I remember fishing for minnows in a muddy creek and watching sadly as they eluded my cupped hands, while Joey laughed uproariously. And I remember, that year, a strange restlessness of body and of spirit, a feeling that something old and familiar was ending, and something unknown and therefore terrifying was beginning.

One day returns to me with special clarity for some reason, perhaps because it was the beginning of the experience that in some inexplicable way marked the end of innocence. I was loafing under the great oak tree in our yard, deep in some reverie which I have now forgotten except that it involved some secret, secret thoughts of one of the Harris boys across the yard. Joey and a bunch of kids were bored now with the old tire suspended from an oak limb which had kept them entertained for a while.

"Hey, Lizabeth," Joey yelled. He never talked when he could yell. "Hey, Lizabeth, let's us go somewhere."

I came reluctantly from my private world. "Where at, Joey?"

The trust was that we were becoming tired of the formlessness of our summer days. The idleness whose prospect had seemed so beautiful during the busy days of spring now had degenerated to an almost desperate effort to fill up the empty midday hours.

"Let's go see can we find us some locusts on the hill," someone suggested.

Joey was scornful. "Ain't no more locusts there. Y'all got 'em all while they was still green."

The argument that followed was brief and not really worth the effort. Hunting locust trees wasn't fun anymore by now.

"Tell you what," said Joey finally, his eyes sparkling. "Let's us go over to Miss Lottie's."

The idea caught on at once, for annoying Miss Lottie was always fun. I was still child enough to scamper along with the group over rickety fences and through bushes that tore our already raggedy clothes, back to where Miss Lottie lived. I think now that we must have made a tragicomic spectacle, five or six kids of different ages, each of us clad in only one garment—the girls in faded dresses that were too long or too short, the boys in patchy pants, their sweaty brown chests gleaming in the hot sun. A little cloud of dust followed our thin legs and bare feet as we tramped over the barren land.

When Miss Lottie's house came into view we stopped, ostensibly to plan our strategy, but actually to reinforce our courage. Miss Lottie's house was the most ramshackle of all our ramshackle homes. The sun and rain had long since faded its rickety frame siding from white to a sullen gray. The boards themselves seemed to remain upright not being nailed together but rather from leaning together like a house that a child might have constructed from cards. A brisk wind might have blown it down, and the fact that it was still standing implied a kind of enchantment that was stronger than the elements. There it stood, and as far as I know is standing yet—a gray rotting thing with no porch, no shutters, no steps, set on a cramped lot with no grass, not even any weeds—a monument to decay.

In front of the house in a squeaky rocking chair sat Miss

Lottie's son, John Burke, completing the impression of decay. John Burke was what was known as "queer-headed." Black and ageless, he sat, rocking day in and day out in a mindless stupor, lulled by the monotonous squeak-squawk of the chair. A battered hat atop his shaggy head shaded him from the sun. Usually John Burke was totally unaware of everything outside his quiet dream world. But if you disturbed him, if you intruded upon his fantasies, he would become enraged, strike out at you, and curse at you in some strange enchanted language which only he could understand. We children made a game of thinking of ways to disturb John Burke and then to elude his violent retribution.

But our real fun and our real fear lay in Miss Lottie herself. Miss Lottie seemed to be at least a hundred years old. Her big frame still held traces of the tall, powerful woman she must have been in youth, although it was now bent and drawn. Her smooth skin was a dark reddish brown, and her face had Indian-like features and the stern stoicism that one associates with Indian faces. Miss Lottie didn't like intruders either, especially children. She never left her yard, and nobody ever visited her. We never knew how she managed those necessities which depend on human interaction—how she ate, for example, or even whether she ate. When we were tiny children, we thought Miss Lottie was a witch and we made up tales, that we half believed ourselves, about her exploits. We were far too sophisticated now, of course, to believe the witch nonsense. But old fears have a way of clinging like cobwebs, and so when we sighted the tumbledown shack, we had to stop to reinforce our nerves.

"Look, there she is," I whispered, forgetting that Miss Lottie could not possibly have heard me from that distance. "She's fooling with them crazy flowers."

"Yeh, look at 'er."

Miss Lottie's marigolds were perhaps the strangest part of the picture. Certainly they did not fit in with the crumbling decay of the rest of the yard. Beyond the dusty brown yard, in front of the sorry gray house, rose suddenly and shockingly a dazzling strip of bright blossoms, clumped together in enormous mounds, warm and passionate and sun-golden. The old black witch-woman worked on them all summer, every summer, down on her creaky knees, weeding and cultivating and arranging, while the house crumbled and John Burke rocked. For some perverse reason, we children hated those marigolds. They interfered with the perfect ugliness of the place; they were too beautiful; they said too much that we could not understand; they did not make sense. There was something in the vigor with which the old woman destroyed the weeds that intimidated us. It should have been a comical sight—the old woman with the man's hat on her cropped white head, leaning over the bright mounds, her big backside in the air—but it wasn't comical, it was something we could not name. We had to annoy her by whizzing a pebble into her flowers or by yelling a dirty word, then dancing away from her rage, revelling in our youth and mocking her age. Actually, I think it was the flowers we wanted to destroy, but nobody had the nerve to try it, not even Joey, who was usually fool enough to try anything.

"Y'all git some stones," commanded Joey now, and was met with instant giggling obedience as everyone except me began to gather pebbles from the dusty ground. "Come on, Lizabeth."

I just stood there peering through the bushes, torn between wanting to join the fun and feeling that it was all a bit silly.

"You scared, Lizabeth?"

I cursed and spat on the ground—my favorite gesture of phony bravado. "Y'all children get the stones, I'll show you how to use 'em."

I said before that we children were not consciously aware of how thick were the bars of our cage. I wonder now, though, whether we were not more aware of it than I thought. Perhaps we had some dim notion of what we were, and how little chance we had of being anything else. Otherwise, why would we have been so preoccupied with destruction? Anyway, the pebbles were collected quickly, and everybody looked at me to begin the fun.

"Come on, y'all."

We crept to the edge of the bushes that bordered the narrow road in front of Miss Lottie's place. She was working placidly, kneeling over the flowers, her dark hand plunged into the golden mound. Suddenly "zing"—an expertly aimed stone cut the head off one of the blossoms.

"Who out there?" Miss Lottie's backside came down and her head came up as her sharp eyes searched the bushes. "You better git!"

We had crouched down out of sight in the bushes, where we stifled the giggles that insisted on coming. Miss Lottie gazed warily across the road for a moment, then cautiously returned to her weeding. "Zing"—Joey sent a pebble into the blooms, and another marigold was beheaded.

Miss Lottie was enraged now. She began struggling to her feet, leaning on a rickety cane and shouting. "Y'all git! Go on home!" Then the rest of the kids let loose with their pebbles, storming the flowers and laughing wildly and senselessly at Miss Lottie's impotent rage. She shook her stick at us and started shakily toward the road crying, "Black bastards, git 'long! John Burke! John Burke, come help!"

Then I lost my head entirely, mad with the power of inciting such rage, and ran out of the bushes in the storm of pebbles, straight toward Miss Lottie chanting madly, "Old witch, fell in a ditch, picked up a penny and thought she was rich!" The children screamed with delight, dropped their pebbles and joined the crazy dance, swarming around Miss Lottie like bees and chanting, "Old lady witch!" while she screamed curses at us. The madness lasted only a moment, for John Burke, startled at last, lurched out of his chair, and we dashed for the bushes just as Miss Lottie's cane went whizzing at my head.

I did not join the merriment when the kids gathered again under the oak in our bare yard. Suddenly I was ashamed, and I did not like being ashamed. The child in me sulked and said it was all in fun, but the woman in me flinched at the thought of the malicious attack that I had led. The mood lasted all afternoon. When we ate the beans and rice that was supper that night, I did not notice my father's silence, for he was always silent these days, nor did I notice my mother's absence, for she always worked until well into evening. Joey and I had a particularly bitter argument after supper; his exuberance got on my nerves. Finally I stretched out upon the pallet in the room we shared and fell into a fitful doze.

When I awoke, somewhere in the middle of the night, my mother had returned, and I vaguely listened to the conversation that was audible through the thin walls that separated our rooms. At first I heard no words, only voices. My mother's voice was like a cool, dark room in summer—peaceful, soothing, quiet. I loved to listen to it; it made things seem all right somehow. But my father's voice cut through hers, shattering the peace.

"Twenty-two years, Maybelle, twenty-two years," he was saying, "and I got nothing for you, nothing, nothing."

"It's all right, honey, you'll get something. Everybody out of work now, you know that."

"It ain't right. Ain't no man ought to eat his woman's food year in and year out, and see his children running wild. Ain't nothing right about that."

"Honey, you took good care of us when you had it. Ain't nobody got nothing nowadays."

"I ain't talking about nobody else, I'm talking about *me*. God knows I try." My mother said something I could not hear, and my father cried out louder, "What must a man do, tell me that?"

"Look, we ain't starving. I git paid every week, and Mrs. Ellis is real nice about giving me things. She gonna let me have Mr. Ellis's old coat for you this winter—"

"God damn Mr. Ellis's coat! And God damn his money! You think I want white folks' leavings? God damn, Maybelle"— and suddenly he sobbed, loudly and painfully, and cried helplessly and hopelessly in the dark night. I had never heard a man cry before. I did not know men ever cried. I covered my ears with my hands but could not cut off the sound of my father's harsh, painful, despairing sobs. My father was a strong man who would whisk a child upon his shoulders and go singing through the house. My father whittled toys for us and laughed so loud that the great oak seemed to laugh with him, and taught us how to fish and hunt rabbits. How could it be that my father was crying? But the sobs went on, unstifled, finally quieting until I could hear my mother's voice, deep and rich, humming softly as she used to hum to a frightened child.

The world had lost its boundary lines. My mother, who was small and soft, was now the strength of the family; my father who was the rock on which the family had been built, was sobbing like the tiniest child. Everything was suddenly out of tune, like a broken accordion. Where did I fit into this crazy picture? I do not now remember my thoughts, only a feeling of great bewilderment and fear.

Long after the sobbing and the humming had stopped, I lay on the pallet, still as stone with my hands over my ears, wishing that I too could cry and be comforted. The night was silent now except for the sound of the crickets and of Joey's soft breathing. But the room was too crowded with fear to allow me to sleep, and finally, feeling the terrible aloneness of 4 A.M., I decided to awaken Joey.

"Ouch! What's the matter with you? What you want?" he demanded disagreeably when I had pinched and slapped him awake.

"Come on, wake up."

"What for? Go 'way."

I was lost for a reasonable reply. I could not say, "I'm scared and I don't want to be alone," so I merely said, "I'm going out. If you want to come, come on."

The promise of adventure awoke him. "Going out now? Where at, Lizabeth? What are you going to do?"

I was pulling my dress over my head. Until now I had not thought of going out. "Just come on," I replied tersely.

I was out the window and halfway down the road before Joey caught up with me.

"Wait, Lizabeth, where you going?"

I was running as if the furies were after me, as perhaps they were—running silently and furiously until I came to where I had half known I was headed: to Miss Lottie's yard.

The half-dawn light was more eerie than complete darkness, and in it the old house was like the ruin that my world had become—foul and crumbling, a grotesque caricature. It looked haunted, but I was not afraid because I was haunted too.

"Lizabeth, you lost your mind?" panted Joey.

I had indeed lost my mind, for all the smoldering emotions of that summer swelled in me and burst—the great need for my mother who was never there, the hopelessness of our poverty and degradation, the bewilderment of being neither child nor woman and yet both at once, the fear unleashed by my father's tears. And these feelings combined in one great impulse toward destruction.

"Lizabeth!"

I leaped furiously into the mounds of marigolds and pulled madly, trampling and pulling and destroying the perfect yellow blooms. The fresh smell of early morning and of dew-soaked marigolds spurred me on as I went tearing and mangling and sobbing while Joey tugged at my dress or my waist crying, "Lizabeth, stop, please stop!"

And then I was sitting in the ruined little garden among the uprooted and ruined flowers, crying and crying, and it was too late to undo what I had done. Joey was sitting beside me, silent and frightened, not knowing what to say. Then, "Lizabeth, look."

I opened my swollen eyes and saw in front of me a pair of large calloused feet; my gaze lifted to the swollen legs, the age-distorted body clad in a tight cotton nightdress, and then the shadowed Indian face surrounded by stubby white hair. And there was no rage in the face now, now that the garden was destroyed and there was nothing any longer to be protected.

"M-miss Lottie!" I scrambled to my feet and just stood there and stared at her, and that was the moment when childhood faded and womanhood began. That violent, crazy act was the last act of childhood. For as I gazed at the immobile face with the sad, weary eyes, I gazed upon a kind of reality which is hidden to childhood. The witch was no longer a witch but only a broken old woman who had dared to create beauty in the midst of ugliness and sterility. She had been born in squalor and lived in it all her life. Now at the end of that life she had nothing except a falling-down hut, a wrecked body, and John Burke, the mindless son of her passion. Whatever verve there was left in her, whatever was of love and beauty and joy that had not been squeezed out by life, had been there in the marigolds she had so tenderly cared for.

Of course I could not express the things that I knew about Miss Lottie as I stood there awkward and ashamed. The years have put words to the things I knew in that moment, and as I look back upon it, I know that the moment marked the end of innocence. Innocence involves an unseeing acceptance of things at face value, an ignorance of the area below the surface. In that humiliating moment I looked beyond myself and into the depths of another person. This was the beginning of compassion, and one cannot have both compassion and innocence.

The years have taken me worlds away from that time and that place, from the dust and squalor of our lives and from the bright thing that I destroyed in a blind childish striking out at God-knows-what. Miss Lottie died long ago and many years have passed since I last saw her hut, completely barren at last, for despite my wild contrition she never planted marigolds again. Yet, there are times when the image of those passionate yellow mounds returns with a painful poignancy. For one does not have to be ignorant and poor to find that his life is barren as the dusty yards of our town. And I too have planted marigolds.

Suggestions for Further Reading

Angelou, Maya. *I Know Why the Caged Bird Sings*. New York: Bantam, 1983.

Baker, Russell. *Growing Up*. New York: NAL-Dutton, 1992.

Baldwin, James. *Go Tell It on the Mountain*. New York: Dell, 1985.

Crow Dog, Mary. *Lakota Woman*. New York: HarperCollins, 1991.

Cunningham, Laura. *Sleeping Arrangements*. New York: NAL-Dutton (Plume), 1991.

Erdrich, Louise. *Tracks*. New York: HarperCollins, 1989.

Hijuelos, Oscar. *Our House in the Last World*. New York: Persea Books, 1991.

Houston, Jean Wakatsuki, and James D. Houston. *Road to Manzanar*. New York: Bantam, 1983.

Kingston, Maxine Hong. *The Woman Warrior*. New York: Vintage, 1989.

Kusz, Natalie. *Road Song*. New York: HarperCollins, 1991.

Leavitt, David. *Family Dancing*. New York: Warner Books, 1985.

Lee, Gus. *China Boy*. New York: NAL-Dutton (Signet), 1992.

Miller, Isabel. *Patience and Sarah*. New York: Fawcett, 1985.

Minot, Susan. *Monkeys*. New York: Washington Square Press (Pocket Books), 1989.

Mohr, Nicholasa. *Nilda*. Houston: Arte Publico, 1986.

Momaday, N. Scott. *The Names*. Tucson: Univ. of Arizona Press, 1987.

Moody, Anne. *Coming of Age in Mississippi*. New York: Dell, 1992.

Njeri, Itabari. *Every Good-bye Ain't Gone*. New York: Vintage, 1991.

Pei, Lowry. *Family Resemblances*. New York: Vintage Contemporary Series, 1988.

Porter, Connie. *All-Bright Court*. New York: HarperCollins, 1992.

Rivera, Edward. *Family Installments*. New York: Viking-Penguin, 1983.

Rodriguez, Luis J. *Always Running: La Vida Loca: Gang Days in L.A.* Willimantic, CT: Curbstone Press, 1993.

Rodriguez, Richard. *The Hunger of Memory*. New York: Bantam, 1983.

Sanders, Dori. *Clover*. New York: Fawcett, 1991.

Santiago, Danny. *Famous All Over Town*. New York: NAL-Dutton (Plume), 1984.

Simon, Kate. *Bronx Primitive*. New York: HarperCollins, 1983.

Snow, Jade Wong. *Fifth Chinese Daughter*. Seattle: Univ. of Washington Press, 1989.

Tan, Amy. *The Joy Luck Club*. New York: Vintage, 1991.

Thomas, Piri. *Down These Mean Streets*. New York: Vintage, 1990.

Weidman, Jerome. *Fourth Street East*. New York: Random House, 1970. (Out of print, but still readily available in many local libraries.)

Wright, Richard. *Black Boy*. New York: HarperCollins, 1989.

Biographical Notes

DOROTHY ALLISON's first novel, *Bastard Out of Carolina*, was a 1992 National Book Award finalist. She is also the author of *Trash*, a collection of short stories that was the winner of two 1989 Lambda Literary Awards. Her fiction, poetry, and essays have appeared in such publications as the *Voice Literary Supplement*, *Southern Exposure*, and *The Advocate*.

JULIA ALVAREZ was born in the Dominican Republic and came to the United States in 1965, when she was ten years old. After receiving degrees in literature from Middlebury College and Syracuse University, she taught at Phillips Andover Academy, the University of Vermont, George Washington University, and the University of Illinois. She has published two books of poetry as well as the novel *How the García Girls Lost Their Accents*. She currently lives in Middlebury, Vermont, and teaches at Middlebury College.

SPIRO ATHANAS's parents were immigrants. Born in St. Louis to an Albanian father and a Greek mother, Athanas grew up in the inner city.

He studied creative writing at Washington University and currently lives in Cincinnati, Ohio.

PETER CAMERON was born in New Jersey and graduated from Hamilton College in 1982. He is the author of two story collections, *One Way or Another* and *Far-flung,* and the novel *Leap Year.* His fiction has appeared in *The New Yorker,* the *Paris Review, Rolling Stone,* and *Mademoiselle.* He lives in New York City, where he teaches at Columbia University and works at Lambda Legal Defense and Education Fund.

FRANK CHIN is the first Chinese American to have a play produced on the New York stage. Known for his distinctive, often humorous portrayals of Chinese Americans and for the incorporation of Chinese mythology in his work, Chin has published a collection of short stories, *The Chinaman Pacific & Frisco R.R. Co.,* which received the American Book Award. His plays include *The Chickencoop Chinaman* and *The Year of the Dragon.* He is also the author of a novel, *Donald Duk.*

WANDA COLEMAN was born and raised in Watts, Los Angeles. She has received an Emmy, as well as literary fellowships from the National Endowment for the Arts, the California Arts Council, and the Guggenheim Foundation. Her published works include *Heavy Daughter Blues* and *A War of Eyes and Other Stories,* and her fiction and poetry have appeared most recently in the anthologies *Breaking Ice* and *Erotique Noir/ Black Erotica.*

EUGENIA COLLIER was born in Baltimore, Maryland, and received degrees from Howard University and Columbia University. She has taught and lectured at numerous colleges and universities, including Morgan State College, Community College of Baltimore, Howard University, Coppin State College, and the University of Maryland. Her story "Marigolds" won the Gwendolyn Brooks Award for Fiction from *Negro Digest* in 1969. Her work has appeared in many anthologies, and she has also written for *Black World, T. V. Guide,* and the *New York Times.* She is currently Chairperson of the Department of English and Language Arts at Morgan State University.

MARY GORDON was born on Long Island, grew up in Queens, and was educated at Barnard College. The author of many essays and articles, she has also achieved critical acclaim for her novels *Final Payments*, *The Company of Women*, and *Men and Angels*, as well as for her collection of short stories, *Temporary Shelter*. She lives in upstate New York.

ARTURO ISLAS was born in El Paso, Texas, and grew up in the desert country that marks the Mexican-American border. He earned undergraduate and graduate degrees from Stanford University, where he later taught English. He was a member of Phi Beta Kappa, a Woodrow Wilson Fellow, and a University Fellow, and he also received the Lloyd W. Dinkelspiel Award for outstanding service to undergraduate education at Stanford. In 1991, at the age of fifty-two, Islas died of AIDS.

GISH JEN, the child of Chinese immigrants, was born in New York City, raised in Scarsdale, New York, and educated at Harvard University and the Iowa Writers' Workshop. She has received fellowships from the Bunting Institute, the National Endowment for the Arts, and the Copernicus Society. Her stories have appeared in numerous quarterlies and have been anthologized in *The New Generation* and *Best American Short Stories*. Her novel, *Typical American*, was published to critical acclaim.

CYNTHIA KADOHATA was born in Chicago. Her stories have appeared in the *New Yorker*, *Grand Street*, and the *Pennsylvania Review*. Author of the novels *The Floating World* and *In the Heart of the Valley of Love*, Kadohata currently lives in Los Angeles, where she works as a full-time writer. In 1991 she received a creative writing fellowship from the National Endowment for the Arts as well as a Whiting Writers' Award.

REGINALD McKNIGHT was born in Germany and raised as an "air force brat" in a number of places. He is the author of the critically acclaimed novel *I Bet on the Bus* and received the O. Henry Award and the *Kenyon Review* New Fiction Prize for his story "The Kind of Light That Shines on Texas." He currently teaches writing at Carnegie Mellon University.

D'ARCY McNICKLE (1904–1977), a member of the Confederated Salish and Kootenai tribes of Montana, was a founder of the National Congress of American Indians. Born in St. Ignatius, Montana, on the Flathead Indian Reservation, McNickle studied at the University of Montana from 1921 to 1925, where his first short stories were published in the university's literary journal, *Frontier and Midland*. In 1925, he sold his allotment on the Flathead Reservation in order to study at Oxford. He later studied at the University of Grenoble in France and at Columbia University. A prolific writer, McNickle completed his first novel, *The Surrounded*, in 1936. He went on to write ethnohistory; a juvenile novel, *Runner in the Sun;* many short stories; and a biography of Oliver La Farge, for which he received a Guggenheim Fellowship in 1963. Another novel, *Wind from an Enemy*, was published posthumously in 1978.

DURANGO MENDOZA was born in 1945 of a Mexican-American father and a Creek Indian mother. He felt an outsider to Chicano, Native American, and white cultures. His stories, he says, emphasize *human beings* who happen to be brown.

NICHOLASA MOHR was born and grew up in the Bronx. She studied at the Art Students League, the Brooklyn Museum Art School, and the Pratt Center for Contemporary Printmaking, often combining her art with her writing. She has written (and illustrated) a novel, *Nilda*, as well as several collections of short fiction, notably *El Bronx Remembered*, *In Nueva New York*, and, most recently, *Rituals of Survival: A Woman's Portfolio* and *Going Home*. The winner of many awards and honors, including the *New York Times* Outstanding Book of the Year and the American Book Award, Mohr has taught at Rutgers University, the State University of New York at Stony Brook and Albany, the public schools of Newark, New Jersey, and in the Department of Elementary and Early Education at Queens College.

CHAIM POTOK was born in the Bronx in 1929 and graduated from Yeshiva University and the Jewish Theological Seminary, where he was ordained as a rabbi. He also earned a doctorate from the University of Pennsylvania. His first novel, *The Chosen*, received the Edward Lewis Wallant Memorial Book Award and was nominated for the National Book Award.

ADAM SCHWARTZ was educated at Macalester College and at the University of Iowa Writer's Workshop. His work has been published in the *New Yorker* and in a collection of stories, *Writing Our Way Home: Contemporary Stories By American Jewish Writers*. He currently teaches at Wellesley and is working on a collection of stories.

GARY SOTO was born in Fresno, California, in 1952. He earned a B.A. from California State University at Fresno and an M.F.A. from the University of California at Irvine and is the author of eight volumes of poetry, nine books of prose (both fiction and nonfiction), and scripts for short films. He has received a Before Columbus Foundation American Book Award, Guggenheim and National Endowment for the Arts fellowships, the "Discovery"/*The Nation* Prize, and the California Library Association's Patricia Beatty Award. He currently teaches both Chicano Studies and English at the University of California at Berkeley.

SYLVIA WATANABE was born in Hawaii on the island of Maui. She is the recipient of a Japanese American Citizens League National Literary Award and a creative writing fellowship from the National Endowment for the Arts. She co-edited *Home to Stay,* an anthology of Asian-American women's fiction, and claims to have started writing because she likes to "explore the forces that bring individual human beings of different cultures together, and to imagine the private struggles that arise from such meetings." She lives in Michigan.

THEODORE WEESNER was born in 1935 in Flint, Michigan, and is a graduate of the Iowa Writers' Workshop. He spent three years in the army after leaving school at sixteen. The author of four novels, most recently *True Detective* and *Winning the City,* he currently teaches at Emerson College and lives in Portsmouth, New Hampshire.

TOBIAS WOLFF is the author of two highly acclaimed collections of short stories and a short novel, *The Barracks Thief,* which won the 1985 PEN/Faulkner Award. His fiction has appeared in such magazines as the *Atlantic Monthly* and *Esquire. This Boy's Life* was recently made into a motion picture, starring Robert De Niro. Wolff lives with his family in upstate New York.

Permissions Acknowledgments